No Badgers in my Wood

No Badgers in my Wood

PHIL DRABBLE

Illustrations by Eileen A. Soper

LONDON
MICHAEL JOSEPH

First published in Great Britain by
Michael Joseph Limited
44 Bedford Square, London WC1
1979

ISBN 0 7181 1853 7

Typeset and printed by
BAS Printers Limited,
Over Wallop, Hampshire and bound by Hunter &
Foulis Ltd, Edinburgh

Contents

Foreword
by 'BB'

In my opinion, this is the best book that Phil Drabble has written. It is also the most important of its kind since Rachel Carson's *Silent Spring* caused such a stir some fifteen years ago, for it tells how ineffective the laws still are relating to the control of pesticides and what really dreadful poisons are still being used on crops and arable land.

Though this may be the most important part of the book, there is, in addition, the account of the author's struggles to protect his deer from fox hounds and the horror of finding one of his beloved badgers in a local snare. When strangers leased a neighbouring shoot and the syndicate employed a keeper he feared might turn out to be a 'good vermin trapper', he makes no secret of the controversial methods he used to combat any threat that might develop.

Phil Drabble is an acknowledged authority on badgers, has spent hours watching them in the wild and has reared them from tiny cubs—not always with pleasing results because, when a badger has lost his instinctive fear of man, he can be a dangerous animal when returned to the wild.

The author was once bitten so badly on the legs that his boots filled with blood, but he accepted it as one of a naturalist's occupational hazards. He bears them no ill will because he knows how badgers think. In the environment of the house, the badger regarded him as dominant and was perfectly safe. But, because he had been hand reared and had lost his fear of man, it was natural to defend 'his' territory in the wood outside from what he regarded as a potential rival. Quite understandable—if you understand badgers!

Phil Drabble was brought up with freedom to roam on a large estate and he draws a delightful picture of the head keeper, 'one of the old school', who could pigeon-hole everyone he met 'with the accuracy of a computer', instantly judging to what class of society they belonged. He describes the last three generations of the squires who owned it and the effect on wildlife as the estate was broken up and the number of keepers dwindled.

I am sure that this book will give great enjoyment as well as sounding a warning about the present threats to wildlife.

'BB'

Preface

The tranquillity outside my study window is sometimes an illusion. Silence and stillness are not always signs of peace because the deceptive calm may be the instant's pause before a predator pounces on its prey, or the interminable time taken to recover from deliberate acts of man. For more than half a century, I have been able to witness, at close quarters, a rural revolution that has changed the face of the countryside and shaped the destiny of wildlife that lives there.

From childhood until I was a man, I enjoyed the freedom to wander on a great estate during the period spanned by the last three generations of the family who had owned it since Norman times. They were typical of so many great landowners who landscaped their estate with woods and coverts and splashes of gorgeous coloured berry-bearing shrubs and rhododendrons.

The superb patchwork that resulted gave England the most beautiful scenery in the world, but it owed little to the aesthetic sense of its creators. Game was their god, and the scenic beauty of their land was mere coincidence, of secondary importance to the pheasants and foxes which provided sport.

As a child, I was tutored by a head keeper whose whims were law over the whole six thousand acres that his master owned. I saw, at first hand, the methods he used to obliterate the enemies, real or imagined, of the pheasants he reared for sport. Knowing no better, I took the carnage for granted and regarded the genocide of predators without emotion.

When the Old Squire died, two-thirds of the estate were liquidated by the avaricious tax man and I saw the first, tentative return of 'vermin' when most of the keepers were made redundant.

The last hereditary owner received, as his birthright, a mere tenth of his grandfather's lands. Luckily for him, he was more of a naturalist than a sportsman at heart. Instead of moaning about his loss, he rejoiced at the gradual return of creatures that had been victims of the keepers' art for committing a crime no worse than being born with hooked bills or canine teeth.

Just as he was succeeding in enriching his lands with wildlife, a motorway plunged through the middle of his estate, so he sold up and went away.

It was typical of events all over England. As the old squires were dispossessed, they were replaced by a new squirearchy, too often *nouveau riche* and ignorant of rural ways. Sport is still their status symbol, but the new tycoons measure success in terms of £.s.d., and are unimaginatively ruthless with anything that hampers shooting pheasants for profit as well as for fun. Mere 'shooters' have supplanted sportsmen.

Badgers have been my lifelong interest. I have always been instinctively fascinated by them and did my first badger-watching on the estate which was my childhood playground. I have kept badgers and reared them by hand to run free in my wood—which I manage as a nature reserve—and have encouraged wild ones to settle, though for a traumatic three years there were no badgers in my wood for reasons beyond my control.

I have chosen badgers as my barometer for several reasons. The most important is that they are a thread that has run continuously through my life, so that I can speak from practical experience. They are so large, and their setts and their workings so obvious that it is easier to be specific about their presence or absence than it would be about more secretive creatures. And they are so tough that, given half a chance, their population soon recovers from the most determined onslaughts of pest officers and keepers alike.

The status of badgers seems to me a fair indication of the prospects for other wild creatures in the countryside. When there are no badgers in *my* wood, it is high time to try to stop the rot from spreading.

CHAPTER ONE

The Old School

The Old Squire was Hannam's hatchet-man. Neither of them was aware of the fact and anybody rash enough to suggest that their relationship was not all it seemed would have touched off an explosion. In theory, they were master and man, and the Old Squire barked out his orders with aristocratic arrogance. This would have been more impressive if his monumental stutter had not slowed down such communication to a limp. Even so, there was no doubt that he was boss.

Hannam was the perfect example of a head keeper of his vintage. He had left school at about the age of twelve, in the 1880s, and had worked for the family ever since. He knew how to be respectful without servility and was a master of subtle innuendo that sowed seeds of doubt about any tenant or neighbour or servant who posed the slightest threat to the game that he preserved.

Head keepers were dangerous men to tangle with, and tenant farmers rash enough to complain about damage to their crops, by pheasants or hares, stood in as much peril as farm-workers who poached them. It was as easy to dispossess a tenant as to sack a labourer. The Old Squire, who was a JP as well as a landlord, acted on suspicions planted in his mind without realising just how often the tail was wagging the dog.

I first met Hannam in the 1920s when I went to buy a ferret. I was aged about ten. He was immaculate in breeches and leggings and a neat tweed jacket of an exclusive design, sold by a firm who specialised in making clothes for keepers. His hair, badger-grey, and his complexion, nut-brown from constant exposure to storm as well as shine, formed the perfect setting for his startling grey

eyes. Class had not yet become a dirty word, and he pigeon-holed everyone he met with the impersonal speed and accuracy of a computer.

Workmen were suspect because he regarded them all as either urban and ignorant, or rural—and potential poachers. They were lumped with shop keepers and clerks who earned their living without soiling their hands, though these 'tradesmen' came from a stratum of society which rarely crossed his path.

Professional men, doctors and lawyers and sporting parsons, were about the lowest class he bothered to store individually in his mental filing cabinet. They were invited for bye-days by his master, when sport was unlikely to attain the quality which would excite the gentry. They plodded round the boundary of the estate, killing game which might otherwise have strayed away to neighbours.

Good head keepers were always scrupulously courteous to such guests. Their civility was fed by the fact that they were really using them as unpaid beaters to drive the bulk of the pheasants back to home coverts for more important folk to shoot. If they reciprocated this solicitude with a lucrative tip, they found themselves in the most favourable spots next time. Otherwise, they got plenty of exercise but precious little shooting.

The gentry came on 'big' days and nothing was too much trouble for them; no pheasants were too high, no sport too fast and furious. Most of them were landowners, often with titles or distinguished army careers. Their common factor was the luck to have so much leisure that constant practice had made their marksmanship well-nigh perfect. Those without the skill to cash-in on their good fortune soon slipped several notches down Hannam's social scale. His reputation was founded on the cold figures of victims recorded in the estate game book. If he didn't produce the pheasants for his master's guests to shoot, his status would slump.

There was no column in the book to show why the bag was large or small; no space to write 'birds failed to show' or 'guests failed to hit them'—and nobody would have been discourteous enough to cast doubt on a guest's competence if there had. So a bad bag, starkly recorded in cold print, was likely to be blamed on the keeper by those who were not there, instead of on the indifferent marksmanship of those who were.

The fact that Hannam did not suffer such fools gladly shone coldly from his eyes—but he was too polite to translate his thoughts to words. He made up for it by the ruthless way he took it out on the less articulate enemies of game.

When I went to his cottage for my ferret, it was the first time I had been at the nerve-centre of a great estate. My father was doctor to both Hannam and the Squire, so he did not give me the short shrift he would probably have meted out to most strange kids.

He took me to see his young pheasants—which were very different from young pheasants today. By modern techniques, the eggs are hatched in incubators, and the chicks reared by the thousand under infra red brooders. They never see a domestic hen, far less their natural mothers, and they are subsequently turned loose by the hundred in fox-proof enclosures in the woods. They are so bored and overcrowded that the tips of their beaks have to be cut off to prevent them plucking one another's feathers to pass the time.

There was nothing fox-proof about Hannam's pheasants. They were in a field of mowing grass through which paths had been cut with a scythe, in parallel swathes about twenty yards apart. Hen coops were spaced along these mown paths in regimented rows. Each coop contained a hen, which couldn't squeeze out between the laths that formed the front, and about sixteen pheasant chicks, which could. The chicks were free to wander over the short turf around their coop and to take refuge in the thick cover on each side. They returned to the voice of their own hen to feed and sleep warm at night.

At one end of the field was a shepherd's hut, on wheels, and an iron boiler, mounted on bricks and heated by a coal fire. There were ten under-keepers, one of whom camped out in the shepherd's hut on the rearing field for most of the summer while the hens and chicks were there. He shot rabbits and cooked them with rice in his boiler for the chicks. Then he cooked food for himself on the embers of the fire.

He was out with his gun from dawn till dusk and he hung paraffin lanterns round the field to keep off the foxes when it was too dark to see to shoot.

Hannam introduced me to this understrapper, who had no way of knowing how unimportant I was, so that he treated me with the deference he would have showed to sons of the boss's friends. I fell for it, as so many of my betters did and, growing bolder as my insignificance shelled off, I plied them with questions.

Their main preoccupation seemed to be the enemies of pheasants. The young keeper showed me, with pride, a female kestrel he had shot that morning. The delicate beauty of the dead bird so enthralled me that I blotted my copybook by expressing sympathy for her. This unleashed a torrent of indoctrination that was the more compelling because both keepers believed it implicitly. They showed me the wicked curved bill, capable of splitting a grown pheasant's skull and the hooked talons, long enough to transfix a young bird to its tender vitals. They told me how all hawks hunt, not just to kill but for sport, and how a single kestrel would have carried off hundreds of young poults on the rearing field—if the young keeper had not been so vigilant.

I had no way of knowing what rubbish this was. It was years before I discovered how lazy hawks are, hunting to eat but too idle to hunt seriously for sport. Nor did I know that, of all our native hawks, kestrels are among the most delightful and the most harmless.

To drive the lesson home, I was taken to see the keeper's gibbet. Like the game book, this was a yardstick of his competence; a physical statement of profit-and-loss, as illuminating to those who could interpret it as a computer load of statistics to a company accountant.

Hannam told me, with pride, that the Old Squire himself called to inspect the gibbet's latest victims every Sunday, after church. Not perhaps what the parson had had in mind when he composed his sermon.

The gibbet was a piece of strong fencing wire, about ten yards long, stretched tight between two trees. Nine carrion crows, in varying stages of decomposition, dangled at one end. The catalogue of their crimes included egg stealing, infanticide of pheasant and partridge chicks, and attacks on young rabbits and hares. I know from my own experience, that the case against them was not overstated. I too am as tough on them as any old-fashioned keeper—not in the interests only of pheasants, but of all the small birds in my wood.

Hannam was a keeper of the old school, and he harboured an implacable hatred of *all* predators. In his eyes, all mammals with canine teeth and all birds with hooked bills were his sworn enemies. To tell him that you had seen a stoat anywhere on 'his' estate was an insult comparable to a slur on his legitimacy.

He hated hawks and owls and badgers and foxes with the same ruthless bitterness that he reserved for crows and magpies and the Huns in Kaiser Wilhelm's army. Nothing was bad enough for them; no death too protracted or severe.

When the Old Squire called on Sunday, to satisfy himself that his keepers had not been slacking in the week, it never occurred to him that the kestrel, crucified with wings outstretched, had hovered harmlessly over beetles and mice. Hannam said that if he had not got his blow in first, it would have killed his young pheasants. Hannam was bred of keeper stock that took such myth as gospel, so there was some excuse for him. His master was

educated and had endless opportunity for observing the facts first hand on his own estate. He really should have known better.

In some ways, I have great sympathy with the Old Squire though. He had learned the 'facts' of rural life from keepers who acted as tutors and, since they were doubtless good—or at least efficient—keepers, there would be no reason for him to doubt the validity of their teaching, because they sincerely believed what they said.

So I examined that first keeper's gibbet with objective curiosity, but no revulsion. I saw jays with jewelled wings next to their arch enemies the stoats and weasels. There were squirrels and hedgehogs and magpies that had misjudged the lethal range of sporting guns, or the skill of the men who set snares and gin traps to lie in wait for them.

It was soon obvious that the old maids of the village, too tender-hearted to deny their pet pussies the moonlight courtship that had eluded them, did not keep their pampered darlings long. No cat trespassed with impunity on Hannam's beat, as rows of multi-coloured tails on his gibbet testified. Irate owners who complained were tersely told to keep their cats at home—or suffer the consequences.

The keeper's cottage parlour was almost an extension of his gibbet, where the prizes of which he was most proud could be

displayed in perpetuity. Instead of a row of rotting corpses, there was case upon case of stuffed animals and birds, all sharing the common distinction of ending their days at Hannam's hand.

A barn owl ('white' owl, he called it) clutched a mouse, whose prominent eyes were caused by a bad taxidermist, though the talons that gripped him doubtless produced a similar expression in life. Three owlets peered from a hole in the trunk that formed a corner of the case and, although my mood was set to appreciate everything I saw, evidence of such slaughter of the innocents did raise qualms in my mind.

There was a stuffed white stoat. No head keeper's cottage would have been complete without one, partly because they were not as rare as supposed, and partly because they never failed to spark off tales of the local mayor and his ermine. It made a social conversation piece.

A whole family of foxes occupied a case as big as a rabbit hutch in the corner, which included a liberal display of evidence that foxes prey on game. Albino pheasants vied with kingfishers which had lost their sparkle and, in one corner of the room, a fearsome collection of clubs and knuckle-dusters bore eloquent testimony that human poachers did not escape unscathed. The confiscated weapons, produced as 'evidence' in court, ended up as trophies to decorate the parlour.

Head keepers of those times were gluttons for protocol and etiquette. The only reason that he had taken the trouble to show me round was that I was 'the doctor's' son. Doctors came well down his scale of precedence as guests of his master's shooting parties, but good manners dictated that the son of his own doctor, visiting his house for the first time, should be treated with respect.

Before being taken through the kitchen to the parlour, where he kept his treasures, I was introduced to Mrs Hannam. She was a large pasty-faced woman, with very pale blue eyes which never synchronised with her lips when she smiled. Humour was not among her charms.

The cause of her sadness sat purring at the side of the hearth. I never discovered his name, but he was the largest tabby tom cat I've ever seen. His mistress was despondent because she had to abide by the same rules as ladies who owned cats in the village. She was quite clearly an ardent cat lover, while her husband admitted that he would rather have a litter of foxes or a gang of poachers at large in his coverts. As a result, Mrs Hannam's pride and joy was not allowed loose in the wood because Hannam refused to refrain from setting gin-traps. The dice would have been loaded against the inexperienced old cat returning home.

It is easy enough to say 'keep your cat at home', more difficult to comply. Poor Mrs Hannam had no illusions about the results of failure. She had seen too many mutilated corpses, with shin bones splintered by the jaws of gin-traps. So she had fitted her old cat with a collar and chain and fastened him to the chimney-piece for his own protection. He is the only cat I ever saw under such constraint and, being the lazy creature most cats are, he seemed to bear his imprisonment philosophically. Whether he ever had spells of freedom or whether his mistress took him for walks on a lead, I never discovered, because he was obviously such a source of friction between man and wife, that to have laboured the point might have festered their disagreement to incompatibility.

Nevertheless the lesson sank in. Hannam was obviously no fool and, if he was prepared to stick his heels in to the extent of denying his own wife's deep wish to keep a cat, except on his outrageous terms, he really must have been convinced that the damage they

caused to game—and other wildlife—was pretty serious. My own observations have subsequently confirmed it.

The most vivid memory of that first visit had an influence on me that persists as strong today as more than half a century ago.

One case, of what I now regard as the stuffed horrors in his parlour, riveted my attention. Two badgers were playing with cubs. There was the same arid grass and leaves as in the other cases, and similar lurid background painting.

I now know that the badgers were exceptionally badly stuffed, their skins had been stretched into a tube as shapeless as the top of an old woman's woollen stocking, so that the poor creatures had the flaccid obesity of overfed ferrets. One of them was carrying a rabbit, while his mate was patting a cub with a paw, and the skins had shrunk as they'd dried, so that huge, un-badgerlike eyes ogled as stupidly as a pet pekinese.

As a tableau of real badgers doing natural things, it was a

disaster. Badgers don't pat with paws like playful cats, nor carry rabbits home—but I didn't realise it then, because I'd never seen a badger before, alive or stuffed. I'd read a lot about them and seen their pictures often enough but, for some reason that I am unable to explain, badgers have always had a natural and irresistible attraction for me.

When once I had seen that tableau, nothing else held out any attraction. White stoats and fancy pheasants, live cats on chains or stuffed foxes, even the ferret that I had bought, sank without trace by comparison.

I made the mistake of asking Hannam to show me a live one. He looked at me to see if I'd gone daft. The very idea of badgers on his beat was too preposterous, but his innate good manners prevented him from saying what he thought.

'I can't', he said, 'and I hope I never can. There are no badgers on this estate and if one puts his thieving snout over the boundary, he don't go back'.

Then he opened the case and showed me, at close quarters, the grinning mask of the sow that was playing with her pathetic cubs. She looked delightful to me, no more fierce than my beloved bull terrier at home, and he never did me any harm, however realistically he acted when we were playing together.

'Look at them jaws', he said. 'Big as a dog's, but more powerful; she must eat as much as a dog. And what does she want great teeth like that for, if it isn't to kill my pheasants?'

It seemed logical enough, but the only difference it made to me was to divert my enthusiasm for badgers along different channels. I had no reason to doubt what I took to be the lifetime experience of keepers, no cause to question either their judgment or objectivity.

Instead of feeling sorry for the wretched stuffed creatures in the case, I should have been perfectly happy to hunt them to help the keeper's cause. It was the beginning of a love-hate relationship which took years to get in perspective for the simple reason that I knew no one who could put the other side of the case. The game-keepers and poachers with whom I grew up knew more field craft than any of the knobbly-kneed academics who taught me biology at school.

Learning my natural history from unlettered men in quiet places built up such confidence in what they believed that it was years before I realised their effect on the game and wildlife on 'their' estates, and on the surrounding countryside. Their dedication and efficiency was beneficial for some species, but catastrophic for others.

Hannam was head keeper for an estate of six thousand acres. That is more than nine square miles and included a large number of tenanted farms as well as the park around the Hall, and hundreds of acres of wood and coverts.

Wildlife is intensely conservative. Birds nest in the same thickets or trees for year after year. Stoats and foxes pass through the same gaps in a hedge or along the same tracks through woodland for generations. Badgers use the same traditional setts for centuries—if they are allowed to.

Observant keepers know such sensitive spots on their beats as intimately as the veins on the back of their own hands. A cunning noose, set in a well-used run through a fence, will hang every fox that tries to pass. The Old Squire liked hunting, and—in theory— any keeper guilty of the heinous crime of vulpicide was liable to instant dismissal. Any keeper who set a fox snare near a public footpath or where a disgruntled farm labourer might see it, asked for what he got, but there was plenty of space, on six thousand acres, where no one but keepers were likely to go. If the Old Squire did stumble across one, he was always prepared to accept the excuse that 'it was set for a poaching cat'. So long as there was a fox or two in evidence when hounds came, he didn't enquire too closely.

Pole-traps, too, were widely used though not strictly legal. They were the most diabolical contraptions and so ruthlessly effective that they could wipe out whole populations of hawks and owls.

Many predatory birds like a vantage point to perch while they spy on their prey, and decide which to attack. So keepers supplied poles for them to perch on in the most advantageous spots. It was as easy to persuade them to use these perches as it is to get garden birds to use a bird table. When hawks and owls got used to the perch, a steel gin-trap was mounted on top which caught every victim that landed on it. There it remained, dangling by its shattered legs, until the next time the keeper passed by and stopped to knock it on the head.

Badgers were easiest of all. Their setts are large and obvious: many keepers did not dig them out because they did not want to disturb the sett by filling the holes in. Left as it was, every visiting badger could be trapped as soon as he arrived. When freshly-dug soil and used latrine pits indicated that tenants had moved in, a large steel gin-trap was set in each hole. Hunger eventually drove the badger to emerge—and the gin caught him by the leg. If he was so suspicious that he excavated a fresh exit, a bait laced with deadly strychnine, or a wire noose where he passed through a fence, were equally effective.

As a result of these various traps, the resident population of 'vermin' was virtually exterminated on the whole estate. The snag was that, when it happened, it left a very large area of superb habitat with plenty of food and no competition. So 'vermin' flooded in from the surrounding area and recolonised the vacuum as surely as water finds its own level.

Hannam and his men were not deterred. They trapped and snared and poisoned and shot until they obliterated the next wave of invaders. And the next and those that followed. It was a continuous war of attrition which eventually had its effect. Where a number of similar large, sporting estates joined up, badgers and hawks and owls and stoats and weasels were wiped out over huge areas of countryside. Polecats and kites and eagles became extinct in England and only survived in remote places which were useless for sport. Gamekeepers—and their masters—changed the whole pattern of our native wildlife.

There was a credit side too. Pheasants were not the only beneficiaries. Blackbirds and thrushes and other songbirds thrived because their foes were controlled. But, on balance, most wildlife suffered.

I never knew the Old Squire well. The circles we moved in never converged—and there was also the matter of about four score years difference in our ages. I saw him perched on his hunter, when hounds were in the district, and heard his autocratic anger with any who got in his way or rode too close to hounds.

The first time I spoke to him was when my father was paying a professional visit and left me in the car while he was in the house. The whole park was alive with rabbits and when I asked if I could have one, he had stuttered his reply: 'N-n-next time you c-c-come, bring some s-s-salt and put it on their tails. You can have all you c-c-can c-c-catch.'

He registered in my mind as a stupid, arrogant old man for so underrating my intelligence, but his offer was couched in terms which precluded losing any rabbits!

When he died, the estate dwindled from about six thousand acres to two. Death duties and mortgages took their toll. Men of his class and generation despised trade and thought it beneath them to talk about money, which they regarded as their birthright. They employed agents—and left them to run their estates because they had neither the knowledge themselves, nor the will to work.

Good and honest agents were rare birds and their inefficiency (and sometimes dishonesty) combined with penal taxation decimated the possessions of many great landowners in a couple of generations. Tenants who bought their farms often retained the shooting themselves without employing a keeper. Vermin increased and pheasants suffered. Hawks and owls reappeared where no predator had dared show a hooked bill or canine tooth for generations.

When the Old Squire died and his son inherited the central two thousand acres or so of land around the Hall, which was all that was left of the estate, he also inherited Hannam and his under-keepers.

Locally known as the Squire—never the Young Squire, since he was past middle age when he inherited—his dwindling resources forced him to cut his coat according to his cloth. He rated Hannam as indispensable, but sacked all but one of the outlying keepers in the interests of economy.

Whatever human misery the redundancies may have caused, they were nothing but good news for the wildlife of the area.

Word soon went round on the local grapevine that the new owner was much more approachable than the Old Squire, so I managed to wangle permission to go rabbiting in the park, an exciting prospect for a fourteen-year-old.

Sometimes I went alone, with my dog and my ferrets and my purse nets. Sometimes the Squire came with me. The park was a picture of desolate decay; a desert of wiry, unpalatable tussocks of grass and reed, interspersed by small woods and spinneys planted long ago as pheasant coverts.

It was the custom, in those days, for landowners not to manage their estates themselves because 'gentlemen' did not have to work and only the vulgar worried about boring routine and detailed organisation. The family had been there since William the Conqueror's time but none of them had ever had a paid job, except in the army or the church, and the Old Squire's great grandson, who now works in industry, is the first in line to do so.

So it was no wonder that bolted rabbits had to dodge and side-step round the tussocks with the agility of a rugby scrum-half weaving through the pack. They never went straight for five consecutive yards, but the Squire had plenty of time to practice, so that he was the slickest shot at rabbits that I ever saw. No star from the farthest-fetched Wild Western could have beaten him to the draw.

He was surprised at my expertise with ferrets and we got on so well that I was always invited back to the Hall for lunch with my host and his lady. They lived incredibly frugally and usually had mince, which I hated.

There were other compensations. Hannam's parlour was a dull side-show by comparison because the old Squire's front door opened into a great hall, as big as his keeper's cottage, floored with austere grey stone slabs. Ancient cannons stared guests and intruders insolently in the eye, and suits of armour still stood ready to protect the owner if he was called to arms. Nobody seemed to have noticed the passage of time, because lances and spears and muzzle loaders stood to attention round the walls, precisely as they had done when some former owner had put them there as spoils of battle.

The star attraction was an enormous stuffed albatross with a nine-foot wingspan, said to have been brought back by an ancestral admiral who had won the battle of Portobello. More to my taste was a huge glass case containing several hundred foxes' brushes, each decorated with a label describing when the original owner was found, how far he was hunted and where he met his gory end. These foxes had shown an extraordinary diversity of colour, ranging from cream through gingery red, to the dark grey of silver fox beloved by blondes. Surprisingly few of them had the traditional white tag so often described in fiction.★

There were plenty of other treasures too. While the keepers were annihilating the 'vermin'—which included all predators, whether harmful or not—their masters amused themselves more selectively. Any innocent rarity straying on to the estate, was shot, stuffed and put into a case to prove its presence to subsequent doubters. Such fashionable status symbols decorating the hall included rare seabirds blown inland by storm, unusually coloured animals or birds, or even common ones if they were beautiful enough. There was a whole family of otters, playing among the rushes by a lurid, cardboard stream, and scores of grinning otters' masks, because the Squire had been a Master of Otterhounds before inheriting the estate. There were kingfishers and corn-crakes, an albino red squirrel, and a charm of goldfinches whose glassy eyes were anything but charming.

The catalogue of wanton destruction would sicken me now, and the effect on the countryside of such large, well-keepered estates must have been truly catastrophic then.

At the time, of course, I was totally unaware of this. Like the Squire himself, I took it as normal and my only regret was that I had not been in the forefront of the hunt, when all those foxes 'paid the penalty' as the sporting writers of the day invariably described it. They omitted to say for what the penalty was paid. Nothing would have excited me more than stalking rarity with a muzzle loader gun, or collecting stags' heads with a rifle.

The Squire himself was very different from his father. For one thing, he was infinitely poorer because his depleted estate fell into his lap together with a pile of debts which it took most of his life to

---

★ The story of the foxes' brushes is told in more detail in *Country Seasons*.

pay off. For another, he was more of a watcher and less of a doer than the old man had been.

He was thin and gaunt, with an aquiline nose that would have out-curved any of the hawks on Hannam's gibbet. His skin had weathered as brown as the bark on the hazel thumbstick he always carried when he hadn't got his gun. My most vivid memory is of an inconspicuous figure in a deerstalker hat, leaning as motionless on his thumbstick as the medieval carving on his pew in church. If he had spent as many happy hours managing his estate as he spent watching over it, his descendants might be there today.

His mother—the Old Lady—moved to the Dower House when the Old Squire died. By anybody's standards she was dynamic, and I shall never forget the time I saw her out hunting. She was about eighty, riding side-saddle to hounds and jumping all before her. From his more stolid mount, the Old Squire was roaring at her to 'Hold hard. You'll b-b-break your bl-bl-blardy neck.'

When she had died and the Dower House was empty, I was asked by the local Master of Beagles if the Squire could be persuaded to let them kennel hounds there for the duration of the last war. I arranged a meeting and, when we went to look round, the brick floors of most of the buildings had been ripped up and left in untidy piles.

The Old Lady, it seemed, had a passion for ratting, and liked to spend Sunday mornings ferreting round the farms and buildings on the estate. When rats refused to bolt and a ferret stayed below to fight—or eat—them, her remedy was simple. She located their approximate position by watching where her terriers were marking—and ordered the floor to be got up so that her men could dig them out. By the time they were successful, it was usually lunchtime, so they all went home and left the debris to look after itself. Had she lived a couple of generations later, she could have minimised the havoc by fitting the ferrets with special collars and locating them precisely by the latest type of electronic mine detector, adapted for sporting purposes. Even so, she would doubtless have left whatever rubble she created as her memorial. Such attitudes were among the last straws that broke up the great estates.

The Squire, however, was very kind to me. When he discovered that my dog was under control and that I could be relied on never to enter his pheasant coverts and disturb his birds, he allowed me to wander freely over his land. I was encouraged to accompany Hannam or his sole assistant, Jim, on their rounds, 'Because', the Squire said, 'keepers bring up young men properly and teach them the things they should know!'

It was, of course, a matter of opinion, because what I learned then would be unacceptable now. I was taught that all stoats must die. They are creatures of compulsive habit and uncontrollable curiosity. Generation after generation used the same runs along hedgerows or the edge of woodland. If a small pit is dug, with a drainpipe as entrance, no stoat that passes that way can resist the temptation to pop down the pipe to investigate. A steel gin-trap, placed unobtrusively in the pit and covered with a stone slab or piece of wood, was an uncommonly patient custodian. It would wait there indefinitely till an animal entered; this would spring the gin and hold it by its shattered leg until the keeper came round to despatch it. Before he hung it on his gibbet, he always emptied its bladder at the mouth of the pipe. Stoats 'mark' their territory as a dog cocks his leg on a lamp post, and the challenging aroma would inflame the curiosity of the next stoat to come that way, so that he would be even less suspicious of what lay in wait for him down the tunnel.

Steel gins have long been illegal here, though they are still made for export to less civilised countries—and I know gamekeepers in

England who still use them. Having seen scores of stoats and
weasels, foxes and cats and rabbits mutilated by their iron grip, I
need no one to convert me to the necessity to outlaw them; but my
own first-hand experience might explain how rats sometimes
escape.

I caught hundreds of rats, as a lad, by setting a steel gin in a 'tunnel
trap', similar to the ones the keepers used for stoats. As so often
happens, familiarity bred contempt and I grew slick at setting a
trap so 'fine' that the least touch on the treadle set it off. At last I got
too slick and the trap went off before I was ready and caught me by
the thumb. It 'bit' me so hard that now, almost half a century later,
there is no feeling in the ball of that thumb, and I get no sensation
of pain if I jag it on a thorn.

In theory, it should have been agony at the time, but in fact I
hardly felt it. Looking down I noticed that the steel teeth had
squeezed my flesh into furrows to match the mesh, but I was able to
kneel on the spring and free my mangled thumb without much
difficulty. It took several hours for sensation to return to inflict a
throbbing agony that lasted for days! But, if I had been a rat, I
believe that I could have bitten off my foot (as many rats did), and
escaped while the limb was still under the anaesthetic of great
pressure.

In many ways the Squire was right. His keepers did not only
teach me to kill the enemies of game ruthlessly. They also taught
me about the habits of many harmless things.

When a blackbird is disturbed, he utters an alarm note. All the
bird books tell you that. Good gamekeepers will tell you much
more. They taught me to interpret the language of blackbirds by
listening to the whole glossary of their alarm notes. I learned the
slow, staccato music they play when a cat or a fox is at large in the
wood. Quite different from their shrill abuse when a tawny owl
comes out at dusk.

Hannam was a wonderful croaker and squeaker. We would sit
still and silent for half an hour or so, hidden under the bushes at the
edge of a woodland ride in spring. Sooner or later the hollow triple
call would echo through the wood as a carrion crow proclaimed
his territorial rights. Hannam always judged the interval precisely,

before the most disgusting triple belches echoed from deep down amongst his vitals, as if he'd swallowed an old-fashioned klaxon motor horn. Thereafter, the wood was never silent long. When the implications of the threats sunk in, the resident crow threw back the challenge. The strident croaks rattled round and Thor, the god of thunder, couldn't have roared out his challenge with more contemptuous arrogance.

Possession is nine points of avian law as well as ours, so that it was only a matter of time before the resident crow sallied forth to see his rival off. He stood no chance against Hannam's fire power and a split second after he showed himself, the crack of the keeper's rifle guaranteed that no nest of eggs would be plundered again by him.

Foxes were more spectacular. I remember one time when we had waited for hours by a public path for a gang of local youths that had been robbing the pheasant nests, and the evening light was just beginning to fail.

Half a mile or so away, on the far side the wood, a jay started to scold. 'Quiet', said old Hannam, 'they'll be coming now'. He listened intently as the diatribe continued. 'That's not people, after all', he said. 'That's the row they kick up when there's a fox or cat in the wood.' With that, another jay took up the chorus and we could hear them gradually coming closer across the wood. The spoil-sport birds were yelling abuse which every potential victim wisely took as a warning.

Suddenly, right at the top of the ride, a gingery shape slid out of the shadows, sat down in the open and calmly started to scratch. It was a lovely fox, so far as any but a dead fox can delight a keeper's eyes, but it was a couple of hundred yards beyond the lethal range of Hannam's shotgun. I have known plenty of men who will let fly at a fox at any range, because there is a popular country belief that foxes are bad healers. If they are wounded, the infection is said to take bad ways and kill them off eventually. Such men will let fly at impossible ranges in the hopes that the most minor prick will develop into gangrene.

Hannam did not subscribe to that. He may have been an unimaginative man, but he was neither deliberately callous nor cruel. He took justifiable pride in his skill and considered shooting quarry out of lethal range to be the action of ignorant incompetents. When his gun went off, he liked to have something to show for it.

So he put the back of his hand to his moistened lips—and sucked. This emitted a high-pitched squeal that would have deceived any rabbit to think that it was listening to some long lost brother rabbit in its death throes. It certainly deceived the fox, which stopped scratching, sat bolt upright and listened intently through ears as sensitive and directional as radar scanners.

At that time, it was common to catch rabbits in wire snares or in steel gins buried so cunningly in their tracks in the open that it would have needed an electronic mine detector to discover them. Such victims made easy, tasty suppers for any passing fox, and they advertised their whereabouts with agonised squeals exactly like the noise Hannam made when he sucked the back of his hand.

The keeper left it to stew in silence for a few moments, then he squealed again. The fox dashed a few yards towards us and then clapped motionless on his belly. Another squeal encouraged another dash, each surer than the last as he got an exact bearing on the source of the sound. It was almost like watching a sheepdog working sheep to see that fox approaching in staccato bursts, interpolated by pauses while he crouched motionless, ears cocked, as a sheepdog does, licking his greedy lips in anticipation of the final sortie.

There was no such victorious climax when Hannam called the tune. The attacker was allowed to advance to just within the lethal limit of his gun, and then a flash and a crack rolled him over while he was still convinced that he was winning. It was a calculated and sophisticated performance—but his remains were not honoured by a position on the gibbet behind the cottage. Vulpicide was a risky business. The punishment for such a rural crime was the sack for servants, or to be socially ostracised for their masters. The remains of 'our' fox were shoved furtively down a rabbit hole, and the entrance crushed in with a hob-nailed boot.

What the Squire didn't see he wouldn't grieve about—and many a pheasant would have cause to rejoice that he would live at least until the shooting season.

However efficient Hannam and his understrapper were, they

were fighting a losing battle. Not only were four out of the original six thousand acres of the estate now unkeepered, but surrounding estates were in a similar position. For better or for worse, they too were crumbling away, but their woods and coverts which had been planted for game and foxes stayed unmolested. Not until the second world war was earth-moving machinery developed on a scale which made it economic to bulldoze such unproductive patches in the interests of mechanised farming. Such juggernauts as multi-furrowed ploughs and huge combine harvesters cannot cavort around in little fields.

As fast as Hannam cleared his patch of 'vermin', it was reinfested from the surrounding countryside. The Squire took it philosophically, for he proved to be less of a fighter than his ancestors, even for his own birthright. Gone were the days when the county arrived for big shoots, bringing their own keepers as loaders. He was content to potter round with a few old cronies, walking-up a handful of wild birds instead of shooting cartloads of driven game, reared and presented by the army of keepers the Old Squire had had in his hey-day.

He probably enjoyed his simple life as much as any of his ancestors—and there was certainly more variety to see on his estate than ever before, because all wildlife had more chance of survival. But when he died, the family fortunes took an all but fatal knock.

His son discovered that it was necessary to sell another fourteen hundred acres to pay for the taxman's greed so that all he fetched-up with was no more than the size of a decent farm.

The new squire never affected the haughty, autocratic manners of his ancestors and, indeed, there wasn't much to swank about now that the estate had withered from six thousand acres to an insignificant tenth of its size. But everybody respected and liked him for it and he was affectionately known as the Young Squire.

It was common practice, when an estate broke up, to sell the land but retain the sporting rights, at least for twenty-one years. Many tenant farmers, anxious to own their farms, preferred to buy them privately, without the sporting rights, than to let them go to auction where the price might jump by at least the value of the shooting, which might be taken by some *nouveau riche* industrialist who coveted it as a status symbol, under the delusion that he could ape his betters and strut around more arrogantly than genuine landed gentry.

So, although the Young Squire no longer owned most of the land, he retained the sporting rights which conferred on him the freedom to wander or shoot wherever the Squire had owned—though, because he was so popular, he would have been welcome to do so in any case.

He was as kind to me as his father and grandfather had been and we were more nearly the same generation, so that I got to know him better. The first thing I discovered was that there was one major difference between him and his ancestors. His mind was not one-tracked on sport, but was filled with the curiosity of real naturalists, who are fascinated by all they see.

Now in my thirties I, too, had long since passed the stage where I wanted to kill every living thing, either because it was traditional quarry for sportsmen, a predator of traditional quarry, or competed for food or habitat. I no longer collected butterflies or birds' eggs and, although I didn't begrudge sportsmen their sport, it held no attractions for me except in so far as I loved to see any good working dog perform, from a greyhound to a gundog, or sheepdog to a ratting terrier. And I still do.

With the Old Squire and the Squire, I had never broken out of the straitjacket of formality. No one of my generation ever got past the stage of addressing them as 'Sir'. Christian name terms were unthinkable. The Young Squire addressed me as Phil from the start instead of the more formal 'Drabble' that his forebears used.

It was a lesser spotted woodpecker that really broke the ice and showed me what depth of interest we shared in common.

There were several great rookeries on the estate, and the farmers annually complained about the havoc the rooks wrought to young corn. So, when the young birds fledged in about the middle of May, tenants and neighbours and friends were invited to come and thin them out a bit.

The Young Squire kept up the tradition and, when I turned up with my .22 rifle as usual, I was told he wanted to see me down by the moat. Slightly puzzled, because I knew there was no rookery down there, I wandered off to find him.

It was a marvellous spot surrounded by the mature trees and shrubs and velvet turf of the gardens of ancient stately homes which, at that time, had not yet surrendered their seclusion to hordes of gawping trippers. The still water of the moat mirrored the evening sky and painted a perfect likeness of the Hall, but it was standing on its head in recognition of the fact that we now lived in such a topsy-turvy world. The Young Squire was at the edge of the shrubbery, and he beckoned me to join him.

There was no doubt about his pedigree. I had so often seen the Squire, standing motionless as a surveyor's tripod, leaning slightly forward on his hazel thumbstick which acted as a third leg to hold him still as a statue.

His son was not standing, but sitting on a log, holding a pair of field glasses to his eyes. When he lowered them to say 'Good evening', there was the Squire's same aquiline nose and weather-beaten skin. Even their neat tweed suits were similar, so drenched

and dried by storm and sun that they seemed to have grown on their owners, rather than being fitted by skilful tailors. And, like their owners, whatever misuse and battering they suffered, there was always a touch of class about them that lesser men and off-the-peg clothes cannot emulate.

High up in a great chestnut tree, fifty yards in front of him, there was a tremendous commotion near a small hole. A pair of lesser spotted woodpeckers, smaller in size than starlings, but shaped as other woodpeckers, were indulging in a most beautiful display, the male bird floating effortlessly from tree top to tree top, showing off to his lady love. After a while, they both settled, rigid and motionless, on a branch by the nesthole they had excavated, content as any lovers to enjoy each other's company without the need for words.

Lesser spotted are probably the scarcest and certainly the least observed of woodpeckers found in England. They are shy and secretive, keeping themselves very much to themselves in the seclusion of high tree tops. So the Young Squire was delighted that a pair had honoured him by nesting across the moat, opposite his study window.

We sat watching them on that May night, with the trees at their freshest and greenest, but too early in the summer for us to be mobbed by midges. The stillness was emphasised by muffled gunfire from the rookeries across the park, too distant to be obtrusive, but an audible warning that there are many ways of enjoying the countryside.

My rifle remained unheeded, propped against a tree, because watching living woodpeckers already held more charm for me than testing my skill against young rooks which had not yet taken their first flight from the nest.

I told the Young Squire about the Old Squire's offer that I could have all the rabbits I could catch by putting a pinch of salt on their tails, and he replied that one of the chores of his childhood was to be sent to the Hall to stay with his grandfather in his holidays. Protocol was rigid, and punctuality and discipline obeyed by all from Morning Prayers, through every mealtime till final escape at bedtime. 'At the end of each holiday', he said, 'the ritual was always the same. My grandfather sent for me, pressed a five shilling piece into my hand, and said, 'Goodbye, my lad. Say your prayers and keep your bowels open!' Only I expect that bowels began with many stuttering b's.

As we got to know each other better, I mentioned Bloody Bill Brock, my tame badger—described more fully in *Badgers at my Window* and named after the famous character in Henry Williamson's short story. I was married by that time, and was in the middle of a long stretch working in industry. I understood the feelings of a bird in a cage, because I too was caged-up in a factory though, in my case, I could escape in the evenings and at weekends.

In retrospect, it seems strange that I should gratify my selfishness by keeping in confinement creatures I should otherwise have been unable to see.

By far my favourite was a badger, which as a cub I reared on the

bottle and which lived ten years with me. It would, of course, now be illegal to keep a pet badger in captivity, and I suppose it was indefensible then. But he didn't have such a bad time, in spite of his restrictions.

Bloody Bill Brock had a large loose box as headquarters, and he came in the house every night after coming for a walk with the dogs. No life for a badger, perhaps, but I know plenty of dogs which get less affection, less comfort and companionship, less exercise and worse food. I learned a great deal about badgers from him and I like to think that the enthusiasm he fired in me for writing about badgers does their cause good by drawing attention to those who persecute them.

The Young Squire shared my enthusiasm and invited me to take Bill Brock over to be introduced.

It is fair to say that Bill was very tame. He had come to me as a naked cub, which had not yet opened his eyes. I reared him on the bottle so that, as he grew up, he developed the fixation that I was his mother. There was a traumatic interlude, when he was about seven months old, well grown, husky and feeling his feet. Badger cubs, at that age, in the first autumn of their lives, are often driven from the home sett to seek a territory of their own. It is nature's way of dispersing the species to fill every suitable natural niche.

Nature is not instinctively kind. I sometimes wonder if her very practical method of persuading mothers to adopt the apparently unnatural course of turning on their own young, is to make certain they will find it preferable to leave the home sett in search of fresh territory.

Certainly my young badger gave me about all the punishment I was prepared to put up with. He only bit me in anger once, when an exceptionally stupid press photographer came. But his normal play grew so rough that the result was almost as painful.

A great many people who have reared young badgers give up at this stage and either have them put down by the vet, because they say they have turned nasty, or set them free to fend for themselves in someone else's wood. Badgers are such territorial creatures that the resident wild badgers nearly always kill such involuntary interlopers so that it would have been kinder to destroy them humanely in the first place—and kindest of all never to have taken them from their own dam.

I stand up to be counted with those who believe that if you keep a young creature under unnatural conditions, for your pleasure, it is your responsibility to see to its comfort and health and food and companionship and exercise till death do you part. So I put up with Bloody Bill's bullying in what corresponded to his tearaway teenage days, and was relieved that he soon replaced his needle-sharp baby teeth with a blunter, more civilised set and that he grew out of his bad habits when he grew up.

I had no qualms about taking him to meet the Young Squire and sample the delights of his estate and, in retrospect, it gives me great satisfaction to think that my badger was probably the first for very many generations to find 'Welcome' on the mat.

I don't think Bloody Bill appreciated it because badgers are so ill at ease when dumped in strange places. His instinct warned that some great, dominant boar badger, twice as heavy as he and well-practised in the art of fighting, might explode from the depths of every shadow. I was the only familiar object and, puny as my support might be, he calculated that I was the best of a bad lot and nothing would induce him to leave my side a yard!

The Young Squire was very amused by this because the result

was that I could stroll nonchalantly around the lawns and shrubbery without the least fear of losing Bloody Bill. He stuck to my heels closer than a spaniel dog, so Hannam was dug out of his retirement and summoned across from his cottage to witness the triumph of his protégé, who could train badgers to a higher standard of obedience than his spaniel dogs.

I felt very sorry for the old man. His eyes had long since lost their hypnotic penetration but, pale and rheumy as they were, they could see, all too clearly, a hated badger on 'his' patch, with no sign that anyone intended to clobber it. He stared at it with hatred but his courtesy forbade him to utter a word out of place. After bidding me 'Good evening', he turned the topic on what methods I had used to 'break' it. The whole of his working life he had produced gundogs for his master and himself—and for sale—not by training them but by 'breaking' them. In his experience, a dog was broken-in when it had its faults thrashed out of it with about as much kindness as Pavlov and the Russians use. Those that didn't make the grade were declared redundant with a charge of shot.

I explained that 'conventional' methods of dog-breaking would not work with badgers. They were tough creatures which would just turn nasty in adversity, and that the man who could handle a nasty badger that meant business was a better man than I was.

My explanation about young creatures becoming fixated on their dams, whether they were human babies and mothers, wild creatures and their dams or any youngster with a foster mother, produced polite, but noncommital grunts. He had never heard of fixation—and the idea went over his head.

When we got onto the subject of territorial instinct, we were on firmer, more common ground. He knew that if you found a badger sett, or a large land drain where badgers lay in hot, dry weather, successive waves of badgers could be trapped in the same place year after year. As fast as one colony was liquidated, it would be replaced by immigrants from the surrounding countryside. He'd trapped them, and the badger-skin hearthrug was there to prove it in his parlour. But he couldn't grasp the idea that *I* could ever be regarded as territory or a sheet anchor of security. Seeing Bloody Bill Brock loose on 'his' patch, even though he had retired and held no further responsibility for it, filled him with foreboding.

What if I were wrong? What if the horrible brute made a liar of me and dashed for freedom in the shrubbery? How could it be trapped or who would shoot it? And what damage might it do in the meantime? Hannam was relieved to find himself free to return home before the onus fell on him—and I was glad that he had gone because my badger stiffened at his approach as if his instinct detected a traditional enemy smelling of death. Bloody Bill then took a liking to an enormous clump of rhododendrons at the edge of the park. Whether there had been a rabbit there lately, or some other delicacy, or whether he was making good his second line of defence, driven by his subconscious dread of Hannam, I shall never know. But he chose to go to the far side of the clump every time I approached and he proved as deaf and obdurate as a dog before Hannam had broken it in, when I tried to persuade him to come out.

I was torn two ways. It was obviously vital to retrieve him before dusk fell or the keeper's worst fears might prove well-founded. On the other hand, I was not anxious to let my host know that there was the slightest danger that I would lose control.

Luck—and cunning—were on my side. I stayed still and quiet till he wondered where I was. When he ambled towards my side of the bush, and discovered me, I ran away. He didn't stop to reason why, but followed me. He had known me all his life. I was his sheet anchor, imprinted on his mind as a reliable friend.

The new-found thicket that he was exploring was a novelty, as yet unproven. My impending departure imposed the risks of relying on devils he didn't know in place of the one he did. So he followed me instinctively, as a reflex, and I scooped him up in my arms, pretending that that was the normal climax to our nightly games.

I took him home and left my host to contemplate the worries that are the price extorted for the privilege of being a landowner. By most calculations, the whole estate was doomed to inevitable disintegration. Its size had shrunk to a tenth in three generations. The family's past glories, ranging from breeding Diomed—the first horse to win the Derby—to victorious admirals, were now no more than oil paintings hanging on the wall. The soil beneath the owner's feet had been tortured and wracked by coalmining, so that the surface sagged in unexpected places. This had left subsidence pools, with dead trees sprouting from the water, as grim memorials of better times.

The Old Squire and the Squire would have been bereft without their sport. They came of generations which took their hereditary privileges as an inalienable right. Even when the outside world could see that things were going to the dogs, the front door of the Hall was always opened by a dignified butler, who seemed ancient enough to have arrived with William the Conqueror.

The Young Squire was different. The disaster couldn't have happened to a better man because he took it philosophically. His sense of humour was such that, when funds would no longer run to servants in the house, he installed a small electric cooker by the sideboard in the dining-room. The punch-line of his joke was a linen napkin draped on the arm of the marble statue in the corner, as a stand-in for the butler.

Instead of mourning the loss of his sporting amenities, he enjoyed the wildlife that filtered back when news got round that hostilities had ceased.

Barn owls returned to nest in outlying farm buildings, and in the numerous shelters in the post-and-rail paddocks, where racehorses and hunters had spent their drowsy summers in palmier days. Although barn owls do nothing but good, living largely on voles and mice, they have bills curved enough to give old-time keepers uncontrollable trigger fingers. Now that no one was there to shoot them, they uttered their traditional ghostly, banshee shrieks at night and fearlessly quartered the paddocks for voles before dusk fell.

Sparrow hawks came back to prospect for nests in the woods, as they had probably done for years. The vital difference was that their ancestors had stopped a charge of shot before they'd done their courting so no one but keepers had seen them. Now they could consummate their marriage with impunity.

In the good old days, the annual two-day rabbit shoot in the park had usually accounted for more than two thousand. Keepers were brought in from all surrounding beats about a week before, and every hole and warren was 'stunk-out' with creosote and the unmentionable concoctions which were every keeper's secret. The havoc such numbers of rabbits could wreak on crops and pasture was incalculable, but any stoat or fox which helped the tenant farmers by killing a few, for food, forfeited his life for spoiling the Old Squire's sport.

Less keepers spelt less rabbits because keepers culled their foes, so now part of the sportsman's job was done by natural predators, all of which delight a naturalist's eyes to watch.

The Young Squire enjoyed them all, especially the day when he discovered some most welcome new arrivals—and telephoned me to go and share his pleasure.

He had noticed that the holes of a huge and ancient rabbit warren, by a secluded wood, had suddenly been enlarged to about three times their normal size. Foxes often open up rabbit holes to use as nurseries in which to rear their cubs, or dig out a 'stop' where doe rabbits make their nests. No diet is as delectable to many predators as a litter of luscious young rabbits.

The workings in the warren by the wood were very different. Immense mounds of soil spilled in cartloads from the main passages, indicating that far more work had been done than simple enlargement. The sheer volume of the spoil heaps was evidence for all with eyes to see that large chambers must have been excavated deep in the heart of the hillside.

So when I was summoned to go badger-watching, I scarcely waited to put the telephone back on its hook. I'd seen stuffed badgers and badger skins; I'd collected Bloody Bill Brock, my tame badger, before his eyes were open, and reared him on the bottle. I'd been badger digging, with terriers, and seen them heaved from their holes with steel badger tongs, and smacked on the snout with a heavy steel spade until they gave up the ghost and died. But I'd never had the chance to see wild badgers in their own surroundings, going about their business undisturbed and naturally.

It was a superb summer evening and the Young Squire and I

sneaked off at about half past eight, to get completely hidden, in sight of the sett, in plenty of time before the cubs were expected to appear.

The holes were in a shady bank on the woodland edge, and there was an old fallen tree trunk overlooking them about twenty yards away but, before we reached it, there was such a medley of bangs and crashes in the undergrowth that it sounded as if a flock of sheep had broken into the wood.

Our muscles seized solid as we froze to immobility, ready to rain down curses on the head of whoever, or whatever, had caused the commotion and nipped our pleasure in the bud. If it wasn't straying cattle, perhaps something had disturbed a poacher or a courting couple. Whatever it was must surely have so alarmed the badgers in their sett that there would be no chance of seeing them that night. As we waited, the crashes came nearer and nearer the woodland edge, always in thickets too dense for either sheep or men to penetrate.

Then the expected took us by surprise. A few yards up the grassy ride, two badger cubs about as big as cats exploded into the open.

Although I had spent so much time in quiet places, this was what I had waited years to see. They were precisely as I expected, carbon copies of the best illustrations in the best books I had devoured all my life. Traditional badger-grey, traditional black and white striped faces, the staccato bounding gait of my beloved Bill Brock when he was young.

Despite this, they were different. They were wild and free, unmolested and unafraid. Instead of going badger watching, as I'd hoped, I'd broken my duck by badger listening! Their fur was fluffed out as rigid as a cat's tail in a panic, and their high-pitched, staccato chittering spoke volumes, not only about the excitement of their play, but about their relaxed sense of security. If they had been in the least disturbed or jittery, they would never have been able to kick up such a din so early in the evening.

It was the perfect way to get a first glimpse of wild badgers and the whole scene etched itself so sharply on my mind that, whenever I recall it, I still recapture the thrill of excitement.

The cubs were gone as quickly as they came. One pinched his

mate so sharply that their boisterous skirmish degenerated into such ill-humour that the aggressor traded valour for discretion, and the other chased him home.

I had been so excited that I must have held my breath in subconscious fear of scaring them. When the drama was over, I sucked in a lungful of fresh-air—but it was anything but fresh. The atmosphere of that cool summer's night was so charged with the stench of musk that the pong was almost tangible. My own badger, when he played, exuded the musky odour of all excited mustilidae. Whether he never got so excited or hand-rearing had civilised him a bit, I shall never know. But he certainly never reeked like those wild cubs.

Although the most vivid impressions of that first badger-watch were not of sight but sound and smell, it was but the beginning of a most memorable evening.

When the two cubs which opened the show had retreated in disorder, we took advantage of the rumpus to slide into the seat on the log. The cubs came out again for the second act, accompanied this time by the sow and the rest of her litter. They romped and rolled and skirmished, and pretended to settle down to work collecting bracken for bedding—but got bored and shed their bundles long before reaching the sett.

I've seen it all—and more—scores of times since, but those first cubs have given me as much pleasure in retrospect as they did at the time.

For many generations, keepers had so ruthlessly trapped any badgers that wandered onto an estate that these new arrivals heralded the dawn of a new era; an era when it was no longer acceptable to obliterate anything and everything which might conflict with game.

The irony was that, as soon as the tide turned in favour of what remained of this particular estate becoming a virtual wildlife sanctuary, an attack was launched on the undefended flank, and planners moved in to do the work of keepers even more efficiently. Their masters decided to dissipate some of the loot they had extorted from death duties by driving a motorway through the heart of the estate.

Seeing the writing on the wall, the Young Squire chucked in his hand, sold what was left of his ancestral home and took himself off to quieter quarters.

The Hall has been turned into a geriatrics' home; the M6 motorway slashed open the belly of the park, and a motorway service station stands within a stone's throw of Hannam's cottage. A wildlife sanctuary was vandalised at birth, but that, I suppose is Progress.

CHAPTER 2

The Boss Badger

The loss of my boyhood stamping-ground fired my own ambition. I had witnessed the destruction of the heritage of an ancient family who had always shown me kindness, and I admired the way they took it on the chin.

It suddenly dawned on me that the smaller and poorer the estate had become, the greater the variety of wildlife it had harboured; that the attraction of an area for shy creatures is not necessarily proportional to its size. All that seemed to be necessary was variety of habitat, and a sympathetic owner who could inspire a sense of seclusion and security—which is an asset that modern times sell short—for man or beast.

The dying embers of the estate I knew so well served to light a flame in me. Somehow, sometime I would have land of my own.

There was, of course, no chance that I should ever inherit an estate, still less that I could make enough hard cash to buy one. So I set my sights realistically low and eventually bought the derelict cottage and ninety acres of woodland I have described in *My Beloved Wilderness*.

The thrill of waking up as owner of a bit of England is hard to describe adequately, though it soon dawns that the pleasure is coupled with the inevitable responsibility of leaving it either better or worse for those that follow.

In the Old Squire's time, it would have been acceptable to pass it on with enhanced sporting potential. The envy of politicians, who covet such possessions, and levy taxes to cripple those who succeed where they fail, made improvement impossible. The Old Squire's estate had inevitably withered, but he died fighting the vermin that threatened his sport. Or commanding those who did! Succeeding generations saw it go further up the spout.

I am not interested in game alone, so that my idea of improvement is to leave my bit as a sanctuary which will support the maximum variety of birds and beasts and flowers.

When my wife and I walked round to hold a roll call of our new retainers, we found fallow deer and foxes and a heronry, as well as a wide variety of woodland birds—but no resident badgers. We were starting almost where the Young Squire left off.

Quite as important—there were no keepers. The whole area had been roamed over for years by men with guns, who had shot anything edible they had seen, on the principle that, if they didn't, the next chap would. When we had walked the ground, before buying it, a highly respectable local, with his gun, had slid sheepishly away, hoping that we hadn't seen him. Or, if we had, that we wouldn't recognise him again. I never let on—till now—that we did!

The absence of game had some advantages from my point of view. It did mean that other creatures, in which I was more interested, had been left in peace and could be encouraged to thrive in our wood.

The status of badgers in an area is a fair yardstick to the welfare of wildlife in general because, being both predators and easy to catch, they are among the first victims of the greed and stupidity which places pheasants above the Almighty in the countryside.

Although no badgers lived upon our land, they came nightly to the wood to feed, so I decided to try to encourage a nucleus by hand-rearing some cubs—two sows and a boar, known simply as Bill to differentiate him from my first Bloody Bill Brock. I established them at full liberty, in an artificial sett where we could watch them.

I have described the first part of this experiment in *Badgers at my Window*, and one of the most useful aids to observation was a mechanical device that recorded their activity.

In the interval between my boyhood when I used to run wild in keepered woods, and the time when we came to our wilderness, I had misspent twenty odd years in the engineering industry. I had been trained as a Time Study Engineer, chasing ineffective work and wasted effort and the rest of the nonsense that industrialists indulge in. You can't work that long in a factory without something rubbing off, so it irked me exceedingly to sit for several hours waiting to see my badgers emerge to frolic and to feed. No work is less productive than idle hours with nothing much to see.

An old friend in the trade built me a complicated piece of gadgetry, mainly from bits of scrap machines, which served my purpose admirably. Basically it was very simple. A flexible lever, made from a stiff spring, was fixed to an electric micro-switch at the entrance to the sett. Any badger entering or leaving deflected the spring, which tripped the switch which was wired to a barograph in my study. So, every time my hand-reared badgers came or went to the wood outside, the precise time was punched-up on the graph. They clocked themselves in and out!

After about a week I discovered that they had never been out before half past eight nor later than a quarter to nine. So hanging around waiting for them from about half past six was pretty ineffective work. The time to get cracking was eight twenty-nine.

But things don't work out like that. Up to sixty per cent of a badger's diet is earthworms which come out onto the dewy grass to mate, presumably because making love in the cramped confinement of their burrows would be such an unromantic pastime. So when the worms emerge, the badgers wander round and chobble them up while they're courting.

On warm and dewy summer nights, the paddock in front of our window positively heaves with worms. Hungry badgers soon have their fill—and full badgers sleep sound. So they are liable to lie in a bit next night.

But if the night is dry and windy, and food is hard to come by, they return to their setts, sharp and unsatisfied, and are likely to be abroad earlier the following night. So it was no good working too closely to the theory predicted by the barograph.

A minor modification solved the problem. I inserted a small pilot light in the circuit and placed it on top of the television. It was then possible to settle down in front of the box until the pilot light signalled that the time had come to switch off synthetic shadows in favour of live entertainment.

It was badger-watching at its best. No tedious waiting because the creatures themselves pressed the button that was the cue for us to drop everything in time to see the curtain rise. Normally, on summer evenings, mosquitoes are out in such numbers that freezing into immobility would tax the endurance of an Indian fakir. Just as some thrilling climax is approaching, a mammoth midge might settle on some tender spot and insert a proboscis that would have won a prize as a persuader in the Spanish Inquisition. A futile slap of self defence would put paid to the tormentor—but it would also scare the badgers for the night.

Not so with our badger-watching. The plate glass window of our sitting-room guaranteed immunity from winged warfare—and a well-charged glass set the seal on five-star status.

After a week or so, I analysed the results punched-up on the graph. As I expected, they showed that the badgers came out somewhere around dusk and finally returned to their sett about dawn. Every badger book had told me that and authorities on badgers, who had been badger-watching hundreds of times, claimed to be able to predict precisely the time of emergence. When you are widely recognised as an 'expert', it is natural to expect people to take your word as gospel—so I believed what the experts said.

Having kept nightly records on my barograph for five consecutive years, I now have doubts. The times my badgers showed up or went to bed varied widely. I plotted them against temperature and rainfall, full moon, light nights, dark nights and every other variable I could think of—and they taught me one thing for certain. I am as ignorant about what influences their decision when to roll out of bed or when to turn in as I was when I started. I learned only enough to teach me how little I know—and I now have my doubts about 'authorities' who claim to know it all.

I did, however, discover something which the experts never mentioned. I had expected badgers to come out at dusk and go to bed at dawn. Or thereabouts. They did, but what surprised me was that at intervals during the night, at perhaps 1 a.m. and 4 a.m., they used to return to their setts, popping in and out like Yoyos. They did not go off for the whole night as I had expected.

For half an hour or so—at unpredictable times—the spring in the entrance was deflected so often by badgers returning and being active at the sett that they punched-up an almost continual line on the graph. A long queue of workers clocking-in or out would have had a similar effect.

Even in high summer it is too dark to see what badgers do in the middle of the night, which may explain why badger books failed to report what my electronic-eye recorded on my graph. My pilot light indicated activity, so I inserted another light in the circuit. This time, it was no midget pilot but a floodlight capable of dispelling the gloom over quite a wide area. When a badger emerged, he would now deflect the spring, close the micro-switch, clock out on the graph and activate both tell-tale pilot and the floodlight on the sett. All that remained was to transfer the pilot to the bedroom—where it proved ineffective, because it failed to wake me!

This was remedied easily enough by including an audible buzzer in the circuit—but I doubt if it would have satisfied the scientists. They would have pointed out that the artificial floodlight might so change the behaviour pattern that the activities might no longer be typical of what wild badgers would do when unobserved.

There is no answer to that—except that many wild creatures seem unafraid of artificial light or mechanical noise. Animals have not yet tumbled to the fatal fact that, in every motor car there lurks a potentially lethal man. Pathetic corpses of rabbits and hedgehogs, foxes and badgers and deer, strewn along our roads at dawn, are proof enough of that.

Any poacher, skilled at 'lamping' with dogs, can tell you that he can creep out to the fields at dead of night, switch on the searchlight beam of his portable lamp, and 'spot' hares or rabbits or deer feeding peacefully on the turf. When he sees one well out in the open, he slips his dog which can get within a few yards of the quarry before the sound of his approach alerts it to the fact that artificial light is dangerous.

So whatever the experts said about the unnatural effects of floodlighting my sett, I was content to continue my evening entertainment by observing my badgers from the bedroom window.

The buzzer awakened me at three or four in the morning when I saw the paddock and sett bathed in light. If I leaped out of bed smartly, I was in time to see the badger that had triggered-off the signal emerge from his tunnel oblivious of the fact that it was his own action that had told me he was coming.

Unfortunately, the entertainment was often a flop. Badgers are fastidious creatures, spending more time prissing-up their homes than the most pernickity housewife. When I tumbled, bleary-eyed from bed, it was only to find my badgers either dragging bedding out of the sett to air, or dragging it back again. The endless succession of entrances and exits punched-up on my graph appeared to be nothing more than bedmaking!

Having been roused out of sleep at 4 a.m., it wasn't worth returning to bed till there was nothing more to see. In order to make sure of missing nothing, I watched until they finished their chores—or often simply messed about—when they either went back to bed or off into the wood or paddock to feed.

After half an hour or so of this, I'd got pretty chilly, even on a summer's night, and the nicest, most tolerant women do get narrow-minded with men who jump into bed, as cold as clams, at four or five in the morning! It became obvious that, if I didn't change my ways, it might lead to a confrontation.

So I put on my Time Study hat and soon came up with a brainwave. A mirror. I fixed a mirror to the top of the window so that, when a badger deflected the spring which tripped the switch and woke me up, I could lie comfortably in bed and watch what happened through the mirror by my window.

That, too, was a failure. I could see movement, but the image in the mirror was too small to be certain precisely what was happening. So I hopped out of bed to find out. And got cold. And got into trouble. I was back at square one again.

So I think, but am not certain, that the purpose of badger activity at the sett during the hours of darkness is mainly bed-making, but also partly play. My failure to be dogmatic spells the difference between the approach of an amateur naturalist who simply enjoys wildlife, and a professional academic who is absorbed only by his dedicated search for knowledge.

I did, however, add another gadget. It was years before Watergate, but we 'bugged' the sett for sound. I sunk a vertical drainpipe, large enough to accommodate a microphone, right into the heart of the sleeping den. A friend fixed me up with an ancient microphone, which we put in the den and connected to a loudspeaker in my study.

As the den was only a couple of feet by eighteen inches, the mike was never more than a foot from the badgers. It picked up every breath and grunt, every chicker of affection or chatter of annoyance. They couldn't even enjoy the comforting luxury of a scratch without my finding out.

The first thing I did in the morning was to switch on the speaker to establish that both had returned safely from their nocturnal expeditions. Bill, the boar, emitted roof-raising, stertorous snores. Louder, I was told, than mine, which I had previously understood to be impossible. The sow, his mate, was more refined.

As the day wore on, their breathing grew shallower as they approached the threshold where sleep slid into wakefulness. The snores subsided and they began to shuffle round and scratch for an hour or so before they emerged for the first time in the evening.

Whenever I heard a noise that was new to me, I pulled the jack out of the speaker and plugged it into my tape recorder. Over a period of months I compiled a fairly comprehensive glossary of their vocabulary on tape.

I already knew, from rearing cubs, that the affection call is a delightful, confidential chicker, not unlike a quiet version of a stallion's whinny. Bill regularly greeted me like this, and I have a treasured tape recording of a 'conversation' I held with him when I opened the lid of his den while he was sound asleep.

Badgers need fear no enemies but man (and other badgers!) so that it is less vital for them to be alert than foxes or hares or other creatures who it is virtually impossible to sneak upon unawares. Bill was sleeping deeply and it was some seconds before he stirred, even after I'd opened the lid and was talking quietly to him.

'Hello, Bill,' I said, very gently, so as not to startle him. Half-asleep, he chickered with relaxed affection. 'Hello,' I said again, and he replied a little louder, nuzzling my hand.

A stranger who might have stumbled across a grown man, head buried in a hole, apparently talking to himself, would have sent for the police or a headshrinker. But our only eavesdroppers were a microphone and my tape recorder, so that I can recall every syllable of that confidential chatter whenever I care to play back the tape. It is a remarkable recording that demonstrates what close accord is possible between man and beast by anyone who will take the trouble to establish mutual trust and security.

At that time, I had two artificial badger setts, one on each side of the paddock outside our window. The two badgers were free to use either, and to come and go as they liked to the wood outside, through a swinging 'badger-gate' mounted in the perimeter fence surrounding the whole enclosure.

They often slept apart, especially in hot weather, and the barograph in my study recorded their precise times of emergence and return to their setts.

We knew when things were about to happen because the pilot warned us in time for us to watch. Bill was usually up and about before his little sow. After a sensual scratch and a call at his latrine pit, he would amble over to the other sett but often halted at the entrance instead of going down the tunnel. After a considerable pause, the sow would emerge to join him.

We wondered what it was he said, so one night, I linked-in another microphone to record what went on *outside* the sett as well as in the den. The sound picture it painted was as vivid as any shadows on the television screen.

It picked up the peaceful background music of a singing thrush and flighting wild duck making patterns on the limpid pool nearby. From deep inside the sett, there was no sound but the steady breathing of the sleeping sow.

The first sign of Bill's approach was rustling as loud, it seemed, in summer grass, as the commotion in the undergrowth made by the first wild badgers that I had ever watched. Although they are such noisy, rumbustious brutes when they're relaxed, an unlocated cracking twig will alert them and hold them, still and silent, till they are satisfied it's safe; they can move with secret stealth when their suspicion is roused.

Bill had no such inhibitions. He came blundering to the mouth of the sett, stuck his head into the pipe and chickered his affection call to awake the sow. The mike in the sett registered rustling bedding as she stirred in sleep, followed by smacking lips and clicking teeth as she performed her toilet. When she was sleek and well-groomed, having satisfied her feminine instinct not to be seen until immaculate, she joined the boar at the mouth of the sett.

Not everything went smoothly. I had originally reared a boar and two sow cubs, but one young sow was hanged in a fox snare on a neighbouring farm.

Fearing for the safety of the survivors, I fastened up the badger-gate in the perimeter fence and confined them to the six acres or so up to the house. The fence was six feet high, secured with concrete around the base. Badgers are superb diggers, more powerful for their size than the latest thing in earthmoving machinery. What is more, they dig for the hell of it, simply because they love digging. So a concrete plinth around the bottom of the fence is treated with disdain by any badger intent on getting out.

I thought so much of my badgers that the mental picture of them vainly fighting for breath in a relentless wire snare made me feel sick. So I took rolls of sheep netting and laid them flat on the ground, lacing them at the edge to the bottom of the fence. The grass grew through this horizontal net and knitted it to the wire, binding it inseparably to the ground.

When the badgers had ideas of getting out, they naturally walked round close to the edge of the fence. When they tried to dig under it, the horizontal sheep netting prevented them. It did not occur to them that the solution was to go back the width of the sheep net away from the fence and tunnel under from there. Or not for a very long time!

One of the recurring problems of getting involved with animals is the conflict between giving them complete freedom, whatever the risks, and restricting their movements for their own good.

When Bill was five or six months old, I taught him to use the badger-gate, which was simply two posts set wide enough apart for him to pass through, with a plank, hinged at the top, to fill the gap. Badgers are bold enough to shove the swing gate out of the way, but foxes and rabbits are not. It is therefore simple to surround an enclosure with wire netting, which will keep rabbits in or out but allow badgers to pass through at will. My objective

had been to make the badger-gate seem as sinister as a trap so that if wild badgers caught my innocent cub on their territory, he could bolt for home without risk of their taking any chances by following him through the 'trap' set in the fence.

It didn't work because when they did catch him, he was so far from home that they would have killed him if I had not heard the commotion in time to rescue him. I then fastened up the badger-gate and shut him in till he grew up enough to take adequate care of himself.

I did not imprison Bill and his sow for very long. If I was living in dread of food poisoning, I should never dine in an hotel; or go out in my car, if my worry was sudden death. By the same token, I calculated that it was better for my badgers to live full lives than to fritter away their freedom in the confines of my enclosure. So I undid the badger-gate once more.

Bill was now a fully developed, husky boar, quite capable of protecting himself against any badger that disputed his right to be there. So I no longer had to worry for his safety if wild badgers were to settle locally.

Every night, the pilot light would flash, and the buzzer buzz to signify that one or both of them had answered the call of reveille. Bill would emerge, scratch, squat to taint his territory and ease springs at his latrine pit, precisely as the text books said he should. But then he would deviate from conventional badger patterns. Instead of going foraging, he would come to one of our sliding windows and do his best to demolish it in his efforts to scratch his way in. The easy remedy was to open it.

Once inside, he would swagger round, with the springy athletic lope that badgers use to signify their insolent contempt for potential rivals but, when he discovered where I was, his superiority would shell-off and he'd chicker with affection for the only equal that he recognised. Our pleasure was mutual. I would stoop to heave him off his feet and land him upside down on my lap, where he obviously enjoyed my caresses.

It was sometimes rather a bore to have to drop whatever else I was doing to make a fuss of him, but it was even more of a trial if I didn't. Having just been refreshed by sleep, his energy would be inexhaustible, his curiosity boundless. If a spring squeaked from the depths of the upholstery, he would rip open the chair cover to see if it was edible. He used to cannon into little tables and upset the ornaments that decorated them, bite visitors' ankles to see them playing knees-up-Mother-Brown, rout the dogs from the hearth to make them play catch-as-catch-can and generally create havoc. All hell was let loose when Bill arrived through the sliding window. The least of all evils was to pick him up and make a fuss of him.

I can't pretend that this was not also extremely flattering. Guests, who had been startled and alarmed by such furry pandemonium, were dumbfounded by the powers of a man who could still the raging tempest. Daniel in the lions' den had nothing on me when Bill subsided on my knee and we were as stilled in mutual admiration as any spinster and her poodle. 'A gift with animals', they used to say. 'Communion with Nature.'

I lapped it up, but was shrewd enough to heed Bill's early

warning. He would revel in his bit of fuss, but he only put up with it till he was bored. Whatever the visitors thought, he was in command and, when the spirit moved him, he'd roll over to recommence playing 'Lights Out' round the house.

Visitors had no way of sensing this, but I would feel his muscles tense and the tempo change from quiet affection to the urge for boisterous play, so I always beat him to the draw and would casually remark that 'He'd go on like this all night, if I let him, but I don't want him to lose his natural instinct. I'll put him out, I think.' So I'd casually get up, open the window and let him wander off into the paddock to join his sow.

When he was about four years old, I noticed a subtle change in his disposition. Superficially, all was the same and he called at the window and came in for a fuss. He undoubtedly regarded me as the dominant boar *in the house*. He played with me, suffered me to pick him up and enjoyed what, I suppose, corresponded with mutual grooming.

But, when I opened the window to put him out, he left me in no doubt that *he* was the dominant boar in *his* territory. If I followed him out into the paddock, he bit me!

Do not take it, from that, that he savaged me. He didn't. If he'd meant business, he could have amputated a finger as easily as we bite through a chipped potato. He only bit me hard enough to warn me that it would be stupid to risk a confrontation. He was quite an artist at this warlike game of bluff because he could grab my hand and hold me in his vicelike grip without ever quite drawing blood. When he decided to let me go, the blue imprints of his canine teeth remained in my flesh as bruises, but never, quite, as punctures.

As a naturalist, I realised precisely what was happening and bore him no grudge for his perfectly normal behaviour. He was not turning 'savage', far less 'treacherous'. The simple explanation was that he was getting as territorial as all wild badgers and would brook no competition, even mine, in what he regarded as 'his' territory. While I was soft enough to allow him to share my territory, all was well. But I could not assume, from that, that I or anyone else was welcome in his.

So many people have been tainted by the stupid anti-badger propaganda that it is necessary to emphasise the point that wild badgers are *not* dangerous. They are shy and secretive and will always retreat if they meet a man. Mine was emboldened to stand his ground with me—if only as a token—because he had been hand-reared and had grown up under the delusion that mankind would do badgers no harm. Domestic bulls and rams and stallions are all extremely dangerous once they have lost respect for man. So are wild animals, and a 'tame' stag can be more dangerous than a tiger.

Bill was just the same. He regarded me as harmless and so was quite prepared to discipline me if I showed signs of contesting his territory. But no wild badger would pose a similar threat.

I took Bill's action at face value. Respecting his territorial instinct, I never called his bluff but evolved a technique to cut out the risks.

When the time came to put him out, I made much of him and

would lie him on his back in the crook of my arm so that I could pleasure him by tickling his chest and his belly. Then I would open the sliding window, still keeping him resting on his back, roll him gently out, curled up like a hedgehog—and slide the window shut before he was sure which way up he was. He used to gather himself up, lithe as a steel spring, and bounce at the thick plate glass, fangs unsheathed in mock attack.

Although his aggression was partly make-believe, it gradually grew more serious so that there was plenty of time for the lesson to sink in that Bill, on his own territory, must be treated with far more respect that any wild badger because he had no fear of man. I accepted this completely and took no chances at all with him except in the house, where he returned the compliment by regarding me as boss.

Meanwhile, as I described in *My Beloved Wilderness*, we got a superb tape recording of badgers mating. It is known that badgers can mate during a very protracted period from spring to autumn, but that the sperm is not embedded in the wall of the uterus until about the turn of the year. Normal pregnancy does not begin till then and the embryos develop in time for young to be born within a few weeks each side of February, irrespective of when the sow was mated.

I knew that my sow had been in season at the time we recorded the noise we were sure was mating, so that anticipation swelled as February approached.

The first clues of changing behaviour were thrown up by the barograph. The activity rhythm of the boar stayed fairly constant but the sow did not venture far past her latrine pit for days on end. I was putting out a nightly ration of bread-and-treacle, which she loved, but even this held no attraction for several nights running. So I waited for Bill to emerge and pass through the badger-gate into the wood, and then I slipped down to bolt it to keep him safely out of the way. This left me free to concentrate on madam.

I had deliberately refrained from getting her as tame as Bill. I wanted any facts I discovered about her behaviour to be immune from boffins' claims that observations on hand-reared animals are not admissable as evidence of 'typical' behaviour in the wild. I was quite aware that such criticism would be levelled but, so long as I was satisfied that my deductions were valid, I was happy to consign to the dustbin the carping of the critics as sour grapes.

As soon as Bill was safely in the wood—and the gate between us was well secured—I took some chunks of bread and honey to seduce his mate. She adored bread-and-treacle, but would sell her soul for honey. Although she was by no means fixated on me, as Bill had been, she treated me with confidence and came out as soon as her sensitive nose discovered the heady aroma of honey. She took some from my hand and suffered me to lift her up without complaint. Her belly was fat and round with young, so that there was no doubt whatever in my mind that the tape which we had made the previous spring had been an authentic record of badgers mating. My main concern, now, was to allow nothing to disturb her.

It would be exciting enough to have badgers which, if they were not breeding in captivity, at least were docile enough to be classified as 'tame'. But plenty of folk have had cubs born in a cage, so that success with ours at liberty would excite nobody but us.

What really would be exciting, however, would be to have cubs born and reared within a foot or so of a microphone, so that it might be possible to get a comprehensive set of tape recordings, literally from the instant the cubs first drew breath, while the sow was rearing them, and until they first appeared above ground so that we could compare their behaviour with the cubs we had hand-reared.

The higher one allows such hopes to soar, the further they have to fall. It is common for boar badgers to leave the sett and take up solitary quarters when cubs are born. This could be an understandable chauvanistic reluctance to put up with the mess and bother of young cubs and the fussiness of their mothers. Or it could be that the sows neither like nor trust crusty boars around when they are nursing—and give them the order of the boot. Even in large setts, containing a colony of badgers which all remain during the breeding season, the sows choose a private 'oven' or den in which to have their young.

So I was rather apprehensive every time I switched on my microphone. The badgers' den was only small, and could not be enlarged by them because I had built it of solid planks into which the earthen entrance pipe fitted snugly.

On the far side of the paddock, between the pool and the wood, was the other artificial sett. If anything, it was slightly larger; it was built in warm dry loam, dredged from the pool, and there was hard evidence that Bill liked it because he spent his time there in hot weather. I wished he'd go there so that his sow could have her cubs in peace.

He didn't though. His obtrusive, coarse snores assaulted my ears every time I turned on the speaker. So I began to wonder if the sow's reluctance to wander more than a few yards from the entrance of the sett was because she didn't trust her mate to be there on his own.

I shall never know. In the middle of February, just when I hoped she'd produce her cubs, she left the sett and started her old routine again as if there had never been a break in the pattern. As soon as I saw her away from the sett, I switched on sound, hoping against hope to hear the whimpering of tiny cubs. Nothing but silence, so for the second time I caught her up and examined her profile.

She had regained her maidenly figure. No distended belly nor suckled teats. No vaginal signs of parturition. I never did discover whether she had cubs or not that year. If she did, and they were stillborn, she may have eaten them when clearing up her afterbirth, as bitches will sometimes do. If they were born alive, Bill may have fancied them for supper.

When I was a boy, I didn't know enough not to remove my hob ferret from his mate, the jill, when her time was up to kit. He certainly ate the litter he had fathered, and badgers are mustilidae, as ferrets are, so that might be one of their uncommon factors. The mystery remained unsolved, but I decided, if there was any chance of the sow being in-cub next year, that I would catch up Bill and cage him till all danger to his cubs was past—whether he had been guilty of infanticide this time or whether I'd misjudged him!

Meanwhile, I had a visit from my neighbour Edward Froggatt. It might even qualify for the title 'Visitation'. He is an extremely

good neighbour who farms the land opposite our house and he lives a quarter of a mile away down the drive. I often pop down on my tractor to borrow his disc harrows or trailer, or a few bales of straw—which he never expects me to return. He calls round occasionally to borrow my ladder or drain rods or any tool I've got that he hasn't. That's what neighbours are for in the country.

So, when he arrived at the back door, I assumed his drains were blocked again but, before I could tell him where the rods were, he beat me to the punch.

'You'll have to do something about that brock of yours,' he said. 'We can't get any sleep.'

Badgers are not noisy creatures, so I asked him to expand. 'He comes in our dairy', he said, 'about four in the morning, and rattles the empty churns about.' Not taking him very seriously, I told him that, if only he'd got a clear conscience, he'd sleep through it. 'I'm not joking,' he said. 'Look at my trousers.' I couldn't quite see what his trousers had got to do with the noise in dairy, and replied that they looked much as usual to me. 'They're not, you know. Your brock ripped them to shreds last night.' His working clothes are never Savile Row, but I made suitable sympathetic noises.

Apparently, getting fed-up with hearing empty churns racketting round the yard and dairy, Edward had pulled a pair of

trousers over his pyjamas and gone down to chivvy old Bill Brock
back home. But, instead of accepting his marching orders with
good grace, it was Bill who did the chivvying, and his host who
beat a retreat, leaving part of his trouser leg in the badger's jaws.

I did my best to get him acquitted. I explained that he was very
playful and that, now he was adult, his idea of a game was rather
rough, but, if the quality of the trousers had been better, I was sure
he wouldn't have torn them! We parted, as ever, the best of
friends—but I was secretly worried. I knew that Bill was extremely
territorial about the paddock at home; even I did not venture into
it. If my badger had decided that, now he was adult and a bit above
himself, it was time to increase his territory, he might well be as
jealous and protective further from home. If Edward's dairy
happened to fall within the territory he had coveted and annexed, I
was quite certain that he might defend it.

Next night, things came to a head. The telephone rang about 2
a.m. and my neighbour sounded slightly testy. 'Your bloody
brock's in my dairy again,' he said. 'We can't get to sleep, so come
and fetch him.'

Jumping in the car, in wellingtons and pyjamas, I was there
inside the minute. The yard lights were on and the whole Froggatt
family had got themselves a ringside seat in the back porch, from
which they could watch through the window with impunity.

As soon as he heard someone in the yard, Bill emerged from the dairy and, without waiting to see who it was, made a bee-line for my feet.

Welly boots offer scant protection and I went smartly into a knees-up-Mother-Brown routine, trying to keep my feet safely out of his reach. The laws of gravity being what they are, this always left one foot on the ground—which he promptly bit! Instinctively, I stooped down and gathered him up into my arms. As soon as he knew it was me, his tense muscles relaxed and he sagged, inert and passive. That would show the Froggatts that it was only a game and, anyway, that I was boss.

Unfortunately, the demonstration so impressed the whole family that they all started talking at once.

The instant Bill heard strange voices, he tautened as hard as steel, wriggled in my grasp—and bit my hand. If he'd meant business, he could have severed a finger, or sunk his great canine teeth into my flesh up to his gums. He didn't do that. But he bit me quite hard enough to convince me that, if I didn't put him down, I was going to get properly mauled. So I put him down and hopped smartly into the car before he started on my feet again.

My hosts thought it all hilarious and, to my pride and credit, I didn't let on that he'd nipped me in anything but play. Once safely in the car, I laughed it off, said I'd told them it was only a game, and that I expected he'd be home before I was.

In fact, I was very worried. I knew perfectly well that no wild badger would ever throw caution to the winds by attacking a human being. But my brock was hand-reared and he had no fear of man. He had lost his natural respect for the human race and was no safer than a bull or a stallion. If I allowed him to continue wandering round and enlarging his territory, sooner or later he would bite someone.

Next morning, I'd got a fist as big and swollen as a prize fighter's—and the only reason I wasn't lame was that it was equally painful to put either foot to the ground. The only thing to do was to bolt up the badger-gate and keep both badgers confined to the enclosure abutting the house.

To my surprise, they didn't object a bit. I gave them a varied and liberal bowl of food every night, to supplement what they could forage for themselves, and they made no attempts to dig out and escape. We still kept the micro-switch going, to monitor their hours of activity and the microphone inside the den. My first job in the morning was to switch on the speaker, just to satisfy myself that they were both safely at home.

When Bill no longer went outside the enclosure, wild badgers grew bolder and came right up to the fence. I believe that, for some time, he had been well able to look after himself and had been enlarging his territory to the extent that he was able to defend it against rival badgers. I reckon that any which crossed his invisible boundary, which would be clearly marked by tainting it with highly personalised musk, got more than they bargained for.

After I had confined him for a while, the outside territory no longer reeked of warning musk so that badgers from the surrounding countryside could spill over the borders into what had been Bill's territory. Meeting no opposition, they got bolder until they came right up to the fence of his enclosure. This went through woodland and scrub, round the pool and paddock, along the edge of the garden until it joined one side of the house.

Within weeks, the strange badgers had worn a visible path—or 'run'—along the outside of the wire netting and Bill had worn one immediately inside. On moonlit nights and as dusk was falling, we could sometimes see him patrolling his side of the fence while a wild badger kept pace with him outside. They could both threaten each other to their hearts' content and, since neither ever got a hiding, each had the luxury of deluding himself that he was master.

In spite of this intense territorial aggression, he still came to the window each night and demanded to be let in. Once inside the house, his extrovert bombast shelled-off and he was his old gentle, affectionate self. The brute that had put me to flight from the farmyard next door, lay on his back on my lap to have his belly scratched!

I still had to be extremely careful how I put him out of the sliding window and was under no delusions about the sort of welcome I should get if I overstepped my mark and trespassed into *his* territory.

Oddly enough, it was not Bill but his mate which discovered how to escape. She began to scratch close at the foot of the vertical fence, but the horizontal sheep netting, laid at right angles to the fence along the ground, prevented her from digging under. Each mesh of the sheep netting was four inches in diameter, so she was able to stick her front leg through and excavate to a depth of about five inches before the steel mesh stopped her. Then she started again in the next hole of the netting and, when it stopped her, the next one to that. Gradually, she had loosened quite a patch of soil under the net laid on the ground until, at last, she came to the edge of it.

From then on it was simple. She just dug a trench right under the flat sheep netting—and on out under the fence.

When I switched on the speaker one morning, there was the sound of only one badger sleeping. The depth of the snores left little doubt which it was, but I decided to open the kennel to find out.

On the face of it, this might seem a pretty hazardous thing to do, for if he regarded anywhere as sacred, one would think it would be his den. When I opened the lid, he never made the slightest protest. He simply chickered his affection call, as he had when still a cub, and suffered me to make much of him. It would have been interesting to have opened it at night, before he had come out, to see if he was sensitive to disturbance during his normal hours of activity but reverted to his behaviour as a cub in daylight hours. Insatiable as my curiosity is, my experience when I had accosted him in the farmyard was far too vivid in my mind to take any more chances with him when night had fallen.

Whenever I discovered that the sow was missing, I would walk the fence to see where she had escaped. I tried all sorts of ruses to prevent her moving the netting, from putting strands of stretched barbed wire along and pegging them down, to fixing suspect patches with barrow loads of concrete.

None of them was effective, but as Bill showed no signs of following her, I usually left her escape channel untouched till she had returned, and then did what I could to seal it off.

Sometimes she would be back the following night, sometimes she would be missing for a few days—and once for four weeks. After a couple of weeks on that occasion, I thought that she had probably been snared and that that was the end of her, so I made good the escape route.

I had built a cage trap into the perimeter fence. It was about six feet long by two feet wide and high, and was covered with very heavy gauge welded netting. It had a steel shutter that closed when an animal entered and stepped on a treadle. There it had to stay till I came round the next morning to release it unharmed or otherwise deal with it, depending on what it was. The treadle needed only the lightest weight to spring the trap and, although I designed it mainly for foxes, it also caught rats and squirrels, rabbits and birds or anything else that entered.

Long after I had given up hope of seeing the sow again, I was delighted to find her sitting in my cage trap in the fence.

Badgers, although they are so aggressive about territory, live in quite large colonies in some old setts, and even the adult males don't fight. This is said to be avoided by tainting each other with musk because it is not done, in the best badger circles, to fight chaps who smell like you!

The sow hadn't been home for just about four weeks so that it was reasonable to believe that any 'colony taint' she had acquired from my Bill Brock would long since have been dissipated. Worse still, from his point of view, she might well have joined a wild colony so that her unfaithfulness would be highlighted by some strange boar marking her with his own distinctive musk.

Prudence suggested that I should keep her safe in quarantine and bed her down in material filched from Bill's own bed. Only when she had slept in hay with his homely smell long enough for its distinctive odour to obliterate all cause for jealousy would it be really safe to reintroduce her to her original mate.

But prudence and curiosity are often incompatible. I had read scholarly papers about badgers being savaged for going into the territory of other badgers, untainted by the correct musk to give them immunity. I had heard learned lecturers going on about it till it almost came out of their ears. The cynical doubt often entered my mind that they might only be echoing the empty theories from books written by others and that few of them had first-hand experience.

I like to test such theories for myself, so I left the sow badger safe in the cage trap and went to the sett where Bill was sleeping in celibate solitude. Having made much of him and been greeted with affection in response, I gently lifted him out of the sett and carried him to the shed where both had been confined while I was rearing them as cubs.

The moment to release the sow had now arrived. I opened the sliding steel shutter that had slammed behind her when she'd touched the treadle and she came out into a small transfer box as easily as sheep are guided into the right pen by a sheep dog. I took no risk of handling her, partly because I didn't want to dilute any strange scent she carried with powerful human pong—and partly because I thought she might bite in defence after spending so long with her own kind in the wild.

I released her within a few feet of Bill's artificial sett and she went straight to the entrance as if she'd left it only the day before. When I had left her in peace for several hours, I switched on the speaker in my study to see if she had settled down. Refined rhythmic snores were eloquent of her contentment, telling of her delight at being home as plainly as if she had put it into words.

The time had come to turn Bill loose so that he could return and find her in his bed. I plugged the microphone into my tape recorder so I could put the theories to the test and confirm them or tear them to shreds.

So far, the experiment had been very stimulating. It is always exciting to make observations on the behaviour of animals in fresh situations, but however easy it is to be objective and detached with strangers, Bill and his sow were my friends.

What if the boffins had been right? What if the crusty old boar went berserk at finding an interloper in his den? For he might *think* she was a stranger if she didn't smell like him. The possibilities were endless and the prospect alarming. He might savage her pitilessly, as the wild boar had once mauled him to the point of death.

If he did, I should be well aware of what was happening because the tape recorder would eavesdrop and give a horrific round-by-round description. Meanwhile, I should be powerless to intervene, because the battle might be fought somewhere out of reach in the tunnel between the entrance and the den. Even if they erupted into the open, parting them would be almost impossible without taking stupid risks, in spite of the fact that I'd had more than enough practice with the bull terriers of my youth.

The sensible thing to do was to introduce them through wire netting which could be an effective barrier to save either from serious harm. I should have thought of this earlier. By the time the extent of my stupidity had dawned on me, it was too late, for I had set Bill free to return to his sett.

Unaware that anything unusual was afoot, he was infuriatingly slow. He stopped and scratched, as if he was lousy, and then he discovered that he hadn't emptied his bowels since the day before. So he selected the precise site for a latrine pit with the prissy precision of a professional sanitary inspector, and took so long about the job that he was obviously enjoying life's simple pleasures to the full.

I was sorely tempted to rush out, scoop him up and return him to the shed where I had confined him, but I knew how touchy he was about welcoming anyone else to his territory and, to my shame, I valued my skin even more highly than my conscience valued the welfare of his sow!

He gave me plenty of time for mature deliberation. Dor beetles had burrowed under the manure heap, so he excavated a few of them and crunched them up with the appreciation of a connoisseur. He found a field vole under a tussock and wasted time vainly poking around for that. Then he got itchy again and had another scratch.

Meanwhile, the tape recorder was crooning a lullaby of soft wheezes and gentle snores as the sow slept on, oblivious either of the threat that approached so slowly or of my nail-biting apprehension about the fate in store for her.

Normally, when he was disturbed by day, Bill would make a bee-line for his sanctuary. This time he seemed to prolong the suspense deliberately. Even when he arrived at the entrance to the den, he showed neither surprise nor anger nor delight. I was certain his sensitive nose must have told him that either a friend or stranger had passed that way and I was in agonies to know whether he remembered the scent of his sow or if it was masked by her sojourn in the back of beyond. He paused, deliberately, at the entrance and had a good shake to flick all dirt and grit and grass seeds from his immaculate fur.

Then the barograph clicked as he entered the pipe and recorded the precise time. It reminded me of policemen taking down particulars of crime. 'At 2.17 precisely, the accused entered the premises . . .' Then the microphone picked-up his shuffling gait along the smooth pipe, gradually amplifying it to the background sibilant wheezes of the sleeping sow.

She slept on in innocence so that it sounded as if he was right inside the den before she sensed his presence. Then all hell was let loose. The crisp, dry bedding crackled and rustled with movement so that, for long seconds, it was impossible to decide whether they were locked in mortal combat or if he had only made her jump with fright. I suddenly realised how impotent I was to help if he didn't recognise her but set about her savagely.

With wild badgers, under natural conditions, it could have been fascinating to watch the outcome objectively, whichever way it went. But I was too involved to be dispassionate. I had warmed them and cleaned them and bottle-fed them as cubs. We had built up a relationship that was almost telepathic and, if harm resulted from the experiment I had set up, I should feel as bad about it as if my carelessness had resulted in injury to a friend.

I need not have worried. When the commotion in the bedding died down, it was replaced by whickers of affection and clicking of teeth, as they groomed each other, that made the slickest castanet players slow amateurs by comparison. They left me in no doubt that their pleasure at being reunited was mutually intense. Ten minutes later, my microphone told me they were sleeping the sleep of the just, as if time had never parted them.

The fact that I was worried that the sow would have been tainted by wild badgers was some yardstick of their presence. I live in good badger country, with ninety acres of my own and a thousand, let to the Forestry Commission, on my boundary. This, in turn, merges with miles of wooded country, because I live on the edge of the ancient Forest of Needwood. It still abounds with wild fallow deer and a wide variety of woodland birds and, at that time, had enjoyed years of freedom from keepers who prey on predators.

Compared to the Old Squire's estates, it was a miserable area for game but rich in the creatures which would have decorated the gibbets of my childhood memories. My only regret was that Bill's aggressive tendencies had forced me to set a limit on where he was free to roam.

It was obviously a wise decision because, as time went on, his temper grew worse, not better. The fence that bounded the enclosure included one side of the house. It was possible to walk out of the sliding windows of my study or the sitting-room directly into the enclosure. It was also possible for the badgers to come directly into the house from the paddock outside.

The yard, on the other side of the enclosure, is also fenced, so that the dogs can run out of the back door into a large yard and small paddock, where they are loose at night, free to discourage intruders. More welcome visitors leave their cars in the safety of the yard and could often see the badgers in their headlights.

If Bill was out when I was seeing guests off, he came to the fence to investigate. This was a friendly gesture while he was still a cub, but I noticed, as the years crept on, that this greeting changed. His

fur fluffed out and any approach to the fence, which was the boundary of his territory, was greeted by low growls that seemed the more menacing because they did not bluster.

By the time I had been forced to keep him in, to avoid further trouble in the Froggatts' dairy, he didn't just amble up to the fence to speed our parting guests, he rampaged up like a tornado. It didn't need the expertise of academics to deduce that he'd be a rough customer to tangle with. As the fowl pen was also in the paddock, I wasn't afraid of having my Christmas dinner pinched!

This deterioration of his temper was very gradual and took several years to manifest itself. I cannot over-emphasise that it was simply because he had lost his respect of man and it would never happen in the wild. Nevertheless, the change was progressive and even I was surprised to discover that it was not always limited to the hours of dusk or darkness.

About this time, I was training Tick, my German pointer, who is one of the most intelligent and faithful dogs of my life. If I was bright enough to show her what I wanted, it was her pleasure to comply. She had hardly ever needed a cross word—and never a blow in anger. I took advantage of this by using her a lot on television and was filming her training out in the paddock. It was a glorious summer afternoon and my wife Jess and a friend were sitting on the terrace as spectators.

Derek Johnson, the cameraman, looked up and remarked casually that 'the badger's watching too, from the entrance to his hole'.

Surprised that he was awake at this time of day, I looked across to see a white striped head, a hundred yards away, with the white-tipped ears showing prominently.

At that distance, I knew he wouldn't be *watching* for badgers are short-sighted. There was no doubt, however, that he was listening and, as I observed him, he sallied forth into the open.

He did not normally leave the sett at that time of day, and I could tell by his attitude that he was ripe for trouble. 'Run', I said. 'He'll have you.' Derek went on filming the dog as if he hadn't heard.

'Run, he'll bite you.' He continued with the job in hand. He'd worked with me a lot and was well used to my warped sense of humour. He thought I was playing a joke to make him look stupid in front of the women, so he wasn't falling for it.

By this time, Bill was well out in the open, coming straight for us. 'Run, you bloody fool', I yelled, 'I mean it. He'll bite you.'

This got him going. He knew I must be in earnest or I wouldn't have sworn at him in front of women. So he ran.

So did Bill—and badgers are much faster than their lumbering gait suggests. Derek had about sixty yards to make the sanctuary of the gate, Bill perhaps twenty more. I stayed where I was with Tick, because it was the sound of his retreating quarry that guided Bill.

It would have been a thrilling race to watch if the stakes had not been so high—and no bookie would have laid more than evens either way.

As things turned out, Derek made it by a short head, literally slamming the gate in his pursuer's face. Bill was furious. He snorted with rage and ripped at the unyielding netting with his wicked canine teeth. The ghost of Hannam whispered, 'Told you so.'

The climax over, I signed to Tick—and we stole quietly away to escape from the paddock through the gate to the wood on the other side. We found Bill, still expressing his contempt for my guest by tainting the ground his side of the gate, masking the stench of cameraman with his highly personalised musk.

The whole episode put the wind up me. I had realised how dangerously territorial he was when he saw me off for interfering with his conquest of the Froggatt dairy, but it hadn't occurred to me that it was necessary to keep out of his enclosure, except at night. So, as soon as Derek had departed, I set to and made a heavy steel grille, which I could fasten over the entrance to his sett and imprison him when any stranger was in the enclosure—day or night.

Next morning I switched on the mike for my routine roll call—and was surprised to hear that only one badger lay there asleep. Judging by the ladylike sighs, it was Bill who had gone missing. I immediately confirmed it by taking the top off the sett and having a look for myself. The next thing to do was to walk the perimeter fence to see where he had escaped—and I soon discovered that he had chosen a spot I had filled in where the sow had tunnelled under the horizontal sheep netting laced to the boundary fence. He had opened it up and left an ugly hole for all the world to see—though fortunately, it was on the side farthest from Froggatts, where the wood joins the paddock.

I didn't want to cause needless alarm, but the least I could do was to telephone my neighbours, saying, 'Bill is out—and I don't think he's too friendly. So I shouldn't hang around if you meet him.'

About seven o'clock that night, in brilliant sunshine, Jess looked out of the window, and said, 'Oh, good. Bill's back!' Ambling quietly down to the pool for a drink was a badger. But it was much smaller than Bill. I should know, I handled him every night.

'No, that's not Bill,' I said. 'That's the little sow.' Besides, Bill would have lain up in part of the wood that was strange to him till dusk. He'd had more than enough time to forget his old haunts since I'd retained him in the enclosure. 'That's the sow all right; I don't reckon he'll show up till dusk falls and everything is quiet,' I said.

'You're wrong, you know. That's Bill,' was the reply.

The connubial wrangle continued pointlessly till I decided to settle it once and for all. 'I'll go out and bring her up, to prove it,' I said.

The nearer I got, the more certain I was right. Bill was a husky virile brock, half as big again as his sow. Eighty yards from the house, at the edge of the pool, I realised she was right and I was wrong. It was certainly Bill. So I set off full pelt for home—and I didn't have the start that Derek had. Bill changed into top gear, but I knew what the stakes were—and Derek had been blissfully ignorant. The incentive got me at full stretch and I held him off till we got to the house and dead-heated on the study steps.

Luckily, Jess had risen to the occasion and was holding the study window open. Bill collared first one foot and then the other, forcing me to put on a star performance of acrobatic dancing. The moment both feet were free, I popped through the window with Bill at my heels. Jess heaved shut the sliding window, pinning his head between the heavy plate glass panel and the frame. Tough as he was, it stopped him in his tracks and when he struggled and freed himself, she slammed it firmly home.

I could feel my shoe filling with blood because the damage had not been caused so much by the power of the bite as by the fact that he had shaken and worried whatever he got hold of, so effectively that the wound took ten weeks to heal.

It was nobody's fault but my own. I knew perfectly well that wild badgers are so shy that under no circumstances at all will they attack a man. But I was equally well aware that Bill had lost his respect for man and was as fearless as a bull.

There was no question of 'treachery' or 'turning suddenly savage'. The whole process had been a gradually growing intolerance of anyone—including me—invading *his* territory. He had given me plenty of notice of his intent and I had been fool enough to ignore it and had failed to check before approaching him in the paddock. So I got what I deserved.

I would have taken it as one of the hazards of my occupation as a naturalist, and been more careful next time—if he had not escaped the night before. But he had demonstrated too clearly, not only that he would brook no interference, but also that he was capable of escaping whenever he liked.

It was only luck that he had savaged me and not a neighbour.

I consider myself entitled to decide what risks I take myself—but that I have no right to inflict such risks on others. So I took my rifle from the rack and shot him.

I have never had to do a more repulsive job. I had reared him, myself, five years before, and worked and played with him ever since. He always trusted me implicitly and was his normal affectionate self when he came in the house. He had made it abundantly clear to me what conduct he liked, what he would tolerate—and what he would not put up with.

His only crime was the natural one of guarding his own territory—and it was no fault of his that companionship with man had eroded his natural shyness. I felt as bad about it as if I had been forced to shoot a favourite dog.

CHAPTER 3

Nice Guys

When Bill was dead, I decided to meet the criticism of the doubting Toms who were always sceptical about the validity of any observation made on hand-reared animals.

I agreed that their behaviour was not always typical of the reactions of truly wild animals in similar circumstances. My badgers had no fear of me so that, if I appeared suddenly and said 'Boo', they came to see what tit-bits I had brought. Wild badgers would have run a mile.

On the other hand, the glossary of badger vocabulary I had encapsulated on my tape recorder had neither gained nor lost anything because of me. And the fact that I could approach unheeded allowed me to make detailed observations that would have been most difficult in the wild.

Nevertheless, I accepted the criticism and was determined to try to prove my theories by repeating the work with wild badgers.

This would have been impossible in the Old Squire's day because the life expectancy of wild badgers in heavily keepered country was so short. But if I had searched far and wide for the ideal area to conduct my experiments, I could not have chosen a spot with better potential than the wood I had been lucky enough to buy.

It is on the edge of a very large area of the ancient Forest of Needwood where badgers doubtless flourished before William the Conqueror was even thought of. It is very banky country, much of it difficult for foresters to work and impossible for farmers—but ideal for deer and foxes and badgers and the woodland birds that thrive in quiet places.

The surrounding farmers mostly set a few snares for foxes before their sheep lamb in the spring—and they catch a few badgers too, some by accident and others by design. But it only skims the cream and makes no permanent dent in the total population.

The land next to me, on the wood side, all belongs to one owner who only visits it occasionally because he lives fifty miles away. This farm, of about a thousand acres, is run by a farm manager, and there is also about a thousand acres of woodland let to the Forestry Commission who have plastered it with the miserable sterility of Corsican pines.

The owner is not interested in shooting and, for the first few years we were here, he was too busy reclaiming the clapped-out parkland to bother about letting the sporting rights. Nobody shot a hawk or an owl, snared a fox or badger, or nailed a stoat or weasel to a gibbet.

From my viewpoint it was paradise, but paradise is a transitory state. The owner of the estate eventually contacted me and said that, although he wasn't going to let the shoot at the moment, he had given permission to some friends to shoot there for the next few years.

It was a nail-biting time. My worst fear was that the friends might turn out to be typical of some of the syndicates I come across in my profession as a writer and broadcaster about rural matters.

Shooting has lately become a status symbol of Big Business. Mini-tycoons make their pile of brass and discover that there are various tax wangles which allow them to flaunt their success by owning or renting a shoot. 'Entertainment' expenses are apparently allowable for foreign customers. So foreign customers are suddenly deluged with invitations to join their suppliers for a day or so's sport. Although many of the wangles don't bear close scrutiny, a lot of business men manage to get their sport at the expense of those who do pay taxes.

Since it is usually something quite out of their sphere, such men are often abysmally ignorant of the customs and ethics of the countryside. They employ a keeper, who usually fills them with whatever tall stories he likes—because they don't know enough to realise when they are being spoofed. They never visit the shoot except on shooting days, so they have no idea what other wildlife shares a livelihood with their pheasants—and many of them couldn't tell the difference between a bull and a bulrush if they saw them side by side. If their yellow Labrador retrievers enter thick cover for a bird, they risk a charge of shot from some oaf who mistakes them for fox. Their main interest is in the number of birds they shoot, what their outlay is, and with what return, for few of them have spared the time to learn the pleasant courtesies of country manners. Small wonder that they usually refer to themselves not as sportsmen but as shooters.

Having seen too many of their species, my terror was that I should get landed with a bunch of such gentry with a Rolls-Royce and runny nose apiece, so it was a great relief when my neighbour's friends called in to make their number.

They were nice guys, in the nicest sense, entirely different from the urban spivs I dreaded. Most of them were farmers, bred and brought up on the land, who liked a bit of sport on Saturdays. Having introduced themselves and told me that they would be shooting up to my boundary, they expressed interest in what I was doing, so that we all decided that, as there is room in the country for all sorts of interests, we could get along very well without doing one another any harm.

They were obviously so knowledgeable that I was surprised that they were even interested in that particular shoot which must be a tremendous problem to run effectively. The answer was the practical countryman's blunt belief that gift horses are not foaled to be looked in the mouth! They weren't paying any rent, nor employing a keeper, so it wouldn't be death and disaster if they didn't get a big bag. The sport was all that mattered.

Even so, I thought they'd set themselves a tidy task. The shoot consisted of a thousand-acre farm which had recently been won from a derelict deer park, choked with rushes and bracken and a feggy grass that wouldn't feed a caterpillar. An idea of its state can be gleaned from the fact that it only fetched £60 an acre at auction in the mid-sixties, when fertile land was ten times that.

In order to make anything of it, the old trees and spinneys had been bulldozed out of the way; the whole area was torn up so that drains could be put in, and then ploughed and limed. When it was done, there were a thousand acres of prairie, with a few shelter belts, planted with an optimistic eye to the future—but nothing for the present.

I calculated that any pheasants they put down would run off to the thousand-acre wood that bordered the park as fast as their legs would carry them. There they would be safe because the Forestry Commission plantations were thickets, about ten or fifteen years old, in which pheasants could skulk all day without ever showing a beak to the waiting guns.

If the Old Squire was looking down from his heavenly coverts, the prospect would have made him shudder in his shroud. No spinneys or coverts from which pheasants could be flushed, but an impenetrable jungle for them to skulk in safety. Even the tons of corn per acre that the 'new' land would produce as recompense would leave him cold. He had come from a generation of landowners who could live in luxury without wringing the last drop of profit from their land.

Modern, money-motivated farmers speak a different language. I reckoned that the chaps who'd got a free shoot didn't have such a bargain because they could easily walk their legs down to their knees and never get a shot. What pheasants they reared had every chance to stray away to neighbours. I was interested to see how they coped.

On shooting days, the drive past our house made motorway snarl-ups seem a picnic. Members of the shoot rolled up in vans and Land Rovers, posh cars and old bangers, and everyone seemed to have a retriever or a spaniel. When the Old Squire had a shoot, six guests were his maximum and Hannam shepherded them round in silent gentility. Even the beaters never shouted, except to alert the guns of the approach of a victim with the single cry, 'Cock over'. The only warning of their approach was the tap, tap, tap of their sticks as they guided the birds in the way they should go. Or should not go, depending on the point of view!

My new neighbours were different. We called them 'the locusts' for I once saw no fewer than forty guns and their dogs spilling out of the assorted queue of vehicles past our drive. Their merriment was so infectious that they reminded me of a coachload of football fans returning from a winning match.

They split into two parties, deployed themselves on opposite sides of the wood and converged towards the centre. Everyone carried a gun, so there were no spare hands for sticks to tap out the disciplined rhythm of the Old Squire's professional beaters.

This didn't inhibit them at all. As the opposing armies of guns approached each other, they hooted and hollered with such enthusiasm that pheasants exploded out of cover to escape the pandemonium. Everyone seemed to have spent his youth watching cowboys and indians at the pictures, and the din they raised would have relegated the Calgary Stampede to a Mothers' Union bunfight by comparison. This shindy ensured that no one could shoot his neighbour by mistake. Although the opposing line of guns approached unseen through the dense cover, everyone could hear precisely where everyone else was. Eventually, they emerged from the thicket and concentrated on stopping any fights that started between their dogs—both those which had been doing all the work and those which had had plenty of time to grow bored with waiting.

Boredom was no hazard of their owners' occupation. As each drive finished, they counted the bag and bickered about who had shot what. There was always a sweepstake on what was accounted for by the end of the day—and differences of opinion about what could and could not be counted. Anything that moved, ran the risk of contributing to the total. Anyone not paying attention was liable to have his cap snatched off and flung high in the air, and, long before it landed, his mates had demonstrated their marksmanship by putting a charge of shot through the crown. When the merriment subsided, they re-formed lines and the static guns went beating, leaving the previous beaters to hang around, waiting for birds to come over them, as in more spacious days gone-by.

Very different from the Old Squire's day, but I thanked my stars that they were my neighbours instead of Hannam or his like. They took what came, reared a few hundred pheasants to augment the wild birds, and never bothered much with what shooting men call 'vermin'. If a fox crossed a ride on shooting days, he got shot—and

serve him right for his stupidity. His relatives earned their reputation for cunning because mugs like that were culled before they'd lived to breed. But they didn't trap and snare and poison and shoot everything that wasn't game, as many keepers do. If there were more like them about, the countryside would be richer and folk would enjoy it more.

Such sportsmen, bred of yeoman stock, have forgotten more about wildlife than most scientists will ever know. They make sure of a good day's Fox hunting by building 'drains'—or artificial earths —at strategic places in their hunting country. Skilfully constructed, these 'drains' attract foxes to live in them as surely as a good nest box will be occupied by tits. Vixens have cubs in the hunting men's drains—and the cubs lie in comfort there in winter.

The anti-hunting fraternity often belly-ache about cruel huntsmen who 'breed foxes for hunting'. They imply that they then liberate them in front of hounds to make sure of having a good day's sport. The only folk who do that are the counterparts of the Rolls-Royce-and-runny-nose brigade in shooting circles. The chaps who hunt only because they delude themselves that this will make them socially acceptable to their better—but usually poorer—neighbours. Strictly speaking, it is not even the nouveau hunting men themselves who hunt 'bag-men' as captive foxes are called. In every hunt there are a few hangers-on, wide boys who

make a good living conning those who have more money than
sense.

It has long been illegal to hunt an animal that has been caught
and liberated for the purpose. The Cruelty to Animals Act of 1911
put a pretty effective stop to it. So it is illegal to hunt 'bagged'
foxes, but I know one wily customer who made a good living
ensuring the deep-pocketed members of his local hunt didn't have
blank days.

He used to pop his terrier down an artificial earth the night
before the hunt and catch the foxes that bolted in purse nets or wire
snares. Next morning, there was always a fox in a milk churn
secured firmly to the floor in the back of his van when he went to
the meet. It was an unusual churn because it had no bottom, and
the van, too, was unusual because it was fitted with a sliding trap
door, operated from the driving seat. When the driver wished to
'plant' a fox in front of hounds, he simply checked the road was
clear, slowed to walking pace and pulled the lever. Charlie fox was
then decanted to run for his life, while his chauffeur remained
unsuspected as one of the followers in cars.

An easy enough trick to play, you might think, but you first had
to catch your fox, which required a good deal more know-how
than most of the riders possess. Certainly more than those who
only go out because it is 'done'.

I had seen scores of 'drains' myself when I was young, but as I
explained in *Badgers at My Window*, the earth I dug to try to attract
badgers to my land was far from successful. My enthusiasm
outpaced my skill and I made it too well. Determined that it should
be comfortable, I had made a sleeping den, lined with thick oak
planks, and connected it to the outside world by earthen
drainpipes, nine inches in diameter. Where I slipped up was when I
tried to make it absolutely water-proof by covering it with a plastic
sheet before putting a blanket of soil and turf over the whole lot. A
moment's thought would have warned me that the plastic sheet
would not only keep water out, but condensed moisture in. And,
sure enough, when I opened it up eighteen months or so later, to
see why no badgers (or foxes) had used it, I found it fusty and
mildewed and quite uninhabitable.

It taught me a lesson and I went, cap-in-hand, to an old friend who made a good living selling working terriers—each in turn advertised as 'the best working dog in England', only to be supplanted, the week after it was sold, by an even more miraculous specimen. As old friends do, in pleasant rural circles, Bert placed the bottomless depth of his knowledge at my disposal.

The first abortive artificial sett had been dug by me with a pick-axe and shovel, oceans of sweat and hours of frustrated bad temper. This time I was better equipped. I hired a JCB digger, to take the irk out of my work, took the earthen pipes to a secluded spot in the wood on my tractor and was ready for action.

It is a very poor job that won't stand a foreman, so I pointed out precisely where I wanted two trenches dug for the pipes—and how deep. They were put in a horseshoe shape, sloping down towards the entrance, so that any rain which percolated in to the newly filled trenches, would drain out, instead of in towards the sleeping chamber. This den itself was most carefully made. The area, about three feet by two, was not critical, but the height was limited to twelve inches and it was roofed and floored with heavy planks—which would not sweat with condensation—before re-covering it with soil and turf.

I knew that foxes would probably use it first, partly because there are so many foxes in such a large area of forest, and partly because they are not so conservative as badgers.

Foxes are unhygienic brutes, given to fouling their own dens and, at the best of times, foxes stink. Badgers, on the other hand, are fastidious as prissy spinsters, despite being so tough and aggressive. If a fox is in an earth and a badger takes a fancy to it, he ejects him with no more ceremony than a bailiff. But, if the fox has fouled the den, the badgers can think of plenty more preferable places and simply leave them to it.

It was therefore vital to my purpose that, if foxes did colonise my sett first, at least they must leave it as they found it.

This is where the critical height of twelve inches came in. It was high enough for either foxes or badgers to lie down and sleep in comfort, even if the badgers have carried in bedding. But it was not high enough for a fox to sit up on his haunches. If he couldn't sit up, he couldn't evacuate his bowels and foul the sett. And if he couldn't do that, any badger that fancied the place as a desirable dwelling would tip him out in the cold!

The first sett we made was in Primrose Dell, one of the quietest spots in the wood, a little over half a mile from the house. I sunk a vertical drainpipe into the den so that I could insert a microphone and connect it to an observation hide on the far side of the dell which, according to the Ordnance map, was once a marl pit.

Intoxicated with my own enthusiasm, I built (or caused to be built) another sett in a large pile of soil about eighty yards from the study window, where the paddock merges with the wood. And, while the JCB was here, I had a number of old tree roots, relics of felling before my time, bulldozed into a pile, about ten yards square and five high. They were put on top of an earth mound and covered with soil, in the hopes that badgers would excavate a sett in the dry soil safe under the root pile.

None of this effort would have been worthwhile if I hadn't had confidence that my sporting neighbours would not treat any badgers that came as ruthlessly as old-fashioned keepers would have done, but such down-to-earth farmers have not yet been contaminated by the competitive custom of double-cross.

In spite of these favourable portents, the experiment got off to a shaky start. I still had the fox-proof enclosure and I had persuaded roe deer to breed there for several years. Although I had been forced to destroy Bill, his sow remained in the sett and when he had gone, I opened up the badger-gate again to let her come and go at will. I had a pipe dream that since she had played truant so often, it was possible that she might have been sleeping around with the wild boars, and that she might cub in my bugged and electronically-recorded sett as a consequence.

I had convinced myself that, though it was no fault of mine that Bill had become so dangerously aggressive, it was not fair on neighbours to keep him. But it wasn't anything I was proud about so I was reticent about admitting my failure publicly. To aggravate matters further, my mauled foot took so long to heal that I was out and about very little for several weeks.

As a result, I never got around to warning my neighbours that the sow was at full liberty—and might appear on their land.

Normally they are very kind. They regard most naturalists as slightly eccentric, but they know the difficulties of dealing with animals well enough to respect the patience and know-how necessary to instil confidence into truly wild creatures.

Most of them keep a few hens for the good of the table and enjoy sport with a gun when work is done. So they are not in love with foxes, and keep a few fox-hangs set in their fences as more or less standard practice. They relied on me to tell them when my badgers were on the loose so that they could set their snares selectively to catch foxes that passed but not badgers.

This is not as clever as it sounds. All wildlife are such creatures of habit that they use the same tracks so regularly that they literally wear paths that are clearly visible to knowledgeable eyes. It is easy to see precisely where they go through fences, cross fields and enter woods so that there is no difficulty about setting a wire snare in the exact spot where the victim will put his head in the running noose next time he comes by.

Badgers have extremely small heads for their size, and the neck tapers smoothly up to the shoulders so that the instant they feel the wire begin to tighten, they usually manage to back out and extract their head before the noose tightens. Gamekeepers and ministry rat-catchers know this and set snares for badgers with such large loops that they literally step into them so that the wire tightens round the belly. No competent trapper catches badgers by mistake.

Therefore, when my neighbours knew my badgers were at large, it was not difficult to catch foxes quite efficiently but do my animals no harm at all.

So I blamed myself for not telling everyone around that my sow was free. My stupid reluctance to admit that I had been forced to destroy the boar, and that I had been careless enough to be bitten by him, probably cost his mate her life. A couple of weeks after he had gone, she also failed to return. It was the first time in more than fifteen years that I hadn't got a badger that I had reared on the bottle.

The keepers and their bosses who affect the wildlife of the

countryside do most of the damage to predators, and sometimes to the competitors, of game. They may kill far too many badgers and foxes, hawks and owls and stoats and weasels. Some of the worst shoot moorhens and linnets because they filch the corn the pheasants might have had. I have even met louts who slaughter kingfishers and herons to preserve a few tame fish for their masters to catch when shooting is out of season. But not all keepers are bad, and the steps they take to foster game help many other species too.

They provide seclusion by chivvying off the trespassers and prosecuting poachers. They provide cover for pheasants to nest—which is also popular for songbirds and many other species lucky enough not to figure on the black-list. They plant berry-bearing shrubs which are equally attractive. And they control predators, which may be bad luck on them, but is as beneficial for other species as it is for pheasants.

Although it is less spectacular and incidental, modern farmers do far more damage with some of the chemical pesticides they use than the bloodiest-minded keepers. Relatively simple concoctions were used until the last few years. One of the difficulties about harvesting potatoes, for instance, was that the sheer volume of potato tops clogged the machinery that was fitted to the tractor to flick the spuds out onto the surface so that they could be picked and bagged by hand.

Some bright spark discovered that if the tops were sprayed with an arsenic compound, they withered and shrank so that the potatoes lay as obvious on the surface as daisies on a tennis lawn. Since they were in contact with the treated foliage, they were hardly as harmless!

So the draughtsmen of government regulations, who probably get no nearer to potato fields than Hyde Park Corner, specified that no potato should be harvested for ten days—I think the period was—after the tops had been sprayed. Such gentlemen presumably relied on the graphs drawn up by weathermen, which probably indicated that there are *never* ten consecutive days without rain in England, so the poison should have been swilled away before the spuds are uncovered.

'Never' is a long time in the country, and a farmer friend of mine sprayed his field at the beginning of a dry spell the bureaucrats said shouldn't happen—not according to their carefully drafted regulations.

Delighted with his crop, my friend fetched a trailer-load of ladies from the nearest town, supplied them with sackbags to tie round their waists as aprons, gave them a piece-work price per hundredweight picked and flashed his eyes in anticipation of some easy profits.

All went well until lunchtime, when the urban ladies perched themselves in a row on a sunny log to enjoy their sandwiches. Presently the toughest and stoutest and most indestructible old duck of all tumbled off her perch. One second she was cracking bawdy jokes, as such female parties do when out on holiday, the next she lay in the ditch, as inert and shapeless as a half-full bag of spuds.

My friend, who is no mental slouch, immediately thought of arsenic. He heaved his employee into the back of his jeep, told the others to stop eating and to go to the house for some coffee, and dashed to the hospital, where they applied a stomach pump—just in time.

Most farmers are unimaginative chaps. You have to be to rear calves, which you know as individuals, and then sell them to folk to be converted to veal under conditions of intensive husbandry more like a concentration camp than traditional farming. My friend was no exception, but the old lady and her arsenic prompted him to action. Back at the farm that night, he brought out all his tins of herbicide and pesticide, sheep dip and other goodies designed by chemists to cut his labour costs.

For the first time, he read the instructions carefully. He discovered, with horror, that for some he should have dressed-up in rubber coat and rubber gloves, goggles and protective headgear before he even opened the tins. There were notices which said: 'Don't harvest for eight weeks', 'Keep away from children, pets and stock'; 'Do not wash tin into watercourse'. It wasn't necessary to be an ace detective to deduce that some of the stuff was about as harmless as an atom bomb.

He decided that he would rather make do with less profit than risk such disaster and he sorted out the most dangerous stuff to chuck it down a pitshaft.

A neighbour, who was currently troubled by magpies stealing his eggs, begged a small bottleful of the devil's brew designed to clear aphids from currants. Interested to see just how lethal it was, we both tagged along.

The experimenter took a hen's egg, made a half-inch hole in one side and shook out about a teaspoonful of liquid. Then he dipped the end of a matchstick in his devil's brew, withdrew it with a single drop adhering to the end, and putting it through the hole in the egg, he stirred it round. He took this perfectly fresh egg, contaminated by only a single drop of insecticide, and put it in the orchard, in front of his window, where he could see anything approach—and drive it off if it was not an enemy.

Within ten minutes his magpie arrived. With typically jaunty insolence, he hopped towards the bait. Every few steps, he stopped and surveyed the scene with suspicious eyes, to check that it was not an ambush. The fresh egg was irresistible so, as soon as he thought the coast was clear, he sidled up and took a peck. Just one single peck of an egg, defiled only by that lonely drop. It was enough. He shook his head, as if a heavyweight had slugged him on the jaw. Then he wobbled away as if punch-drunk.

All predators are always on the look-out for sick and weakly prey. Within seconds, a carrion crow was on the scene, delighted by the discomfort of his rival. Before he could decide what to do, he was joined by his mate. The magpie had done them no harm, except perhaps to compete for eggs, but nature is ruthless and the chance to kick him while he was down too good to miss. They set about him and, broken by this last straw, he tumbled over dead.

Not being a scientist, I hadn't timed the drama, but we discussed it with our host who had conducted the experiment, and he reckoned the whole thing was over in less than a minute.

The old crows were obviously delighted with themselves at having vanquished their adversary so easily. To celebrate, they queued-up and each had a triumphant sip from the egg. Within two minutes they had joined the magpie in eternity.

The experiment was wholly reprehensible—and it is quite illegal to lay poison in the open. But although it was conducted almost twenty years ago, it is as vivid in my mind's eye now as it was then. Nor shall I ever forget the farmer's reaction as it dawned on him that the whole obscene drama had been played with a single drop of liquid, of which he had spewed out gallons on his fields in the course of his professional career.

At about this time, Rachel Carson had alerted the world to the suicidal dangers of similar chemicals used in America, in her book called *Silent Spring*.

Our chemists were cheerfully brewing satanic concoctions in the name of intensive husbandry which bid fair to annihilate wildlife first and then, perhaps, us. Slick salesmanship persuaded farmers to use them, and another of my friends, who fell for their patter, is now an invalid with Farmers' Lung. That is a polite way of saying that he accidentally—probably carelessly—inhaled some of the obscene stuff which atrophied one lung entirely.

I was well aware that the use of such substances was common practice in modern 'efficient' (?) farming but, like so many of my fellows, I battened down the thought in the back of my mind, and what I didn't see, I didn't grieve about.

My friend the farmer, less critical of boffins, believed what they said and profited by the increase in crops their new technology made possible. When the results were not as good as he expected, he was not above slurping—in double the quantity—to make sure.

Largely due to Rachel Carson's book, conservationists took up the cudgels and really made rude noises.

They were labelled cranks, but the publicity that ensued forced the politicians at least to pay lip-service to the rumpus and slap on a few controls just in time to save sparrow hawks and other common species from extinction. But although they have banned some of the most dangerous chemicals from farms, they still allow them to be used in gardens. Now dear old ladies, spraying their roses in all innocence, probably do more damage to suburban birds than farmers with thousands of acres of crops.

Anyone who doubts the dangers of the stuff that is poured for profit on our fields should read about the agricultural chemicals approved by the Ministry of Agriculture. They do a booklet called *Approved Products for Farmers and Growers*★—and it includes the safety precautions necessary even to use the stuff.

I find this booklet one of the most obscene horror stories I ever read but, even so, the ghastly demonstration with the magpie and the crows etched the message in my mind so vividly that nightmares about it plague me still.

The use, often innocent and usually legitimate, of these poisons on the land certainly does more damage to a wider variety of our animals and birds than all the Hannams, past and present.

Meanwhile, my badgers had gone, partly because of my own carelessness, and new badgers had not yet colonised my setts. But things had been going much better with my deer.

Almost ten years earlier, I had bottle-reared a delightful roe kid which had arrived as an orphan a few weeks old. Roe are smaller than fallow and far more elegant, real woodland sprites that do not live in herds, but family parties. She grew up with complete confidence both in me and all my friends.

As she had no means of knowing that all strangers were friends of neither me nor her, I kept her confined in the enclosure by the

★ Available from HMSO

house. She didn't seem to resent this at all because it allowed her to enjoy sweet, fresh grass and clover in the paddock, and the broad leaves of hazel, oak and birch in the wood. There was a dense reed bed for her couch by the pool and thickets in the rest of the six acres where she roamed.

She was as greedy as she was beautiful and was willing to sell her soul for chocolate digestive biscuits. She gave every indication that her life was happy and complete.

Nevertheless, I hate being under constraint myself, and I sympathise with fellow prisoners, human or not. I eventually managed to get a pair of wild roe deer which I put to join her, under the delusion that I was doing her a good turn which she might repay by presenting me with a kid of her own.

She never took to her guests, and although the buck chased her half-heartedly when she came into rut in the July, I never saw her let him mate her. Certainly he never provided any evidence that he did, and she eventually died, still a virgin so far as we could tell, at the respectable age of ten.

The wild doe showed no such inhibitions. She was already in kid when she arrived and reared a youngster the following summer. In July she mated with the buck we had brought with her.

It is fascinating to be a voyeur at such nuptials. Like other beautiful females, roe love playing hard-to-get. Every time the buck approaches, his darling runs away, not just anywhere, but

always by the same circuitous route. The ritual continues for days on end, till the pattern of her denial cuts visible paths in the turf and through the undergrowth. Prosaic countrymen call them roe-rings, the more romantic know that they were really made by the fairies to be followed by the daintiest deer on earth. So they bring up their children to believe they're fairy rings, and who is to say which is right?

It takes the female several days to be in full heat and receptive after the scent she exudes has first put ideas into her master's mind. He goes on chasing her up her chosen garden path till both are out of breath and all but the most ardent would be out of patience too.

At last his compelling faith is justified. The shyest deer is far from unattainable; she stops in her tracks and allows him to mate her and the experience seems to be so rewarding that they repeat it thirty or forty times.

It is not common for roe to consent to breed except in the unfettered freedom of the wild, so we were naturally delighted by the compliment ours paid us, not only by breeding annually, but by rearing the second generation, born here, to have kids of their own.

The original wild doe died of worms, for roe are exceptionally subject to internal parasites, but we thought we'd conquered the complaint with a worm medicine that was mixed with their food, avoiding the traumas of capture and forced dosing.

Then it gradually became harder to rear the kids; they thrived at first, but gradually faded, and I decided we had kept roe on six acres too long, and the ground was possibly 'deer sick'. I had resisted turning them loose in the wood at first because Miss Roedoe, my original hand-reared roe, was so absurdly trusting that she might have wandered and been worried by a dog, or run over or shot or even stolen as a pet.

I am as unsentimental as any farmer when the time comes to kill and dress a duck or fowl I've reared for table. It is only one of a flock, which I don't know individually—and I look forward to meeting it again when it emerges from the oven. But when I have experienced hour upon hour of the intimate contact necessary to feed and keep clean and give confidence to the helpless youngster I am rearing on the bottle, I cannot help getting personally involved. It upsets me as much, if tragedy befalls, as it would if harm befell my favourite dog.

When my tame deer died, my feelings for the others did not approach the same intensity. It was quite obvious that they were no longer thriving and that, if I wasn't to lose them, I had to take quick action. The obvious thing was to turn them loose in the wood outside and let them take pot luck. If conditions suited them and they thrived, the area was quite large enough to avoid all risk of overstocking. If they strayed away and came to a bad end, they would be no worse off than if they remained and suffered the effects of continuing to live on land that was deer-sick.

To give them a sporting chance, I caught them up once more and dosed them with the latest jollop for the internal parasites that play such havoc with their species.

A pleasure of my life is that such experiments always teach me something new and unexpected. There were between twenty and thirty fallow deer in my wood, very much larger than roe. I wasn't certain if they would ignore each other, as they had always done when chance had made their paths converge each side of the boundary netting.

Interspecific aggression—as the boffins grandly call a spot of aggro between different species—is not common with deer. A fallow buck will charge and chivvy another fallow buck which trespasses on his territory. Roe are as bad with roe and red with red. Red and roe deer often seem to live happily together in the same wood but I had had no experience of what would happen with roe and fallow. I was interested to find out and hoped the larger fallow would not bully them too much.

At first, it seemed, they planned to ignore each other. The roe buck had lived in the enclosure for five or six years and he obviously regarded *that* as his territory. The others had been born there and knew nothing else. So for the first few days they paced up and down, miserable as tigers in a cage, not trying to break through the fence to the outside world, but back to their own familiar surroundings! As time wore on—and they grew hungry—they gradually sampled the food further from home so that, when we went down the wood, they appeared all over the place. They never seemed to be at loggerheads with the wild fallow deer.

When they had fed and wandered to their hearts' content, they always 'homed' back towards the paddock, tested the fence to see if we'd left a gate open, and settled down to rest and chew their cud in the belt of woodland opposite the house.

It so happened that this included the heronry, where nobody— including me—is allowed to trespass. It is thick and secluded and has always been a favourite harbour for wild deer. As it is only about a hundred yards from the house and bordered by two wide grassy rides, pointing at the window, it is also a marvellous place to observe anything that uses it.

Soon after the roe deer adopted it as their sanctuary, we noticed that the fallow deer seemed to keep away. It could have been coincidence, or that the scent of roe offended them, but we could see no positive reason.

As time went on, and the roe grew more confident, we saw that we were wrong. The little roe buck had a pair of wicked antlers, only about nine inches long, but sharp as stilettos, with protruding brow tines and branched at the top. Not the sort of weapons I should choose to have thrust into my vitals. It was soon obvious that the fallow didn't relish the prospect either. The roe had apparently staked a claim to this new territory and, if fallow came anywhere near, the buck exploded from his lair and spurred them away to more distant places.

This did not dovetail with my plans. I'd observed roe at very close quarters for several years—and my favourite was dead. I'd let the others out for their own good but had hoped they would wander all over the wood and give me the chance of some concentrated work with fallow instead. It hadn't occurred to me that they would trump my ace by driving off the fallow.

Luckily, I heard about a man who had been trying to get roe for years. He owned a very big estate and was happy to make a generous enclosure for them if I gave him my roe. So we opened the gate, fed them into the enclosure with flaked maize, caught them up and packed them off to pastures new.

When they had gone—and Bill was dead—there wasn't much point in the enclosure. Although the netting was blacked and unobtrusive, we had to look through the enclosure to see into the wood. It gave the illusion that we, ourselves, were caged so I took it down in the hope that wild fallow would come close to the house and replace the tame roe.

It offered other prospects. If badgers did oblige by taking to the sett I'd made at the edge of the wood, opposite the window, we might be able to persuade them to feed near the house, as Bill and his mate had done. Meanwhile, the removal of the fencing made all the difference to the prospect from the windows. While it was there, it was obvious that we were detached observers, looking at the wood outside, as aridly objective as boffins with a microscope. Now that the offending barrier was gone, we felt that we were *in* the wood, personally involved with whatever happened; psychologically detached, not from the solitude we shared with deer and birds, but from the artificial world outside.

The village is more than a mile away, but there are refugees there from the city grime and smoke who know little about the ways of the countryside. They think it is a marvellous playground where they and their doggies can wander at will—and, if a dog chases a rabbit or a deer or a hare, it will give him some exercise and a good time will be had by all.

When such folk go off to work in the morning, it is not uncommon for them to shut dear Fido out to amuse himself while they're away. The more irresponsible of them let him out last thing at night and go to bed before he returns, persuading themselves that he's probably doing a spot of courting with the nice little bitch down the road.

Dogs that are allowed to chase rabbits and hares at will soon discover their latent instinct to hunt, which may have been smothered by generations bred for the false standards of the show ring. Although they may be too physically flaccid to overtake a deer, they soon discover that sheep are far more fun. So, almost every spring, we have to deal with a few sheep-worrying dogs.

About a thousand ewes are lambed on the farm above us; they are safe for a few days because they are wintered in covered yards. As soon as the lambs are strong on their feet, they go out with their mothers to grass and are dispersed so widely over the thousand acres that it is difficult to keep them closely supervised.

The first sign of trouble is on the shepherds' morning rounds— tell-tale tufts of wool where the ewe has struggled free at the beginning of the chase. The climax is painted by her corpse beside the fence where she was finally cornered. Her lambs are usually torn and mutilated a few yards away.

Our drill is well-established. David Core, the manager of the farm next door, comes round to tell his neighbours and we take it in turns to patrol while dusk fades into night, and again when dawn is breaking. Sooner or later our quarry—they usually hunt in pairs—fall to the crack of a rifle. It is hard luck on the culprits because there are no bad dogs, but too many bad owners; but only fools would give them a second chance.

When the dogs have had a killing, foxes move in for the feast and, if they are not satisfied, may kill a lamb or two themselves. Because the area was unkeepered, there had been an explosion in the fox population, so one year the owner sent a keeper over from his other estate to thin them out a bit.

He was one of the old-fashioned sort who despised men who used poison because it was so indiscriminate. He was fond of saying that any unskilled lout could 'dope' an egg or lump of meat, and that proper keepers selected their victims and took pride when they triumphed.

Unfortunately, he was old-fashioned enough to class badgers as well as foxes as vermin, because both had the canine teeth of meat eaters. His method of 'selection' was to use wire snares which he set where foxes (and badgers) came through the cattle netting or under sheep fences. Whatever he said about skill, it didn't take

Sherlock Holmes to see from the hairs on the fence exactly what passed where. And it didn't need the precision of a watchmaker to hang a noose which would draw tight when anything put its head in it.

He came at the odd hours keepers use, but since the estate where he worked was twenty miles away, he didn't come very often. He excused this by using self-lock snares, which he said were bound to kill their victims so that it wouldn't really matter if he couldn't 'look them' every day.

Old-fashioned free-running snares are made of multiple fine wires twisted into a thin, very strong cable. One end is woven round an eyelet, like shoe-lace eyelets, and the other is fastened to a strong cord or pliable wire for anchor. A running noose is made by sliding the eyelet along, and the skill is in pegging the noose so that the victim puts its head in it and draws it tight as he passes through the gap. Although it may sound pretty lethal, it doesn't always kill the captive, especially a wily fox, because he will stop struggling and wait when he discovers it will hang him if he doesn't. So good keepers check their snares every few hours.

The difference between that and the latest self-lock snare is that the self-lock mechanism is a toggle, like the one fitted to the guy rope of a tent. When the newly-caught captive struggles for freedom, it pulls up tight, exactly like an ordinary old-fashioned snare, but it doesn't free-off when the pressure is relaxed. If it does catch a victim round the neck, strangulation is virtually inevitable.

But it is difficult to catch a badger round the neck because it is wedge-shaped and the noose slides off over his small head if he backs out of the gap. So keepers who don't like badgers set the noose so large that he literally steps through it past his forelegs. His body is so relatively large that the noose tightens and holds him round the belly.

A few days after the first snares had been set for lamb-eating foxes, David was at the door by breakfast time. A badger was caught in the fence by the wood, so would I come and see it?

I arrived to find a sow badger which was, justifiably, very cross indeed. The snare had her firmly round the belly, but she was free to move in a semi-circle about two feet in radius, limited by the length of wire anchored to the fence. As I approached, she retreated to the extent of her tether, turned to face me and coughed in agony and anger. She had struggled so long and so hard that wire had bitten into the soft flesh of her udder and belly, which had lapped over it like a spare tyre till it was buried and invisible.

Anticipating trouble, I had taken a pair of wire nippers about the size of powerful toenail clippers. It would have been simple enough to cut the anchor wire and let her go. If the snare had been free-running, this might have been a reasonable thing to do because, when she got to the safety of her sett, she would have scratched and worried at it until she could grab the buried wire, pull it through the eyelet and liberate herself.

This toggle self-lock contraption was different. It would have been just as easy to cut her adrift at the anchor but, when she got home, the toggle would have held-fast relentlessly and, however ruthlessly she bit and worried at the wire, it would never have freed her unless she had severed it inside the loop. As time passed, the agonising wound would have festered and she would have died of gangrene.

It was soon obvious to me that the sow badger I'd been called to help had set me a difficult task. She was free to move over quite an arc, her snapping jaws were anything but impotent and she regarded human beings as the lowest form of life—with considerable justification!

I returned to the farm for a two-pronged pitch fork with which I straddled the wire cable close against the sow's body. This reduced her potential movement from a two-foot circle to almost nothing. Then I 'tailed' her. Badgers have a tail about six or eight inches long with a core about as thick as man's little finger. Once I had immobilised her with the pitch fork pinning the snare, it was therefore possible to grab her tail and lift her clear of the ground at the full extent of the snare that held her. All that then remained was to get it off. All!

There was no way of getting at the toggle which was buried out of sight beneath rolls of flesh. Brutal as it seemed, the only way was literally to probe under her skin for the wire with my nippers, and sever it with a shrewd pinch. Since this increased her pain, the badger took it as an unfriendly act but, in her own interests, I persisted. At last I felt the cruel wire between the jaws of my nippers—and squeezed. The wire parted, and the sow swung free, hanging head down from my precarious grip on her tail.

So long as I kept hold, I was safe. But I had no means of telling whether she would beat a hasty retreat when I dropped her, or wreak a misguided revenge on me. I swung her gently, like a pendulum, gradually increasing the arc till I felt my grip was slipping. Then I slung her several feet in one direction—towards the wood I calculated was her home—while I ran like hell in the other.

It was an extremely dangerous thing to do, but I had little alternative since I was not happy to see her die in agony nor to shoot her, which I suppose would have been more sensible. Indeed, I have repeated the exercise several times since, with various modifications to limit the risks. But the experiences have filled me with implacable hatred for these barbarous snares which also catch deer and sheep by the leg, and dogs and cats and other wildlife. They catch everything, unfortunately, but the men who set them and yet, I suppose, because there is no blood and the victims are rarely able to scream, there is little public outcry about them.

Luckily, somebody soon shot the raiding dog and it was not considered economic to bring a keeper twenty miles to catch a few foxes after the lambs had grown too big for them to kill, so the keeper returned whence he came and left the badgers in peace.

The yardstick of success, in managing a wood as a wildlife sanctuary, is the degree to which shy species lose their fear of man. Our heronry has increased during out tenure, from fourteen nests to over fifty.

This year two pairs actually nested in the oak trees in the fowl run where I go twice a day. The great grey birds have lost their fear of me and when I rattle my corn bucket to call the poultry to feed, the herons don't panic away to the next parish, as theory says such shy birds should. They simply stretch their sinuous necks to peer over the edge of the nest and satisfy themselves it's only me. Then they settle down again, to brood their eggs, as if they were sole occupants of a desert island.

There are other fringe benefits. A few girls from the local boarding school do projects in the wood. One year they almost sweated blood to dig an artificial earth, overlooked by an observation hut, in the faint hopes of seeing fox or badger cubs there some time in the future.

It didn't look very promising to me because the sleeping den was only six inches below ground level and the two piped entrance tunnels were less than eight feet long. Any animal lying in the den would be troubled by the smallest external sound, and I had my doubts about the construction giving enough sense of security to attract a rabbit, far less badgers.

I paid lip service to it, because I didn't want to discourage their efforts in excavating such heavy, daunting clay. In any case, it was in the best spot I could devise, in the side of Primrose Dell, so I sited my own five-star sett I dug with a mechanical digger a few yards away. Mine was the sett to end all setts and I had no doubts about badgers queueing up for it. When they did, the girls could share my pleasure because both were overlooked from the observation hide they'd built.

Such pride deserves its fall. There were badgers in their sett several months before they even bothered to inspect mine! And, over the years since, they have demonstrated their good taste by preferring the sett made by feminine hands.

Anyone who has nailed up a bird-box for blue tits or a robin will share the thrill of our success. The first glimpse of birds prospecting the site puts it out of bounds to anything which might disturb it for days on end. No neighbours' cat can get within yards of it without risk of being drenched by a bucket of cold water.

It suddenly becomes vital to be up hours before breakfast to watch the birds carrying nesting material, count the journeys they make in an hour and make abstruse—and probably inaccurate—calculations about the volume of nesting material they use.

It was like that with our badgers. Once they took to the girls' sett, that side of Primrose Dell was out of bounds. I grew more aggressively territorial than any badger and would cheerfully have chucked any stranger, who trespassed near the sett, clean into the pond. I examined the tracks through the undergrowth, trying to deduce, from the footprints, whether my visitor was boar or sow, old or young. And I was so careful not to contaminate the bedding they brought with human scent that I analysed it with binoculars from the far side of the pit hole.

The temptation to badger-watch nightly was well nigh irresistible—but I curbed my curiosity in the interests of engendering a long-term sense of security. Whenever I went to the area, I 'dropped' the dogs fifty yards away, made my circumspect inspection alone, leaving them lying motionless till I was out of the danger area again.

The trouble paid off because when the badgers had got used to the girls' sett, they explored mine next door. Although I say it, it was a right and proper sett. Long curving tunnels, sloping to the entrance for perfect drainage. A dry and airy den, and the only unconventional feature—from the badgers' point of view—was a vertical pipe, three inches across, down to the centre of the den. This pipe was covered with a paving slab on the surface of the ground, to prevent rain seeping to the den, and it acted as a chimney for ventilation. Its real purpose was so I could insert a microphone which could be connected to a tape recorder in the observation hut. This would give warning when they were coming out and I hoped to be able to repeat the glossary of badger language I had made with Bill and the sows.

As things turned out, it was a dead loss. By the time the cable had been trailed inconspicuously round to the tape recorder, about thirty yards had been spooled out and, for some reason I do not understand, it acted as a radio aerial and recorded Radio I! So, instead of hearing cosy snores, rustle of bedding and clicking teeth grooming shiny fur, some screeching pop star was forever blathering about coons and moons and suchlike balderdash.

Engineers, more qualified than I am, were always promising to cure it by obscure technical abracadabra. So far, they have not succeeded, but I hope they will before the need arises again.

It was not surprising that the badgers took to our setts in Primrose Dell. It is more than half a mile from any building, the setts are built into a bank, there is always water in the bottom of the Dell, woodland on two sides, corn over one boundary, and pasture over the fourth. They would have difficulty in finding anything better.

Although I was scrupulous about not disturbing them, I often saw them coming and going from a distance. One day I was tempted to make an exception. We have a lot of BBC producers here, often professionally, but most of them personal friends with common interest—and knowledge—of natural history.

On one occasion a stranger came who wished to discuss a

possible series involving our reserve. I took him round, to show
him what there was, and we saw deer and hares and rabbits and a
lot of woodland birds. At Primrose Dell, he asked to see the layout
of the two setts. I had noticed, for some days, that there were few
signs of fresh working so rather assumed the badgers had moved to
another sett.

Taking him over to the slab, I lifted it up and saw a badger
curled up asleep in the den from which the pipe protruded. 'A
badger,' I whispered. 'Sound asleep. You'll be an old man before
you see the likes of that again.'

He leaned forward, booming out that he could see him plainly.
The brock woke with a start and bounced into the tunnel—and my
guest asked what else there was to see. The fact that he had been
within two feet of a wild badger—which only woke up because of
his loud-mouthed inanities—impressed him not at all. My
expression may have conveyed emotions I was too polite to put in
words, for whatever ideas he had for a series were strangled at
birth. I never heard from him again.

Once the badgers took to Primrose Dell, they foraged all over
the wood and were not slow to find the sett by the house. It was of
entirely different construction and looked, from the window, like
an outsize compost heap.

Badgers love lying under tree roots. They are dry and give a
satisfying sense of security against men with spades. If a terrier is
sent down the hole, they can retreat into an awkward corner. The
poor dog has to thread his way through inaccessible crevices where
quick retreat is so difficult that every attack on him inflicts severe
punishment. In Hannam's day, I saw a lot of dogs sent to ground to
badgers and there was usually far greater cruelty inflicted on the
hunter than his prey. If unintelligent men are successful in digging
him out—which is now illegal—they often wreak terrible
vengeance on him in retribution.

My sort of sett was proof against such vandals because nothing
short of a mechanical digger could move the roots. Before the
roots had been piled-up and covered with soil, we had placed two
tree trunks parallel, about a foot apart. Another log or two on
top of these prevented the space between them filling with earth

and stones, so that there was a clear entrance to the heart of the pile, deeply covered with earth and roots to soundproof it and keep the weather out.

The first optimistic sign of use was a pile of freshly dug soil outside the entrance. A badger had obviously crawled along between the tree trunks and, liking what he found, decided to improve it.

Each morning the pile of soil outside gave an accurate indication of the amount of tunnels or dens he had created out of sight. As time passed on, the dense undergrowth of the wood near the sett was worn bare by criss-cross paths which showed how much and how regularly badgers were using it. To heighten the attractions, I put out nightly dollops of bread-and-treacle and thanked my stars for my luck to have neighbours only marginally interested in knocking-off foxes, and showing hospitable tolerance for badgers.

As the winter wore on, there was every sign that three of the setts I had constructed were regularly used. The soil of our wood may be heavy and offensively clammy but it provides a varied diet and I provide a sanctuary which is guaranteed against disturbance. The surrounding woodland, a relic of the ancient Forest of Needwood, naturally supports a high density of badgers so that they seemed delighted to move in over my boundary as soon as I provided residential attractions.

The following spring, I went away for four days to the Mammal Society conference. It is my annual holiday, where I meet a whole gaggle of fellow eccentrics with similar tastes. When I returned, Jess was over the moon with excitement.

'What do you think we've seen?' she said. And, knowing that I wouldn't guess, she went right on to tell me.

'Cubs,' she said. 'Three badger cubs in the sett right below the house here.' It was the pinnacle of my ambition, something which I had been working for years to achieve, so that the next few hours, till dusk, were an eternity.

We settled with field glasses by the window, and a glass of something stronger at our side. This was the right and proper way to badger-watch. If cubs emerged, it would, indeed, be cause for celebration.

Long before dusk fell, the gloom at the mouth of the hole was splintered by the white wedges on a badger's head. The sow had come up to check that all was well. She emerged into the open to have an obligatory meditative scratch and disappeared through the nettlebed to her latrine pit at the edge of the wood. I have watched badgers hundreds of times and it still gives me as much kick as the first I saw, with the Young Squire, so many years ago. They are always predictable—yet they never do the same thing twice. However precisely they fulfil expectations, there is always something fresh to see, something new to learn.

When this one came out, a rabbit was grazing the herbage almost in her path. In theory, it should have run for its life before such a savage predator. In practice, it scarcely bothered to hop two feet away. Some would say that this was a good indication that badgers are not as black as they are painted. Every blackbird and jay in the wood raises hell when a fox comes out, because foxes are so much more dangerous than badgers. It is a human generalisation that wild creatures are far too wise to fall for. I have watched foxes go through a bunch of rabbits which have hardly twitched their whiskers. They are uncomfortably aware how dangerous foxes can be—but they also know enough to perceive when they are, and when they are not, hunting. A marauding fox is spotted for what he is, and every rabbit thumps the ground to warn his fellows before he dives for cover. When the same villain has his belly full and is simply passing by, they seem to know and scarcely pay him the compliment of taking his presence seriously.

The fact that the rabbit ignored the passing sow badger might simply mean that it knew the predator's mind was more occupied with emptying her gut than filling it. It isn't a theory to which I subscribe because, of all the badgers I have watched, I've never seen one that really put the wind up the local rabbits. Except, of course, young rabbits in a 'stop'.

Rabbits usually leave the communal warren to have their young. They dig a single, short tunnel, often no more than five or six feet long with the end hollowed out in the shape of an Indian club. They leave their kittens here, filling in the entrance to the hole behind them and only return to suckle and clean them. They

are safe from other rabbits, which are spiteful, aggressive brutes, but particularly vulnerable to badgers, which dig them out and eat them.

So, in theory, rabbits ought to be terrified of badgers, but in practice they are not. Most of the danger is past by the time they are weaned and can outrun the swiftest brock.

Within a few minutes, the sow badger returned and disappeared into the sett. I had no means of knowing what went on below ground because it had not been possible to bug that sett, but seconds later the gloom was lightened, not by one set of white stripes, but three.

The month was April and the cubs were almost as big as half-grown cats. Not as long, perhaps, or as lithe, and certainly shorter on the leg. They were well-fed, rotund and full of fun.

Almost as soon as they came out in the open, one of them began rocking from fore feet to hind, bouncing around as rhythmically as a miniature rocking horse powered by perpetual motion. His brothers or sisters immediately joined in the fun, rolling and gambolling, resilient as rubber balls and the more playful and excited they grew, the more their fur fluffed out, as frightened cats' tails do, and the higher pitched their squeals and squeaks of mock anger became.

Judging from their size, the cubs were about three months old and I still can't understand why I hadn't seen them before. It was certainly not the first time they'd been out, because they had the bold air of self-confidence of creatures who knew the territory as well as the fur on their well-groomed coats. If the sett had lain vacant and unused all winter, I should have thought the sow had been disturbed from the nursery of her choice and brought her youngsters here for peace and quiet. But the sett had been used continually and I can only suppose the cubs were born there and simply hadn't come out while we'd been watching.

Whatever the explanation, I was more than satisfied. All young wild animals are beautiful, none more so than badger cubs, and only the most callous louts would harm them. So far as this litter was concerned, I was thankful that they had chosen to accept my hospitality and that I was in a position to see that no one interfered with them.

CHAPTER 4

The Outsiders

For the next week or so, the cubs filled our eyes with pleasure—and lulled us into a false sense of security.

In theory, they should not have distracted me in working hours because the books say that they are crepuscular creatures, active only at dusk and dawn. It should have been possible to concentrate from before breakfast till after supper but it didn't work out like that. At lunch time one day, I looked up from my desk in time to see such theories toppled. Halfway down the tump a grey, furry form was somersaulting as if some unseen hand had pitched it from the top. I couldn't believe my eyes. Badgers abroad at midday? Impossible.

As I sat transfixed, the 'unseen hand' rocketted over the summit, turning out to be another badger cub. It ricocheted after its brother (or sister) down the slope, bouncing from tussock to tussock with the resilience of a rubber ball. The first cub, lying in wait at the bottom, zoomed-in for its revenge and the two cubs rollicked and roistered as carefree as if dusk had fallen in the heart of secluded woodland at the back of beyond.

I was torn between the practical urge to stay rooted to my chair, determined not to miss a trick, and the less selfish reaction of fetching Jess to see the fun. We have shared so many thrills—and so many disappointments—in the last forty years that for me to hog such an unrehearsed performance would have been unthinkable. Within fifteen seconds, we were both settled by the window but, in my absence, the cubs had disappeared.

We couldn't decide what had induced such apparently uncharacteristic behaviour. When keepers kill a sow which they see is suckling cubs, they patrol the area of the sett two or three days afterwards and are often able to catch the cubs as well, when starvation drives them into the open in search of their mother. Apart from starving cubs in search of food, or badgers disturbed or diseased, it is unusual to see them out except at twilight. I had certainly never seen cubs out in the open in the middle of the day, though adults occasionally lie out to sun themselves, as foxes do, and countrymen sometimes see them staggering home in the morning after a night on the tiles.

There was no means of knowing where our cubs had gone in the few seconds I was out of sight. They could have wandered off into the rhododendron thickets or into the oak wood—or returned down the hole under the roots. Lunch was forgotten, we had to wait and see.

Five minutes later, the dark hole facing us was suddenly split by the familiar white stripes of a badger's mask. A large mask, which turned out to be the sow doing a reconnaissance to check that the coast was clear. She stayed motionless at the mouth of the hole, testing the breeze for enemies and I wondered why the warm, steamy April weather did not cause convection currents to belch up the tunnel from the den and blot out faint scents outside with the familiar fug of badgers underground.

As soon as she was satisfied, she emerged completely and allowed herself the luxury of a searching, meditative scratch.

We were not, of course, close enough to hear any slight sound she might have made but she seemed so absorbed by her toilet that it was unlikely that she would concentrate on routine domestic discipline. We couldn't decide whether it was with or without permission that the cubs erupted to join her.

This time all three paraded. One bit his mother's tail—without producing the faintest sign that she had noticed—while the other climbed to the top of the tump and resumed the boisterous game of king of the castle.

All young things are delightful to watch at play—young badgers more than most. Although they lack the lithe grace of foxes, their rampant enthusiasm seems to power them with steel springs instead of mortal muscles. They rolled and gambolled for

ten minutes or so before the sow suddenly tensed, presumably at some sound or scent she didn't like. One second, she was relaxed at ease outside the hole, the next, both she and the cubs had vanished.

It killed any ideas we may have had about starting to badger-watch after tea. Having once seen the cubs playing, when text books said that they should be asleep, we were determined to discover whether daylight activity was the exception or the rule. It is hard enough to concentrate on writing with no distractions but irrelevant thoughts milling round the back of my mind. When there is the real possibility of breaking new ground, my discipline disintegrates.

The joy of watching those cubs playing in broad daylight, not once, but for several consecutive days, held out prospects which had so far been confined to the never-never land of daydreams.

Badgers had frequented our wood ever since we came, ten years before, and they had taken to the artificial setts we had provided almost as readily as tits to a tit-box. The fact that we had had a garrulous gang of sportsmen on our doorstep without upsetting them or us had encouraged the belief that it is the rule rather than the exception for conservation to march hand-in-hand with sport.

The sudden arrival of a litter of cubs within a stone's throw added a new dimension to potential perils over the boundary fence. I had spent so much effort in persuading badgers to live where I could easily observe them whenever they moved in daylight that it was no longer possible to take anything that posed the faintest threat for granted.

At the end of the previous season, the farmers who had enjoyed the shooting as guests of my neighbour for about ten years, had been replaced by a conventional syndicate paying big money to rent the sporting rights. Until the arrival of the badger cubs, I hadn't worried much about them, but their possible effect on the cubs suddenly concentrated my mind.

Suppose that the new syndicate did not turn out to be as co-operative as the last? Suppose that they brought a keeper with no greater tolerance for 'vermin' than Hannam had had. Although they had been renting the shoot for the last three months, I knew nothing whatsoever about them. This, in itself, was ominous. When the previous shoot started, the first thing they had done was to make their number with their neighbours. It is a civilised country custom to tell folk who you are when you arrive. That is the way to get their permission to go over their boundary, on shooting days, to retrieve wounded birds and put them out of their misery.

I hadn't bothered, till the cubs appeared, because I knew that the new syndicate wouldn't shoot till October—and there was plenty of time before then. All that I knew so far was that I sometimes saw flash cars sizzling up the drive and, once or twice, I had seen enormous vans, twice as big as furniture vans, going past the house in convoy. The name painted in huge letters on the sides proclaimed the fact that their normal use was to carry the stuffing used for chairs.

Anything so out of context raises rural eyebrows. Every stranger in the country is the focal point for gossip at the local inn. Such rumours had it that these pantechnicons belonged to a magnate who had made his brass in bedding. Irreverent wags down at the local jumped to the conclusion that the shoot had been let to 'some sort of furniture-stuffer from Glossop'.

Discounting such tattle as the rubbish it probably was, I made enquiries in more reliable quarters. I gathered that the mammoth vans had been used to transport the netting and pens, incubators and brooders and other contranklements now considered indispensable for rearing pheasants by the thousand. That sort of sophisticated gear would be useless without a professional keeper, and my second discovery was that the new syndicate's keeper was installed in a house about a mile away, at the other side of the farm.

This inspired niggling doubts about why neither he nor his masters had ever called, as the previous syndicate had done. Was it because they didn't know what country manners were, or was it simply because every flying visit was so jam-packed with action that it left no time for social calls? It was a question I should normally have interred at the back of my mind to wait and see what happened in due course.

The badgers opposite my window gave the whole question urgency. Whoever the new syndicate were, and whatever their views, it was vital that they should know about my work with badgers so that, if harm befell them, it could not have been by accident.

Deer, not badgers, were my introduction to the keeper. Among the harsh realities of spring, as already mentioned, is the seasonal urge of straying dogs to worry sheep. Our dogs have the run of the yard and paddock by the house and the first indication we often get of intruders in the wood are the high-pitched, almost hysterical barks ours utter when strange dogs are on the rampage. They often strike up this staccato malediction when hounds are hunting locally, long before the cry of the pack or the notes of the horn are audible to human ears.

So, when the dogs chimed out at dead of night, I went to the window to discover what was afoot. It was far too dark to see and the shindy our dogs were kicking up would have drowned the sound of foxhounds in full cry. So I confined them in the comfort of the kitchen—which calmed them—and went out into the yard myself. Half a mile away, deep in my neighbour's wood, a rhythmic yapping warned that somebody's dogs were hunting something. It was far enough from our land to pose no immediate threat so, selfishly perhaps, I tumbled back to bed.

Next day, a forestry worker found the body of a deer fast in the fence. She had tried to jump over, but got a leg stuck between the top of the netting and the barbed wire, six inches above it. The dogs had torn out her throat, feasted and gone home. Two days later the same fate befell another deer.

Although it was on the keeper's beat and, in theory, nothing to do with me, it had been far too close for comfort. My profession entails a good deal of filming for television and a few deer that are steady enough for reasonable filming are high among my assets. If the dogs got into my wood and chivvied my deer around, they would soon get far too spooky to allow any cameraman within a hundred yards. Quite apart from the fact that, having spent hundreds of hours getting them comparatively tame, I am not prepared to allow anyone's dog to chase them with impunity. So I rang up the keeper, told him that dogs had killed two deer on his beat—and would presumably extend their services to pheasants. If he would call at my home, I would tell him where they were.

Half an hour later, he arrived at the gate. Although we had been neighbours for three months or so, we had never met, so I introduced myself.

'Oh! I've heard about you,' he said. 'You're the man that harbours badgers.' My hackles rose. 'Harbours badgers!' The phrase rankled in my mind so that I was torn between a slanging match and courtesy.

I try never to be rude except on purpose, so counted ten. He had an efficient Land Rover and respectable keeper's suit and the air of authority that keepers acquire through holding the power of life and death over huge tracts of countryside. He had presumably been charged with producing large bags of pheasants from most unpromising terrain and, in my book, the odds against success were pretty long. So I had some sympathy with his resentment against anything which might knock-off a pheasant, except members of his syndicate. The implication conveyed by his choice of words posed similar threats to my badgers. 'Harbours' badgers, indeed. The words stuck in my throat, but nothing was to be gained by responding to the challenge until the time was ripe.

I invited him into my study, gave him a cup of coffee and showed him some photographs of the badgers I'd been working with for the best part of a decade. He was unimpressed. I gave him a copy of my book *Badgers At My Window* and added my signature to the title page. 'I don't read books,' he said. 'I haven't time.'

Hannam would have treated a similar stranger with more finesse. So would lots of keepers I know who have been brought up to believe that the only good predators, with hooked bills or canine teeth, are dead predators, but realise it doesn't always pay to say so.

As gently as I could, I explained that my badgers were, by his standards, very ignorant. They didn't understand the boundaries on a map and there was nothing that I could do to deter them from passing from my ground, through the fence, to his.

I honestly believe that, in wooded, heavily foxed country like ours, badgers probably do pheasant shooting more good than harm.

Pheasants are idle birds that rarely fly when they can run. By the same token, they prefer to roost, or 'jug', in a warm tussock or reed clump on the ground to flying up to a draughty perch aloft. If a fox prowls round, his sensitive nose locates a pheasant jugging in thick cover as easily as a pointer would. He stalks it carefully until he has pin-pointed it precisely, and pounces on it to ensure it never runs the risk of being shot. A badger, on the other hand, bumbles around in search of worms and slugs and beetles. I have watched badgers cannon into sitting bantams—which recover from the shock more quickly than the badgers, and fluster away to safety. Only if they are stupid enough to panic into wire netting or dense cover is their mobility so impaired that the badger will capture them. It is hard to protect fools from their folly.

Pheasants are more mobile than fussy bantams. When badgers disturb them roosting on the ground, they make a clean getaway — and roost aloft next night. If a pheasant happened to be sitting on a clutch of eggs, the badger who stumbled across her and drove her off, might eat her eggs as a bonus. Good luck to him. If a fox had found her, he would have stalked her first and made certain that she didn't live to lay a second clutch. Then he'd have had the eggs for pudding.

So I explained to the new keeper that I reckoned that badgers did him more good, by making pheasants roost safe from foxes, than harm by stealing eggs, especially as most modern shoots do not rely on wild birds but hatch eggs, by the thousand, in incubators, and release the poults to freedom in the woods only when they are large enough to fly up to roost.

I could see that I was getting nowhere. I was also getting very cross. 'All right,' I said, 'If we can't co-operate, we'll do it the hard way. You see that mound over there? There is a sow badger and three cubs in it. Rightly or wrongly, if she disappears, I shall assume it was because of you. Then I will have more of your pheasants than all the foxes and all the badgers would have taken.'

He could not believe his ears. No decent fellow in the countryside would touch his neighbour's birds. They are stupid, wandering brutes and, even with luck on one's side, it is hard enough to persuade them to hang around until the shooting season. To have anyone so ill-disposed just over the boundary would tip the scales unfairly.

He blinked in silence, then he asked me to repeat what I said. The steam had had time to go out of my rising temper, so I back-pedalled a bit and explained that, living on the far side of his beat, I could be of great benefit in warning him of trespassers and poachers—so long as he let my badgers alone. But I repeated the fact that I was doing serious research on badgers, and that if he was not prepared to reciprocate by leaving them in peace, I would make certain that the shoot near me was as uneconomic as possible.

This time he heard alright—and I don't blame him for trying to discover whether I really was as eccentric as he obviously thought.

'And how would you do that?' he asked. 'Are you a poacher?' I told him that I had been brought up with keepers and poachers and that their techniques were not unknown to me. But I assured him that he would not catch me poaching on his beat. I had no need. My wood was the only oak wood in the area and, every autumn, pheasants gathered from all around to reap the acorn harvest. Up to then, I had never done them any harm and they had wandered off to return to the estate unscathed. But, if the litter of cubs in the earth by my window disappeared, and I had the faintest suspicion of foul play, any pheasants that visited me would have a one-way ticket. I would not shoot them once a fortnight but trap them seven days a week.

My threat was unfair, uncivilised and unforgiveable. But I had come to the conclusion that my visitor was a tough customer of the kind who frequently advertise their services in the *Shooting Times's* 'Situations Wanted' columns as 'good vermin catchers'. I calculated that, if he thought I was as soft as his idea of a fuddy-duddy naturalist, he might practise his art as a vermin catcher at the expense of any predators, in fur or feather, which strayed onto his beat. My one chance seemed to be to talk to him in what I construed was his own language, and convince him that it simply would not pay to kill my badgers.

The message failed to find its mark. 'I'm very hard on badgers,' he said. 'I won't have one on my beat.' And he took himself off in deep dudgeon.

At that stage, I did what I should have done at the beginning. I contacted the agent who had let the shoot and obtained the telephone number of the man who was renting it. Introducing myself as his neighbour, I told him that his keeper and I had got off to a bad start and that our views on badgers appeared to be poles apart. I hadn't had time to discover how, or if, he proposed to control them, so I played safe and asked his boss to forbid the use of poison—which is indiscriminate as well as illegal—and to arrange for the keeper to catch his foxes in free-running snares from which badgers could be released if they were caught accidentally. I suggested that a meeting between us might iron out the problems. My neighbour seemed very co-operative so I confirmed our conversation by letter and enclosed a copy of my book, which gave a detailed account of my work with badgers for the previous decade. He could then judge for himself what a serious set-back it would be for me if the badgers in my wood were sacrificed for his sport.

A couple of weeks later he wrote to say that he had asked his keeper to avoid killing badgers. He added that he had been in the area the weekend before but didn't have time to call in because he hadn't returned to the shoot after lunch. He hadn't had chance to read the book but thought the style attractive.

Meanwhile, the cubs in the sett by the house were pure delight. When we had bulldozed the roots into a pile and covered them with earth, I had had enough faith in the project to erect a rough wooden observation tower, about twelve feet high, within ten yards of the sett. This gave the option of watching at close quarters from above or through binoculars from the house. The magnification of the binoculars brought the subjects up to about the same apparent distance.

One of the main difficulties in watching badgers on the edge of woodland, as these were, is that convection currents are quite unpredictable. The wind may well be coming from the south so that, in theory, the proper place to watch them is a few yards to the north. But the wind twists and swirls through the trees and wayward eddies play along the woodland edge so that, it seems, the whole area is polluted by the taint of human scent. It is easy enough to put this to the test by lighting a scrap of paper and making a mental plot of the path of the smoke. The fact that my high seat was raised above the ground was of tremendous help. As evening approached the air cooled faster than the ground so that, whichever direction the wind was from, there was always a chance that the warm air rising from the ground would hoist my scent in eddies out of reach of any earthbound badger's nose.

A venerable clump of rhododendrons conceals one end of the tump from the window, so that it was possible for cubs to emerge and forage off into the wood without alerting anyone watching from the house. This gave the high seat an advantage but, once we had discovered that badgers are not as restricted to dusk as we thought, there was an obvious risk of scaring them if the moment I chose to climb into the high seat happened to coincide with their emergence.

I should really have liked to have fitted up a spring and micro-switch at the mouth of the sett as I had done with Bill, my hand-reared badger. They are such creatures of habit that they cheerfully shoulder aside heavy 'badger-gates' mounted in fence lines, provided that they are sited where they would normally pass. The snag was that I just didn't dare take any risks of scaring them over my boundary. The shooting tenant had promised to be co-operative but he lived so far from his keeper that the proof of the pudding depended less on the master than on the cook. Only time would tell whether the keeper was prepared to pay more than lip service to his orders.

The possibility of disturbing the badgers by messing about at the mouth of the sett while fitting up a micro-switch, did not seem a

sensible risk to take, so I abandoned the idea of monitoring or bugging by conventional methods. Modern burglar alarms are activated when an intruder 'breaks' a ray, which carries no tell-tale scent, but when I enquired how much it would cost, it scared me off. The only safe—and cheap—way of enjoying the cubs was to sit by the window with our vision enriched by a powerful pair of binoculars.

It was astonishing how fast they grew when once they were making regular appearances above ground. They were as noisy and boisterous as bad-mannered kids and it was a relief to see them knocking hell out of each other instead of biting my tender fingers and wrists as my otherwise delightful hand-reared cubs had done. Although they were far from weaned and broke off either work or play for a snack from the dam's dugs, they seemed to start foraging for themselves earlier than Bill and his two sows had done. This, of course, was precisely what the boffins had predicted, and the prospect of being able to test the theories I had evolved by observing the behaviour of these wild cubs was very exciting.

Although animal play is entertaining for us to watch, it has a deadly serious purpose. A kitten pirouetting round the floor with a table tennis ball is limbering up to capture prey without which it might, in future, starve. Our fallow deer follow close on each other's heels in spectacular zig-zag flight over terrain that seems certain to break their fragile legs. A casual observer might visualise it as a primitive ballet dance, dreamed up by some divine choreographer. They rocket round, often through thick cover, for sheer joie de vivre, stopping at last to allow their heaving flanks to pump in fresh breath. It is tempting to be anthropomorphic and believe that the winner will be crowned victor ludorum.

The truth is more likely to be that such play teaches the physical layout of territory better than any other. A deer that knows the precise hazards in the wood can go flat-out between the trees faster than a pursuing predator which is a stranger. A hare, hotly pursued by a greyhound, will sometimes aim directly for a tree but jink to one side at the very last split second. If she is successful, the dog's momentum will be too great for him to take similar evasive action by the time he realises what has happened. Many a good dog has died that way.

So, in fairness, has many a deer. My favourite white fallow doe Honey, which I bottle-reared six years ago, has had four dark fawns by wild bucks. Then, for the first time, she had a very light

coloured dappled doe which was the apple of her eye, and mine. When she was about a month old, this fawn could outstrip all the other fawns in the wood, and her dare-devil dashes nightly caught our breath. Her tiny cloven hooves propelled her through the trees at breakneck speed.

One afternoon, Jess noticed that the old doe had been standing in the middle of a ride all day and, when I went to investigate, I found her fawn stiff in death with a blotch of blood staining her muzzle. A post mortem revealed that she had either been kicked in the ribs, which is unlikely, or had cannoned into an unseen branch or root or stump hidden in the undergrowth. Her whole ribcage was bruised and her lung was badly lacerated.

Badger play has an equally serious purpose. The cubs don't chase each other as practice for escape from other predators, for no predator but man need exercise their minds. Nor are they playing in preparation for catching food to eat because there is no need to be a sprinter to catch worms or slugs, or to eat laid corn or fruit or baby rabbits too young to leave the nest.

There was no doubt about the objective of the cubs we watched. They were indulging in mock fights, and thoroughly enjoying it, but they would be fierce opponents when they were adult. They puffed out their fur, to exaggerate how formidable they were and tainted the air with the virility of their anal musk. They rolled each other over, attacking their opponents' tails, pretending to paralyse them by mutilating the bases of their spines. They tenderucified each other by savaging their victims' private parts. All good, strong drama to watch from our sitting-room window, far better and more immediate than anything on the box.

Sadly, there were too few repeat performances. Just as we were getting the hang of the timing of their programme, they wrapped it up. One night, there was a gala show; the next, the curtain never rose. In the morning, when I went out to investigate, everything looked normal. The soil to the sett entrance was padded flat with constant wear from many feet. The latrine pits contained fresh dung and there was a pile of crumpled bracken bedding that had been left out to air. Nervous that I should taint the place, I didn't go too close but crept away when I was satisfied that everything looked normal.

Perhaps, instead of playing on our side of the rhododendron, in the open, they were growing up and exploring deeper into the wood. I had noticed lately, that their play was interspersed by much grubbing and digging with their snouts, as pigs and hedgehogs do. Several times, I had seen a cub actually foraging with the sow, making a grab to poach it if she caught a large and juicy worm. Rather than risk disturbance, I decided to spend one more night by the window. If I saw nothing then, I'd perch myself in the high seat and have a look at what went on in the wood.

Next night was blank and we never saw a badger. In the morning, the path to the sett was pitted with rain but not over-trodden by returning badger feet. Far worse, the pile of bedding, left out two nights before, was lying untouched, sodden and limp as flowers by a grave when the funeral feast is over.

In the ordinary way, there would have been no great cause for worry because it is not uncommon for badgers to leave a sett for weeks or months and take up their abode somewhere else. An old country saying claims that nobody ever sees a dead donkey. It is obviously an exaggeration, but it is certainly true that, road accidents and trapping apart, very few people ever see a dead badger either.

My own theory about this—and I have no proof to substantiate it—is that the worst enemy of a badger is another badger, so that they must be in some danger of meeting their end as a result of fatal fights. I have not the least shred of doubt that Bill Brock would have died from wounds suffered during his battle in my wood, if I had not happened to hear the commotion and rescued him in time. I don't think that his adversary would have killed him outright. Being the tough creature badgers are, he would probably have managed to crawl back to his sett, where he could have died alone in dignified agony. Had he done so, the stench of putrefaction down the hole would soon have been horrific.

If there had been plenty of alternative accommodation, my guess is that the other badgers would have moved to a sweeter smelling sett. I dare say that this is one of the reasons why badgers suddenly change their living quarters. So perhaps there were originally not three cubs but four in my sett. And perhaps the reason I had never seen the fourth may have been that he was dead. When he putrefied too much for comfort, perhaps the dam and siblings had left him to rot alone.

It is idle to speculate how long they would normally have taken to return. That would depend partly on whether the local population was sparse or overcrowded. If it were sparse and there were plenty of desirable alternative residences, it could have been months before they were back. If the area was heavily populated, so that territorial competition was intense, a 'high' badger in the sett might have been the least of many evils.

The animals could easily return and control the stench by the simple expedient of walling in their comrade. In due course, when he was desiccated and odourless, his remains would be excavated and would end up in the heap of soil that characterises the entrance to 'worked' setts. It may well be that this habit of clearing out the mortal remains of their ancestors along with used bedding gives rise to the theory that badgers conduct their own funerals. The men from the Ministry of Agriculture might be able to confirm this. They have had unrivalled experience in killing badgers, and have gassed one sett in Gloucestershire more than twenty times. They found that it was repopulated by wave after suicidal wave of badgers from around who walled up the corpses of their predecessors.

The next few weeks were nail-biters. The cubs had gone, and I had absolutely no reason for suspecting foul play apart from vague impressions gained from my solitary conversation with the keeper.

The two setts near Primrose Dell, at the far end of the wood, were occupied by adults which I believed to be last year's cubs that hadn't bred. My curiosity prompted me to spend long hours watching to discover if the sow and cubs had joined them. Commonsense dictated a policy of leaving well alone lest I disturb them and drive them over my neighbour's boundary. Commonsense won, but I never saw the cubs again and have no idea what happened to them. Within a couple of months, the badgers had also left the sett in Primrose Dell and, for the first time since we had come to live here, there were no badgers in my wood. A pipe dream that had taken years to compose was shattered overnight.

There was no hard evidence as to the cause of their disappearance, and I tapped the local grapevine without any great success. So I was gratified, a few weeks later, to receive a letter from the shooting tenant to say that he had now had time to read my book and knew a little more about badgers than when he started. He added that his keeper was doing his best to see that my badgers came to no harm and that, so far, only one had been caught in a snare, but it had been set free 'and had apparently run off quite happily'.

Bitter personal experience of disentangling badgers from snares had taught me that they are unlikely to 'run off quite happily' after being trapped, so I thought this rather over-optimistic. I hoped that it hadn't been my sow from the sett beside the house. The idea of 'my' cubs starving because their mother had been snared was too repugnant to contemplate.

Since my new neighbour appeared co-operative but seemed to have no practical experience with badgers, I repeated my invitation to him to drop in for a chat.

The following Sunday, a Rolls-Royce glided up to the back door, followed by a Range Rover and an E-Type Jag. Few country folk bother about the formality of using front doors, so I had left the yard gate open. Their prestigious machinery elevated us to the status of the stockbroker-belt at cocktail time.

Our visitors exuded an air of opulent prosperity and the boss-man's opening gambit was, 'My word, Mr Drabble, you've got a fine pad here. If you're thinking of parting with it, will you give me first refusal?' I have every intention of staying here till I'm carried out feet first, and felt that my rejoinder hardly matched his geniality. I said I hoped to live longer than he did.

We walked round the wood and I recounted my fears for my badgers which had disappeared. I showed them the artificial setts I'd made, demonstrating the fact that there were a nice lot of wild pheasants, in spite of the fact that, for several generations they had been forced to share their habitat with such reputed predators as badgers. They sized-up my potential acorn crop, presumably assessing the temptations to any of their birds that strayed over my boundary—and we indulged in a little lighthearted verbal fencing.

The whole bizarre episode demonstrated the almost unbridge-able gulf between different legitimate interests competing for the countryside.

I earn my living with my pen—and if my pen runs dry I shall go hungry and thirsty. My overheads are almost nil and I depend not on what my workforce does for me but on what I do for myself. I suppose it must have seemed to them eccentric that I should dedicate such a large slice of my life to conserving predators that are useless for any legal sport. They doubtless worked just as hard as I did and probably measured their success by the quality of leisure they enjoyed. To see their point of view more clearly, I did a few sums to get some idea of the cost of a shoot like theirs and to see how much was at stake if it turned out to be a flop.

I had a fair idea of the rent because, when it had been put out to tender, I had written for particulars. I knew that the asking price was in the region of £2,500 a year and I reckoned the keeper's wages would double it at least. The depreciation and running costs of the keeper's Land Rover would add another £500 and sporting rates, perhaps another £300. Six acres of land on the farm were fenced, cultivated and sown with a game mixture of sunflower, rape, buckwheat and kale, as patches of holding and feeding cover to keep the birds where they could be driven to the guns. That would add about £300—topping the £6,000 mark. The keeper's house was heated with oil, the incubators were electric and the brooders powered by bottled gas, which would add another £300 or so, while the working capital involved in pantechnicon loads of brooders and incubators and other game rearing equipment would take more pennies from the pile. All this before the cost of a single pheasant (or its food) was taken into account. At a conservative estimate, I reckoned the shoot must have cost between £7,000 and £10,000 a year.

The man who carried the can for its success was, ultimately, the keeper. The game book, in Hannam's day, was the yardstick which propped up a keeper. If bags were good, everybody loved him. If too many invited guests had blank days, he was liable to find another man in possession of his cottage when he came in off the beat.

I doubt if things are very different now. Some men claim their shoots as allowable expenses for entertaining foreign customers. Others run company shoots, paid for out of profits, with keepers on the factory payroll as security men, and similar gimmicks which the tax man can sometimes be hoodwinked into examining through his blind eye. Any honest man who has ten grand to spare out of what the taxman leaves is unlikely to dilute his shrewdness with much sentiment. A keeper who doesn't deliver the goods can expect short-shrift from him.

When I totted-up the size of stake we were playing for, it was difficult to be optimistic. I had done half a lifetime's work to buy a place I could manage as a nature reserve. My visitors sweated it out in factories five days a week—and wanted to enjoy a day or so's sport in the country when they stopped to breathe. I had seen my point of view, with clarity, all along. Now that I assessed theirs, in £.s.d., I could see that too.

Things turned out better than I had expected at this first meeting with the tenant. He promised to tell his keeper that he would not hold the loss of a few pheasants against him. He must spare the badgers and, if they were proved to do great damage, we would work out the solution between us. This suited me fine, because I had every confidence that badgers, if they returned, would behave themselves, so I promised to do my part as a watch-dog for trespassers my end of the shoot, and to rear more pheasants to put into my wood than I took out, so that there would be no question of 'milking' theirs. We parted with protestations of mutual goodwill and high hopes for the future.

There are wild fallow deer in our wood which I have tamed by feeding with tit-bits and never disturbing. My bottle-reared white doe, Honey, acts as a decoy and persuades even the new arrivals, from the wood across the drive, that it is perfectly safe to feed close to the house. The result is that our deer are a substantial asset to my work as well as a pleasure to watch.

This is only possible because I protect them from disturbance and give them a solid sense of security. It is therefore very important to me that they are not chivvied round by foxhounds

and, the first time it happened, the master and I had what politicians would call a full and frank discussion! The master, who hunted them himself, was a competent professional and, when he realised a tame and steady deer was worth as much to me as a prize bull to a farmer, he took effective measures to see that his hounds did not trouble us again.

All went well for some years until the hunt acquired a new master. The day his hounds met in the district, I happened to be involved with a journalist and his wife who were doing a story about conservation in my wood.

Although they were obviously more accustomed to the city smoke, we had a pleasant day, wandering in quiet places, watching deer and birds and discussing the badger setts and my plans for the future. The article was for a government periodical produced for old folk and they wanted an evocative picture summing up my attitude to wildlife.

Honey, the white doe, is incurably greedy and, when I rattled a bucket of corn, she came straight up to the house to feed from my hand. Most photographers seem to me to take an excessively long time fiddling about before they take their shot—and these were no exception. I had seen it all before so I turned myself off, and left them to it.

Imperceptibly, a sinister sound etched itself into the back of my mind. Although the country is superficially so quiet, there are always background noises, which I subconsciously register—and ignore when I know what they are. One neighbour calls up his cows night and morning with such banshee yoicks and yells that strangers visualise murder and rape. Since I know what it is, I never notice them. Another neighbour keeps valuable pigeons and a squad of guard dogs to protect them. They have sounded as if they are savaging intruders so often that I should no longer hear them if they did. Yet, if I am out in the wood, the faintest rustle or crack of a twig rivets my attention.

The message that filtered through my mind while the man was shooting pictures, raised the hairs on my neck seconds before I was conscious of the sound that tapped it out. All that I knew was that every nerve was jangling and my gut convulsed as the adrenalin started to flow. I was aware of danger by primitive animal instinct, though I could not have put my finger on the cause. Then the penny dropped. Far in the distance, faint as a muted sigh, was the unmistakable voice of hounds lusting for their prey. 'Quiet,' I hissed. 'Listen.' But my companions were unable to disentangle the voice of the hounds from farm dogs barking in reply or the incessant throbbing of a tractor, ploughing in the valley.

The fence around the yard and dog paddock is high enough to keep in our dogs, so it was reasonable to suppose that it would also be high enough to keep foxhounds out. I opened the wicket gate on the corner of the house and rattled my corn bucket to entice Honey in. If the hounds did come in our direction—and I hoped they wouldn't—there was absolutely nothing I could do to stop them entering the wood because the fence around it, though cattle-proof, was only four feet high. It would be bad enough if they chivvied the wild deer round but unthinkable with Honey, who had been brought up with the house dogs and regarded all dogs as her friends. Having made a quick decision about getting her safe in the yard, it was soon obvious that it was easier said than done.

Honey is hand-tame and, I repeat, extremely greedy, but she is still, at heart, a wild animal. If I take a crowd of visitors towards the wood, she will trot up, confident as an old sheep, to nuzzle the corn bucket—provided that she does not imagine anyone is trying to cut off her retreat by getting between her and cover. But the least threat to her escape route galvanises her to evasive action.

By the same token, she doesn't like gates. She came so far, but no further, and it was obvious that nothing that I could do would make her pass through that narrow wicket gate. The matter was urgent because the voices of foxhounds in full cry was now no more than a mile away across the wood. Fifty yards along the fence is a ten-foot gate through which we drive the tractor. I thought that perhaps it would look less like a trap and she might be tempted through it.

I rattled my bucket and moved along the fence. The doe was dilatory as a woman playing hard-to-get. She pretended that the few grains spilt her side of the wicket were ten times sweeter than the plenty in my bucket. The fox must have pointed his mask in our direction because the cry of the hounds swelled every second and they were now within a few hundred yards of the wood and rapidly closing the gap. They crossed the drive a hundred yards above the house and came into my wood in full cry. Once they got the scent of deer, they forgot all about the fox that had led them here. Honey heard them then and realised they were strangers. She stood tense, for a second, sizing up the situation, and then bolted up the ride opposite my study window.

Hounds converged towards her diagonally, and I feared they would run right into her at the first cross-ride, a couple of hundred yards up the wood. I reached for my rifle, put a bullet up the spout and dashed to her rescue. If they had pulled her down I would have shot every hound attacking her but, by the time I arrived, she and her pursuers had disappeared into the thicket.

She had fled to a ten-acre neck of the wood which is very dense cover. I rarely disturb it so the majority of the deer choose to lie up there and, since it juts out from the main body of the wood, we can observe and count them crossing the main ride, which points down to the window, as they enter or leave their sanctuary. The area is relatively small and the cover too thick for rapid movement.

They could not have chosen a more dangerous patch for hounds to corner her.

They had been in the wood about five minutes and I expected the huntsman to arrive at any moment. Meanwhile I marshalled my two journalists so that we were spread out along the ride to try to keep as many hounds as possible in the main compartment of the wood. This was partly because they would have more difficulty catching deer there and partly because, if they succeeded, at least Honey would not be their victim.

The journalists were hopping mad. They thought all hunting was obscene and should be stopped—deer hunting more than most. They rattled on about class privileges and idle rich and noble beasts and all the usual old claptrap, but I was far too busy with the practical task of heaving stones at any hound I saw to worry about their theories.

At first, it had seemed quite practicable to hold the fort until the huntsman arrived, simply discouraging hounds with a stick or stone aimed at their ribs when there was the opportunity, and filling their ears with verbal abuse when they were too elusive. It was like stopping a sieve with ten fingers. We were spaced so far apart along the ride that hounds treated us with disdain. As my companions grew more and more emotional, a chilling objectivity engulfed me. The naturalist's basic curiosity took control of my anxiety and I was filled with dispassionate interest in the way those deer coped with the peril that engulfed them.

It is easy to imagine that all hunted animals stampede and rush headlong in flight, evading their pursuers only so long as they are able to outpace them. Literature is full of terrified stags plunging over cliffs and foxes panicking into tight corners, from which there is no escape. It isn't like that in real life. Certainly not with deer.

Hounds had been rampaging round the isolated neck of the wood and I could hear them hunting directly towards me. I cocked my rifle, in case it was Honey they were after, but it was now an old black doe which belonged to the wild herd in the big wood across the drive. She wasn't even galloping. She minced along, prissy as a spinster, watching and listening over her shoulder, trying to make up her mind if she really was being followed. At the

edge of the ride there was a large, sprawling bramble bush, and she came out in the open to put this bush between her and her pursuers. Her icy calm bolstered her willpower to freeze immobile till hounds were no more than four or five yards away—but out of sight on the far side of the bush. As they veered to the right of it, she side-stepped silently to the left, leaving them to blunder on past her into the main part of the wood, speeded by a volley of tangible abuse from me. As the old doe slipped safely back to her chosen sanctuary, I thought that I had never seen a more impressive example of an unflappable cool head. If I could keep as balanced and think as effectively and as fast in a crisis, I should be a better man. It was an object lesson in pure survival.

I suppose that living as close to wildlife as I do makes me fairly fatalistic. Life is never cosy in the wild and I am forever seeing its tragedies and setbacks as well as its pleasant side. So long as I am doing what I can, I take things as they come. For this reason, I was less het-up about hounds getting into the wood than were my two companions. I knew where Honey was and I was doing my best to divert hounds to less vulnerable parts of the wood. That was more than enough to monopolise my concentration. When I did meet up with the master, I would enjoy the luxury of discouraging a second visit.

The journalists who had escaped for the day from the Big City could not understand this. They delivered a lecture against blood sports without realising that, at least for the moment, they were preaching not just to the converted, but to a High Priest of their creed. In order to give the tired theme a rest, I asked one of them to go to the gate from the drive to my wood and wait for the huntsman to come—which he should have done long since—and tell him where I was so that I could help him get hounds out.

Meanwhile, I made the best of things by learning more in an hour about how prey avoid their predators than I could normally learn in a year. Every time the hounds approached, the deer played a sophisticated game of hide-and-seek, allowing them to blunder past within a few yards time after time.

Professional huntsmen must get the chance to observe these mechanics of survival every time they draw a wood and I sometimes wonder how many foxes hounds would catch without the superior mental skills of a huntsman to help them. The rest of the field, the mugs who pay large subscriptions to be marshalled like school girls in a crocodile by a Field Master who won't let them get within a hundred yards of hounds, would see more by watching Gone to Earth. So in spite of my anxiety for Honey's safety, I was absorbed by the drama unfolding around her.

At this point, my journalist visitor returned from his sojourn at the gate to say that there was no sign of anyone on horseback but that he 'had given a piece of his mind to a rough looking customer in an ancient woollen cap, who seemed to be following on foot'. This subsequently turned out to be a farmer-neighbour who had seen half the pack enter the wood and kindly come over to try to divert any stragglers somewhere else. Next time he saw me he was forthright about my 'funny' visitor who had blackguarded him for trying to help. 'I had to walk off,' he said, 'or I should have put one on him.' Which would have been an experience the victim would never forget!

Meanwhile the hounds in the wood had split up and were hunting in bunches of four or five. Their voices echoed from every corner and, because they were now coming from several sides at once, deer were at last beginning to panic. We had been coping alone for almost an hour with no sign of men on horseback and my temper was approaching the point of no return.

The first follower to turn up was no pink-coated huntsman, perched in arrogance on his horse, but a vintage colonel in an ancient Morris Minor. 'Have you seen anything of hounds?' he asked. It was not a good beginning.

'The bloody things have been in my wood, hunting my deer, for more than an hour,' I said. 'Where's the bloody master?' The master has an unlikely name for such a traditional sport, and I deliberately mispronounced it as an oblique expression of my opinion.

The colonel put me right, adding that there were no hounds in my wood. Two creatures, with bloodstained jowls crept out as he said so, and he eyed my rifle with mistrust. 'Be quiet,' he said, trying to distract me, 'and listen. I can hear the horn.' The wood was silent except for the hoot of a far-off tawny owl, so the poor old man took the brunt of my pent-up emotion. I was unpardonably ungallant, because there was obviously nothing he could have done about it from the cockpit of his flivver.

Huntsmen eventually turned up when dusk had fallen and they apparently deemed discretion the better part of valour. They halted at a safe distance, hollering and tooting on their hunting horns till the last hound slunk back towards the sound.

When daylight came, I found a dead fawn and an unrelated doe. Her ears were torn off, a foreleg and her bowels had been eaten and it was evident that she had still been suckling a fawn of her own, which now stood small chance of survival as an unweaned orphan. Thankfully, Honey had escaped, though it took many weeks for her and the other survivors to recover from the shock.

The master turned up later in person to apologise. He explained that he had lost half his pack and taken over an hour to find them. Unimpressed by the feat of losing hounds in full cry, I wondered who had been in charge of which, and although he promised to try to avoid a repeat performance, I doubted his competence to control his hounds and prevent them rioting onto deer any more effectively next time. So I grudgingly forked out the cash to buy three thousand yards of heavy wire netting to raise the fence round my wood from four feet high to six.

If hounds get over that to chase my deer, it will have been an unprofitable exercise for me—but it will be distinctly unhealthy for them.

That winter the prospects for badgers in the wood showed signs of improvement. The sett opposite the house, where the cubs had been, was not re-occupied, but the one at Primrose Dell was and there were plenty of signs of work in the wood. Gamekeepers do most of their trapping in the spring, after the shooting season and before they get involved with hatching eggs and rearing poults. They are so busy stopping pheasants straying, or being poached while shooting is in progress, that there is time for little else.

I had no means of knowing whether the reappearance of badgers was a result of my meeting with the tenant at our house, whether his keeper had had a change of heart—or even if he had been connected with their disappearance in the first place, which I only suspected and could not prove. So long as they were safe now, I didn't care.

It was a marvellous opportunity for watching the repopulation of territory at first hand. The badgers I had observed in the wild had always lived in established setts, so that I had no means of

knowing how or when they first decided to live where they did. Text books are conspicuous by their silence on the matter, possibly, I suspect, because the experts who write them rarely live in badger-country and so concentrate on established setts they visit when they have the chance.

I had been lucky only because I provided purpose-built setts, with piped entrances and observed them daily till they were occupied.

I had made clearings in the wood, as deer lawns, to provide additional grazing. I sold the timber and bulldozed the roots into piles so that I could cultivate the space, and I had had these roots covered with a foot or so of soil before the bulldozer left.

The first animals to take possession of this residential paradise were rabbits. The stench of diesel had scarcely drifted away before rabbits were scratching in the soil and disappearing into the root pile underground. When they bred—which is at almost any season—foxes heard or smelt their kittens, enlarged the entrance tunnels so that they could follow underground and make a meal. The intrinsic attractions of safe refuge in dry tree roots are as great for foxes as for rabbits and, every spring, there is a litter of cubs in one or other of the root piles where a vixen has enlarged a rabbit burrow. She doesn't often survive till autumn because the fewer foxes there are in my wood, the less temptation there will be for hounds to follow them.

Whenever I am out in the wood, I cast my eye over the root piles. I know the patterns of rabbit holes, pockmarked over their surface as accurately as the pictures on a familiar puzzle. I scrutinise the new ones and ponder the cause when cobwebs appear across the mouths of holes, or seedlings decorate well padded runs with greenery. The tenants have obviously gone and the puzzle is whether the cause of their demise is natural predation or yet another wave of man-spread myxomatosis.

It is an obscene disease in which the head swells to almost twice its natural size and the eyes and private parts disintegrate with suppurating pus. Scientists developed the disease in their laboratories and it is deliberately spread in Australia as a 'control' of rabbits. In this country, the vector is the rabbit flea, which innoculates 'clean' rabbits after feeding on the blood of infected specimens. Since these fleas don't fly, it is difficult to see how isolated pockets of rabbits catch it. Some countryfolk suspect that infected rabbits—at a blackmarket price of a tenner or so apiece— are dumped in healthy stock by disgruntled farmers or officious pest officers. It would be quite illegal to do so and no successful prosecution has ever been brought so that such theories are no more than speculation.

Occasionally, when I'm investigating the rabbit buries in the wood, my eye is caught by a hole far bigger than the rest. It may only be an enlargement made to extract a fox's supper, or a den opened up by a vixen to have her cubs but, just once in a while, it is the jackpot. In that case there will be a barrowful of earth to indicate that a badger has taken a fancy to it and opened it up to make a survey. That is usually all that happens for a while, but within a week or so, the spoil heap at the entrance will spill out another mound of earth when, with luck, the badger will have extended a visit to full residence.

The big tump on the far side of a glade contains several hundred tons of roots and earth which, having proved irresistible to rabbits, had been occupied by a vixen which had left it in favour of fields of standing corn. That November it was claimed by badgers which I believed to be surplus cubs from a lovely well-drained sandy sett on a farm down in the valley. Although it was four or five hundred yards from the house, it was in full view of the window and we looked forward to happy hours with binoculars in spring when evenings lengthened but, long before such dreams came true, the seasonal sheep-worrying troubles started.

I heard dogs several times hunting in the big wood across the drive but nobody reported finding mutilated deer. Then, in broad daylight, the familiar high-pitched voices of dogs about to kill chimed out across the forty-acre field opposite the house. Knowing his sheep were there, I telephoned my neighbour and then dashed across to join him. We were just too late to save a ewe which was being savaged by two sheep dogs. The farmer killed them both with a right and left and we found another dead ewe ten yards away. One dog had a collar bearing an address three miles away, but when the police called round, the owner said the collar was his but not the dog. His dog, it seemed, had died, so he put the collar on a stray which immediately ran away. It was such a good story on the spur of the moment that I suppose it might have been true!

Two days later I thought I heard a dog hunting on land leased by the shoot but, when I got there, it was much further off than I had thought. On the way back, I noticed a circular patch, about a yard in diameter, worn in the ground on the edge of the field. It was typical of the efforts of a badger to get out of a snare and investigation showed badger hair scuffed off on the post used to anchor the snare. I found two more self-lock snares set further down the fence line. On enquiry, I was told that a badger had got in a fox wire but had been liberated. Judging by the efforts he had obviously made, I doubted if he had 'run off quite happily'. To make a bad job worse, the snares were only about two hundred yards from my boundary.

We had agreed in the summer that only free-running snares would be used for foxes—but these were self-lock, from which it is both difficult and dangerous to liberate a badger, even if the will is there.

I said nothing at the time but decided to have a good look round for myself. I knew that the keeper used a Land Rover—which was a double-edged tool. It may have transported him quickly from place to place but the noise of its approach gave unauthorised visitors plenty of time to disappear quietly into cover until it was past. The self-lock snares that I had seen proved to be no exceptions, and I eventually came across one on the furthest boundary of the shoot; it had also been sprung. This time there was no chance of the victim running away happily. In her efforts to escape, a lovely sow badger had gone round and round the anchor post, winding herself in with each revolution until she applied the immense pressure of a tourniquet. The wire had bitten into her flesh and crushed out her life. When I found her, she was cold and stiff in death.

I wondered how long it was since the snare had been inspected, how long the sow had struggled before she died. Droplets of milk had been squeezed from her teats and her udder was still distended so that I knew her orphan cubs were doomed to die.

Feeling sick, I stood in contemplation, torn between legal action and an almost overwhelming urge for violence. I settled for the law. The 1973 Badgers Act had made it illegal to take, injure or kill badgers, or to cruelly ill-treat them. This seemed to fit all four criteria. So I fetched the police, showed them the untouched badger—and other snares not far away—and suggested that the rest was up to them.

They would take no action because there was no hard evidence who had set the snare. Even if there had been, they said that the defence of setting it for a fox and catching a badger 'by mistake' would have been unanswerable.

There never was, of course, any proof that it was the local keeper who had caught the badger. As his master rightly pointed out, if I could walk round the shoot and find it, I could also have been there before and set the snare. Or so could anybody else. It seemed a fairly remote hypothesis but there is no argument about it being theoretically possible.

To my regret, the matter was never tested in the courts because, like so much modern legislation, the 1973 Badgers Act is not worth the paper it was printed on.

It throws a sop to conservationists by beginning with a·clause making it an offence 'if any person wilfully kills, injures or takes, or attempts to kill, injure or take, any badger'.

That is concise, clear and wholly admirable—except for the word *wilfully*. There is no reason to read any further because if you catch a badger 'by mistake' in a snare set for a fox, or if a badger is gassed in what you 'mistook' for a rabbit bury, you didn't kill it 'wilfully', and have committed no offence.

But, just supposing there happens to be a conscientious beak upon the bench, who is cynical about such carelessness, you only have to skim down the Act to clause 7, which deals with 'authorised persons'.

An authorised person may kill, take or injure a badger, and so may any servant the authorised person authorises! It may also be anyone authorised by the local authority or the Natural Environment Research Council or the Minister of Agriculture. It would be hard to find someone who would not qualify. The reasons given for such 'authorisation' are that it is believed it would prevent serious damage to 'land, crops, poultry or any other form of property, or for preventing the spread of disease'.

The only possible cause for confusion might be the word 'property'. You may authorise the killing of a badger on your land if you suspect he might dig a hole in your lawn, make a latrine in your crops, bite your bantam or chivvy the pheasants in your release pen. If the pheasants were free to wander where they liked, it might be argued that they were no longer 'property' but wild animals, and you might not be covered under the Act for clobbering badgers interfering with something no longer defined as 'property'. Never mind, set your snare for a fox and catch the badger by mistake. Then you would be home and dry. What a load of rubbish!

Perhaps Peter Hardy who piloted the Act through Parliament was well satisfied with his success. Especially as he subsequently inserted a clause into the Wild Creatures and Wild Plants *Protection* Act (my italics) to allow Ministry of Agriculture Pest Officers to gas badgers which had been one of the few methods of exterminating them to be prohibited.

Finding the dead badger in a self-lock snare had convinced me, rightly or wrongly, that my suspicions had not been without foundation. During the next few weeks, my remaining badgers dwindled until there was no trace of one anywhere in my wood.

Convinced that the law is an ass, I decided to have a go myself. Feeding birds into my wood, as I had threatened, or dropping a fox into each release pen, might have settled the matter, but that strangulated badger and her abandoned cubs—with the implied danger of similar treatment to those which might re-colonise my wood—had done the trick. So far as I was concerned, it was war— and no holds barred.

CHAPTER 5

Interim

Field sports are basic and earthy enough to inspire positive points of view. The old school of keepers genuinely believed that they were justified in annihilating anything that preyed on game or even competed with it for food or habitat.

Hannam's gibbet was an ostentatious record of his skill at outwitting hawks and owls, badgers and stoats and cats. The Old Squire's generation remembered with nostalgia the days when the penalty for poaching was transportation to Australia.

There are still keepers around who cling to the old traditions and I recently took part in a television programme which included a gamekeeper's gibbet displaying, amongst other trophies, the rotting corpses of five polecats. 'Polecats'—even if some of them are only feral ferrets, as I suspect—are rare by any standards. The

keeper who had caught them certainly *believed* them to be genuine pure polecats and so did a scientist who examined one of the skulls. This did not alter the fact that both the keeper and the members of the syndicate involved regarded it as perfectly acceptable to 'control' polecats in the interests of intensively reared pheasants. The only chink in their armour appeared when they criticised the programme's producer for showing the gibbet on the screen, on the grounds that millions of viewers might 'misunderstand'! (Or understand too much?)

I know fishermen who shoot herons and trap otters, both of which enjoy theoretical legal protection, and fish farmers who do not even draw the line at shooting kingfishers on the grounds that they might prey on trout fry. Foxhunters are equally contemptuous of the 1973 Badgers Act and some of them still kill badgers which take possession of their artificial fox earths or which open holes which have been 'stopped' to prevent hunted foxes taking refuge.

On the other side of the fence are those who not only take no part in field sports but do everything in their power to prevent anyone else doing so. Most of the anti-blood sport fraternity have no personal experience of what they are trying to stop. They have never seen hounds catch a fox and they get more excited about men who shoot pheasants than when cattle are carted half across Europe to be killed by uncivilised foreigners who have never heard of laws to ensure that slaughter should be humane.

The fact that the pheasant lives in convivial surroundings, is well fed and dies suddenly, while the cattle are kept intensively, and transported in discomfort to be bled to death to make white meat, worries them not at all. They are more concerned with the fact that sportsmen *enjoy* shooting than how much cruelty is involved. They get hot under the collar because rich men can afford to spend hundreds of pounds a year on shooting—though many of them spend as much on holidays abroad. Hunt saboteurs froth on their beards in their efforts to prevent other people going foxhunting or shooting a pheasant.

For many years my hobby was ratting and I have always preferred going out on Sunday mornings with a bag of ferrets and a dog to being bored by the parson in his pulpit. I have no doubt that rats feel pain and terror at least as acutely as foxes, but I was never threatened with violence because I enjoyed the sport for the stupidly illogical reasons that ratting is a 'working' man's sport and that rats are 'nasty' and no help to those who are hell-bent on catching votes by exploiting socially divisive topics.

I can see both points of view but consider that the ways others choose to enjoy themselves is no concern of mine. If they wish to hunt foxes—or rats—or go shooting or fishing, I would not raise a finger to stop them. However, I did all in my power to get otter hunting banned because the otter population has declined till there is real danger of extinction so that disturbing them with hounds, even when they are never allowed to kill their otters, could be the last straw.

The irony is that the cause of the otter's decline was not otter hunting. Records of otters found and killed between the 1850s and 1950s are remarkably consistent and indicate a fairly steady otter population. The decline then set in, so dramatically and severely

that otter hunters themselves were the first to be worried and they took action by calling-off hounds before they killed. It now seems that the major damage was caused by chemical pesticides used in agriculture which killed fish and frogs and birds and small animals. Otters suffered secondary poisoning by eating prey which was already dying of poison.

At about the same time, the Ministry of Agriculture and the River Boards took it into their heads to 'reclaim' a few acres of marshy land by dredging rivers and sluicing water, which should be conserved, straight down to the sea. In order to fulfill their ambition of turning rivers into drains, they bulldozed trees from the banks, ripped out the roots and destroyed the habitat that is vital for otters—and many birds—to breed. The damage was intensified by disturbance by the public. Shy otters were simply prevented from breeding and their numbers dwindled.

Positive steps to arrest the damage have been taken but may be too late. The otter has been placed on the list of Protected Species and, in theory, is protected by law—except in Scotland, which was also years behind the more civilised parts of the country in banning the gin-trap.

Gin-traps in drains and culverts and the secret places where keepers and river bailiffs hold sway are almost impossible to discover. There are those who say that hunting actually helped otters survive because landowners forbade their bailiffs to kill one, so that there would always be a 'find' on their stretch of river, and because the hunt would tip the bailiff when they enjoyed good sport. Without that incentive, it is said, there are always enough men of evil intent towards any predator to catch every otter that ventures along a river bank.

But what the law can't control may yet be done by logical persuasion. The Otter Trust, founded by Philip Wayre in East Anglia, has already persuaded landowners on seven East Anglian rivers to form Otter Havens which are not only protected from huntsmen but also from disturbance by walkers, boaters and fishermen.

The Trust has also brought pressure to bear on the bureaucratic River Boards to desist from destroying the habitat along the banks of these havens, so that otters may again have sufficient suitable breeding cover for their survival. The intention is to spread the good work to other parts of England. Since members of the Trust are prepared to back their ambitions by putting their hands in their pockets to the tune of up to £70,000 in a year, there is solid ground to take their actions seriously.

My own problems were more immediate and local. The badgers had gone out of my wood and, since I had found evidence of snaring over my boundary, I thought I knew the reason, however circumstantial the evidence was. I had spoken my mind, as is my habit, and proposed to make a counter-attack on the local pheasant population on the assumption that, if the shoot did not prove an economic proposition, the shooters would go away and we would start with a new lot who might be more sympathetic.

There was an acre or so of bracken near the edge of my wood which had grown so dense that it had smothered the little pine trees the Forestry Commission had planted when they were my tenants. I had managed to persuade them to disgorge the lease of my land and return control to me, so that I could run my reserve with a management committee of the ideal size. One!

I detest a monoculture of Corsican pines because their close-packed sterility crowds out other vegetation and provides neither

food nor breeding habitat for birds. Bracken is almost as bad, without the compensation of being a saleable crop and, in the past, I had used pigs to clear patches of bracken and scrub. If enclosed within a fence, they consume most plants that can squeeze a living in competition with bracken. They grub up the roots with their irresistible snouts in search of anything else that is edible, from bulbs to beetles. They do not give up hope, even when reason would tell them that the efforts they are expending have no chance of reaping a fair return. They simply turn over the same patches of ground again and again, leaving the soil in perfect tilth for seedlings.

My plan was to fence a bunch of pigs in an enclosure surrounding the bracken patch, supply water, a comfortable shelter and a subsidiary diet of commercial pig nuts to supplement the natural food they would get by grubbing up the patch.

When they had done the job, I could send all but one to the butcher, and put the odd one in our deep freeze. They would have a good life (while it lasted)—far better than their relatives in super modern piggeries with air-conditioning, artificial light and chains dangling from the roof. Chains are necessities in intensive farming because conditions are so boring that the pigs will bite off each others' tails to pass the time unless they are supplied with something else to chew.

I should reap my reward for supplying tolerable conditions because the pork would taste much better than factory farm meat, as free-range eggs do compared to pallid supermarket tack.

I had no intention of allowing the clearing in the wood to sprout with self-set birch and oak, bramble and blackthorn thicket, as I have done with other clearings the pigs and I have made. This time I would plough it and sow it with wheat.

Nor had I any intention of reaping the crop. When the grains shed, the local pheasants could do that, and it would be so much more rewarding than even Hannam's old-fashioned stubbles which, after all, had only been the surplus after the harvest had been reaped. My crop would be partially protected by the straw—since that would not have been gathered either—and the generous grain would be the reward of hard labour as the birds could spend their winter working for it.

Hannam would have hated my neighbour's shoot. The birds skulk in vast tracts of forestry firs and pines, which provide shelter from which it is virtually impossible to dislodge them. Instead of haphazard little fields, with berried hedges and stubbles, under-sown with clover, or fields of swedes and mangolds and turnips, the farm next to me was a prairie of plough. Desert, Hannam would have called it, because there was little natural food and less cover.

Although our wood is at the edge, it must seem like an oasis, with forty acres of oak trees, laden with acorns, supplemented by blackberries till the devil puts his hoof on them in October, and sloes and hawthorn, mountain ash and alder. A proper English wood except for the piece the Forestry mucked up—and that is beginning to sprout English trees again, for I clear the pines round them, as weeds, to help them grow, instead of the other way round.

When the acorn crop falls, pheasants drift in from all sides and stay, undisturbed, until they have skimmed the cream before returning to the grain hoppers and feed points on the shoots they came from. I calculated that, if I grew a crop of corn, and didn't harvest it, they would be stupid to stray back to be shot. Not that I planned to give them much chance because, once they have been released, pheasants are classed, in law, as wild birds and belong to anyone on whose land they are at the time. Our visitors would have a one-way ticket.

Although the wood was throbbing with life, it seemed strangely empty now the badgers had gone. I try to get round it three times a day when work does not chain me too tightly to my desk. I feed the poultry and wild duck either before or after breakfast, depending on the time it gets light and, while I am out, I take the dogs with me round the wood. Now that I had decided to encourage visiting pheasants, I took a bagful of corn with me and scattered a few handfuls in likely places.

Jess usually comes for a walk with us after lunch and I go out again about dusk. There was an additional motive for this now that I had developed an interest in game because it might be useful to know precisely where they roosted; cock pheasants are most stupid birds, which advertise their whereabouts by crowing as they fly onto their perches and leaving patches of droppings on the ground below that are an open invitation to all with eyes to see.

I hadn't appreciated before just how aware of the badgers I had been. My observations had, to some extent, been subconscious, but I must have noticed every well-worn run and latrine pit and the precise gaps in the fence they used when they passed or returned from my land to my neighbour's.

There was one particularly well-padded run, a veritable badger highway, from the sett by the house and through the heronry. I don't disturb the heronry when the great shy birds are breeding, so I went round the grassy ride, that surrounds their sanctuary, to see where the badgers emerged. Well-worn badger tracks were as clear as roads on a map where the ride intersects the wood near a high seat that I use as an observation tower. On the far side of this ride, the track continued under an old Forestry sheep fence and there was nearly always a tuft or so of grey hair caught in a jagged bit of wire netting.

It gradually dawned on me that this main run was blurring-up.

For years it had been padded so regularly in all weathers that the clayey soil had been polished smooth and shining. Now that the badgers had stopped using it, the coarse woodland grasses encroached from the edges and a skithering of puny plantlets pushed up tentatively where the earth was least compacted. Time was already beginning to soften the harsh outline. Stopping to look a little closer, in the forlorn hope that I was wrong, I examined the gap in the fence. A tuft of hair was still entangled in the wire but, instead of being grey and shining with sleek health, it was now brown and brittle and unkempt.

The sett at Primrose Dell had still got a great mound of excavated soil spilling out from the entrance, but it was no longer blanketed with fresh bedding, dragged out to air. Now there were rabbit droppings where some insolent old doe had felt it safe to sit and sun, confident that she wouldn't be disturbed. Wherever I went, such little signs caught my eye and rammed home the fact. The absence of 'vermin' in my wood would have won full marks from Hannam. The animals that had filled my eyes with pleasure had not been my way lately. They had probably been hanged in a snare for trespassing. There was no point in being sick with anger because there was nothing I could do about it anyway. Not in the immediate future.

Meanwhile, my attention was drawn to vermin of a different kind. Every year I rear a dozen cockerels for the good of the house and one or two to give to friends. These day-old cock chicks are bred for the broiler industry and would normally be killed for the chicken-in-the-basket trade at about ten weeks old. They are grown so fast that the flesh is pappy and insipid but this is not surprising since they have spent their short life-sentence in a broiler house, never even seeing God's fresh air or a blade of green grass.

I rear mine under a broody hen and run them on free range to the age of five and a half months. About ten per cent die because they have been selectively bred to achieve their required size by ten weeks old—and the geneticists who produced them couldn't care less if they drop dead within another week. Longevity is not a quality they are striving for. But most of mine live and grow to enormous (if uneconomic) size so that they are between twelve and fourteen pounds—as big as small turkeys—when I kill them for Christmas. Far from resembling tasteless cotton wool, their active life, scratching for insects and worms in the paddock, produces texture and flavour that makes me drool to think of it. Although I do not shut them in a pen at night, I do keep them in a wire netting enclosure, high and strong enough to keep the foxes out.

Looking out of my bedroom window just as it was getting light one morning, I was puzzled to see one of the best cockerels executing the most extraordinary capers. He was leaping about, shaking his head as if he'd got a mouthful of hot potato and then, to vary the routine, he fell flat on the floor, twitching with violent convulsions. The light was not too good, but it eventually dawned on me that he was being attacked by an enormous stoat, which had pinned him by the throat as effectively as old-fashioned bull dogs held their bulls.

Rushing downstairs in my pyjamas, I grabbed a shotgun off the rack and went to salvage a potential Christmas dinner. The wretched bird was staggering round the enclosure with the stoat still locked on to his jugular, ripping and tearing to enlarge the wound and let the life-blood out.

I had the choice of rushing up to frighten the predator away—and possibly saving the bird's life—or shooting the stoat, and almost certainly the bird which was bound to share the shot. The bird seemed to be on his way out anyway. If the stoat had not actually severed his jugular or damaged his spinal cord, the shock would probably have been enough to finish him off. If I only frightened the stoat away, he would almost certainly return to attack the rest, so I took careful aim—and got the worst of both worlds.

Gamekeepers say that the reflexes of stoats and weasels are remarkable. Both species love hollow tree trunks and stone walls where they can seek cover. Both are insatiably curious. So if a keeper sees one dive for cover, he 'squeaks it up'. All he has to do is to purse his lips and suck in air to imitate the squeal of a rabbit or the squeak of a mouse. Within seconds, a serpentine head will poke from a crevice to locate what he believes may be his dinner. The head and white chest make a perfect target, but I have heard keepers say that a stoat's reflex is so good that he can duck to safety when he sees the flash, and be safe before the shot arrives.

I never believed it, of course. Keepers are full of such tall stories, so I took careful aim at my cockerel's head—and his attacker—and gently squeezed the trigger. The bird fell dead all right, but the stoat was nowhere to be seen—though I'll never know how I missed it!

Conservationists prattle endlessly about the iniquity of killing predators for the sake of sparing the lives of game. When I realised that my cockerel enclosure was within the hunting territory of an obviously competent stoat, I knew I was on the same spot as a keeper. The fence I had erected was adequate to exclude badgers, and although foxes could, in theory, scale it, they rarely did. Netting of small enough mesh to exclude stoats would be prohibitively expensive—and they would climb up it in any case.

So it was vital either to kill that stoat or suffer the loss of the rest of my poultry as well as the bird I had shot.

It brought home problems a keeper faces every time he puts his birds out from the security of covered rearing pens to an open-topped release pen. His livelihood depends on being able to produce adequate birds for his masters to shoot. So, in self-defence, he puts tunnel traps round the perimeter of his pen and traps every rat or stoat or polecat that comes to investigate.

The keeper who took part in the television programme I mentioned earlier, had killed five polecats, and was proud of his expertise. Nobody was more surprised than he was that there were many among the millions of viewers who found his action indefensible.

Popular objections centre on the fact that some people disapprove of shooting for recreation, or killing predators in the interests of sport. How then, would they react to me killing stoats to protect my cockerels reared for food? It is a fine dividing line that has more in common with sentiment than logic. All right to kill a stoat attacking domestic poultry but not game? All right to kill a rat, even for eating the food of either. Wrong to kill a badger on either count because it is easier to make an enclosure that badgers can't enter? Or what about otters, which would attack poultry or game as ruthlessly as any stoat or fox and far more certainly than badgers? Or should *all* predators be protected by confining poultry in secure houses where they may be safe from sudden death only because they have exchanged natural freedom—with its perils, for the 'security' of the broiler-house.

I cannot answer for anyone else, but I would not kill an otter under any circumstances because I would not want it on my conscience that I had added a straw to the load that threatens the species with extinction. And if I couldn't keep my poultry safe from badgers, I would deserve to arrive when only the parson's nose was left, because badgers are so easily excluded, and only take poultry in exceptional circumstances anyway.

So far as stoats are concerned—there are plenty of stoats and I leave them in peace in our wood so long as they keep away from the domestic poultry pens. They are welcome to a few pheasants, as many rabbits as they can catch and to their tithe of small birds, which breed a surplus as a crop to feed the predators. But I am not starry-eyed enough to allow them to take the food out of my own mouth, so I put down a tunnel trap in the cockerel pen which was soon more effective than my gun in preventing further loss. My success gave me no satisfaction. There is nothing either skilled or sporting about tunnel traps, and stoats are beautiful creatures, even in death.

In life there is no animal more sinuously graceful. I have had two hand-reared tame weasels and one stoat. If taken young enough to know no fear of man, they are as affectionate and playful as kittens.

When I had had my last bitch stoat for a few weeks, I came across some research that indicated that stoats reproduce their kind by delayed implantation as roe deer and badgers and various other mammals do. The female is mated in the normal way but the fertilised egg does not immediately become attached to the uterus wall and develop into an embryo. It remains floating free for a time before the delayed implantation takes place.

Roe deer, for example, mate in July but there is no sign of an embryo developing until midwinter. Badgers can mate at any time

between April and November, but the cubs are normally born at the end of January or in February, irrespective of when mating took place.

I was not surprised that stoats also bred by delayed implantation but their case was exceptional because, I was told, they were so precocious that bitch stoats were mated before they were weaned.

This seemed a pretty tall story even for the boffins to dream up. My stoat had come from a keeper who had seen the dam carrying a helpless kitten across a woodland ride by the scruff of its neck. Not having his gun, he chased the stoat, which dropped the kitten to make her escape more certain, so the keeper picked the kitten up and put her in his pocket for his children to see before he killed her.

They entreated him to spare her life but, beautiful and attractive as she was, he didn't want to keep her in case she escaped and got into his pheasant pen. So she came to me.

She spent her days in my study and her nights in a large aviary I built for her outside. As the result of a broadcast, I was given a young dog stoat as her playmate but I was careful never to leave them alone together because I wanted to test the validity of the theory that stoats are mated before they are weaned. If there was any truth in the theory, she might already be in kit.

The following April it became obvious that she was pregnant so

I ceased having her in the house and left her alone in her aviary. Ferrets will eat their own young if put under mental stress, so I was determined to do nothing to upset her.

By mid-May I knew that she had kitted but had no means of knowing if any of the litter had survived without opening the nest box up, which might have tempted providence too far. Most naturalists develop a protective shell of stolid bovine patience to discipline their curiosity so I stifled my enthusiasm, deciding that it would be prudent to wait till the kittens came out to play. If there were any kittens.

I thought there were because the bitch stoat came to the edge of the netting when I approached, not to utter the high-pitched affectionate greeting I was accustomed to, but to chatter with ferocity to warn me off. Something had changed her mood from playful companionship to protective rage. She was no longer a tame stoat, fixated on man by being hand-reared. She had grown as wild as the stoats in the wood and she never allowed me to handle her again.

When I stopped outside the aviary to examine her at close quarters, she climbed up the netting to bare her fangs at my eye level, exposing her belly to view as she did so. Now there was no doubt about it. Two rows of enlarged pink teats proclaimed that a litter of young were suckling her. A couple of weeks later, when I judged them to be four or five weeks old, they began to come to the entrance of the nest box and play on the aviary floor. Ten days later they were chasing after their mother, nose to tail, as sinuous as a serpent in a hurry.

I put the dog stoat in a cage on the aviary floor to test the bitch's reaction. She was obviously extremely excited, chattering continuously, though I could not decide whether in rage or invitation. This time, my curiosity did get the better of me so I opened the dog's cage door to see what happened.

All hell was let loose and the two adults went round the aviary faster than dry leaves in a hurricane. It wasn't clear, at first, whether they were threatening, sparring or fighting in earnest. Then the dog got the bitch stoat by the scruff of the neck and I knew that copulation was only a matter of time. Ferrets often take hours

mating, which is the nearest thing to rape to anything I've ever watched.

Stoats do not pair in the conventional sense. They have separate territories which they are prepared to defend vigorously. According to the research I had read, although it had not been published, the bitch stoat has a post lactation oestrus, coming into season when her young are ready for weaning. A wandering dog stoat smells her from afar and comes to mate her. When he has done so, he also mates her immature daughters. I was fascinated to see such an unlikely theory put into practice and was delighted, next season, when three of the bitches had litters of their own.

The old bitch died before she was two from the usual nematode parasite, which produces fits in stoats and weasels by making cavities in their skulls. This results in increasingly recurrent fits which eventually prove fatal. It is an agonising fate, far more cruel and prolonged than a tunnel trap or gamekeeper's bullet, but without some such natural control, there would obviously be a stoat population explosion.

I gave the young females away, and the original old male also died of fits, so that I was eventually left with an untamed and untameable young male. A zoo specializing in British mammals asked if they could buy him, but eventually I swapped a couple of pairs of harvest mice for him.

There are no wild harvest mice in our part of the country, so I

was delighted to have the opportunity of trying to breed them in captivity to liberate in the wood, since I reckoned it was useless to try to establish a wild colony that did not start large enough to stand normal predation by hawks and owls and weasels and still leave a viable breeding stock.

Harvest mice are the smallest British mice, rich gold in colour, with tails as prehensile as monkeys'. They used to be common in the days of the small fields Hannam loved for his game, and they made their nests, as spherical as tennis balls, from grasses skilfully woven to the stalks of standing corn. Their agility, aided by their grasping tails, enabled them to spend most of the summer aloft in standing corn, swinging from ear to golden ear as easily as monkeys in the jungle.

I arranged five glass aquaria in a line along the back of my study cupboard, and covered them with lids which were connected by tunnels through which the mice could pass from one aquarium to the next. I set out alternate aquaria with a deep bed of peat, with pieces of buried bark and planted them with bilberry and reed and grasses to resemble natural habitat as closely as possible. Between the central and end tanks I put tanks much less densely planted, where I could feed the mice and supply fresh water. The purpose of a long row of interconnected tanks was to give the mice a chance to establish and defend their own territory and to visit neighbouring areas for food and water.

This proved a wise precaution because the appearance of harvest mice is very deceptive. Being able to watch them at close quarters, I was instantly captivated, not only by their diminutive size, but by their agility because they were active by day, so that I could watch them skithering around their territory with the speed and grace of Olympic gymnasts.

Their habits did not fulfill the promise conveyed by their dainty appearance. However beautiful they looked, their hearts were villainous and black. They were spiteful and aggressive and the mice at the top of the peck order chivvied the lesser fry unmercifully. They didn't just chase them from the food or out of the bit of territory they reckoned was theirs. They followed up the attack by chasing the loser round and round from one tank to the next, half across my study. When they did get in close, they attacked the victim's tail about half an inch from the body, nipping it right round, as vandals ring-bark ornamental trees.

The result was similar. When the skin was cut right round the tail, the end withered and dropped off. In no time at all, I found myself with bob-tailed harvest mice. Not only did it disfigure their beauty but, far worse, it hobbled their agility so that, in the wild, where climbing at speed could spell the difference between life and death, they would have been at a mortal disadvantage.

The remedy proved fairly simple, I planted up the tanks far more densely, deliberately providing thickets impregnable enough to shield the weakest from attack, and waited, impatiently, for them to breed.

They multiplied as rapidly as a colony of tame white mice would have done, so I took thirty-five of them and let them go in a patch of wood that is dense with wild roses and thicketty plants that bear seeds. There was masses of cover for them there and plenty of food, while the sanctuary should have been as impregnable to predators as a fortress.

There didn't seem much point continuing to breed the remainder in my study for, if the experiment was a success, the colony in the wood would now thrive and multiply. The only reason I hadn't put them all out was that the survivors in the study were all warriors whose battle scars included shortened tails and I

thought that too great a handicap to give them much chance when they had enemies to elude.

At about that time, a friend who had always admired them, asked if I had a pair to spare so that he could repeat my experiment and liberate any surplus they produced into the countryside where he lived, so I gave the rest to him.

He turned up, a few weeks later with an offering in return. From a bag in his pocket he produced no fewer than fourteen grass snakes, ranging in size from threadlike midgets, no bigger than large earthworms, to a huge grandmother, almost a yard in length.

At Primrose Dell, there is a little pool in one corner of the wood which has a small bog, of about half an acre, at one side, and is surrounded with exactly the sort of dense cover grass snakes would choose for themselves. Frogs and newts breed in the shallows and I have often wondered why it is that I have never seen a wild snake since we came to live here. Perhaps the heavy clay soil does not suit them, or they may be scoffed by the herons as soon as they show themselves, for I have no doubt that grass snakes would suit their palates as well as eels. Thickets of wild rose have flourished there since the Forestry Commission departed for I have grubbed out their little pines to let light and air into the margin.

So we took the grass snakes down to the dell and wished them success as they slithered their way furtively into the undergrowth.

One Sunday morning, a man arrived at the door to see if I wanted a sparrow hawk. He had found it hanging in the hedge by the leather straps upon its legs which falconers call jesses.

Falconry is one of the most spectacular sports in the world and the sight of a peregrine falcon stooping at grouse flying across heather-clad moorland on a bright autumn day is unforgettable.

Falcons and hawks are not trained. They perform their function as naturally as any wild predator hunts its prey. They are 'manned'—which simply means accustomed—to the falconer until they are no longer afraid of him. They are also lazy birds, hunting more for food than sport, so that falconers get a sharp edge on their appetites before flying them, so that they can catch them again because they are ravenous for food.

Not only is it a very skilful pastime, it is exceptionally time-consuming too. I know rich men who employ full-time falconers and I know others, so obsessed with the sport, that they devote their own lives to it to the exclusion of work or social contracts.

Trained, or manned, hawks are flown in exhibitions at the Game Fair, the falconers dressing themselves up in medieval costume so that the whole display fills casual observers with the ambition to participate in a nostalgic pastime that will ferry them back on a magic carpet to the Middle Ages.

The result is that the most unsuitable people buy hawks. They think that they can leave them tethered by the legs to their blocks while they are at work all week and take them out for a bit of sport at the week-end. The lucky hawks either die or escape and fly

away, though they have as little chance of survival with a leather thong trailing from each leg, as the wretched sparrow hawk had when he was brought to me. If the farmer hadn't found him entangled in the hedge, he would have died of exhaustion or starvation.

The farmer didn't live far away and he asked me if I knew who owned it. I had a shrewd suspicion but, if I was right, I feared the same thing would happen again if he were returned. Hawks are such truly wild birds that I don't really like to see them tethered by the legs, even by proficient and sympathetic falconers. Ignorant or callous amateurs make me sick. I once met a dealer who had imported fifty falcons from India in November and said, with some pride, that he 'had managed to sell twenty-five of them before they died'. It is with some pride that I say I was instrumental in having his import licence revoked, and it would give me even more pride if I could have had him convicted of cruelty to animals. It cured me, once and for all, of giving active help to anyone who may transgress, even in ignorance.

So I said, with half-truth, that I didn't know where it had come from and suggested cutting off its jesses and turning it loose to take pot-luck.

I suppose that one of the attractions of hawks is the almost hypnotic power of their eyes. That hawk had never seen either of us before, so that there is no reason to believe that he associated the man who brought him any more with his rescue than with the discomfort which preceeded it. He had far more reason to regard us both—and all other human beings—with mistrust and suspicion and fear than with gratitude or affection. But he perched boldly on the fist that brought him and suffered his legs to be touched and the thongs cut without losing his dignity for a second. When he sensed he was free, he took stock of his bearings and flew off to the end of my wood, farthest from where I guessed he had been imprisoned, as if he had lived with us all his life, as 'wild' as the wildest hawk of legend.

The whole question of licensing people to take hawks for falconry, when they are on the schedule of protected birds, seems bureaucratic nonsense. Peregrine falcons fetch £500 and more from oil-rich natives of the Middle East, so that the temptation to trade in them is more than many can resist. Yet it is possible to get a licence to take and keep a wild hawk for falconry.

I know one keeper of the 'Bob-the-killer' school who had a hawk in a pen in his back yard, where it was ruining its feathers by bashing them against the wire netting that imprisoned it. He took great pride in being a good vermin trapper and, knowing that he had no love of hawks and owls, I concluded he had caught one which he could convert into cash the tax-man wouldn't know about, instead of hanging it on his gibbet where some conservationist might see it and report him for killing a bird that is (theoretically) legally protected.

One of the best ways of discouraging such men is to bring a successful prosecution for illegally destroying a protected animal or bird—and then take action against the employer for 'causing' the offence.

The chances are that the landowner or shoot manager will know nothing about it but, if the resulting publicity is embarrassing enough, he will sack the keeper who brought him into disrepute and set more effective terms of reference for his successor.

Accordingly, I raised the matter of the hawk I knew about with the authorities concerned with issuing licences. I gathered that they rarely refused licences to keepers because, if they antagonised them, they would shoot or trap every hawk on their beats but, if they became interested in falconry, their local birds would have more chance. It transpired that the man I had enquired about had permission to *take* and keep only one hawk on his premises. He had no licence to sell one.

How alarming to find such stupid faith in human nature! If the bureaucrats concerned could prise themselves from their office stools and get into wild places to see what really goes on, they would find that a licence to keep *one* hawk simply means that the one hawk an inspector would find on the premises when he called, is not always the same hawk that was there last week! As soon as the owner gets a customer, he sells it to him for an enhanced price, since the customer may not be able to get a licence to keep one and therefore could not purchase one legally. When that hawk has gone, the keeper can catch another and another to complete an endless series of illicit deals. If bureaucracy had the guts to use the law vigorously against anyone who causes danger to threatened species, there would be more chance for endangered species to survive. I hope that it was a long time before anyone had the chance to put the sparrow hawk we set free up for sale again.

One of my most treasured experiences in the wood had nothing to do with rarities, badgers or gamekeepers. For several years I introduced a programme for children called 'Animals Unlimited' on steam radio. We ranged widely from prehistoric monsters to modern pets, and from bird song to butterflies. Towards the end of the series, we included a competition to discover the boy and the girl who could identify the most tape recordings of wildlife sounds. In addition to book tokens and record tokens, one prize was to be a visit to our wood where the producer would join us to make a programme about what we saw and the winner's reactions to it.

Since I was charged with the task of making sure we didn't draw blank, I was naturally worried when I discovered who the winning boy was. His name was Peter, he was twelve years old and he had been totally blind for eleven years. Not easy, I thought, to devise a programme to which he would enjoy contributing.

I need not have worried. He turned out to be one of the nicest, most natural kids I had met in years. He brought his own cassette tape recorder which he manipulated with professional expertise, and announced that he did not spend much of his time in woodland so, while he was here, would I help him to tape the songs of a few woodland birds?

I had already made up my mind to try to give him a few experiences he was unlikely to have had before, so I kicked-off by introducing him to Miss Roedoe before taking him in the wood. Miss Roedoe was the old roe deer I had bottle-reared eight or nine years before and there was no doubting the fact that the way to her heart was through her tummy.

Roe deer are among our shyest deer and tame ones are not common so I was not surprised when Peter said that he had never met one before. 'Switch your recorder on and cross your fingers, then,' I said. Dilys Breese, who was producing the programme, switched her recorder on too.

I rattled a tin of chocolate digestive biscuits, for which Miss Roedoe would have cheerfully sold her soul and, within seconds, a dainty russet form drifted into view through the shadows at the edge of the wood.

'She's coming, Peter,' I said. 'She's about eighty yards away where this paddock melts into the trees, and she has obviously heard the biscuit tin.'

She paused for a few seconds at the edge of the clearing, making as sure of an impressive entrance as any old trouper on the stage would do. Then she came delicately mincing towards us, nostrils slightly flared to catch the first whiff of the food she coveted.

'She's coming, Peter,' I said. 'Hold out your hand with some biscuit—and don't make any sudden movements or you'll scare her off.'

His face lit up as he felt her nuzzling his hand and he asked if he could stroke her. 'While she's eating, you can,' I said, 'but, the moment she stops—you stop. And keep still till she regains her confidence and starts eating again.'

From her nose, he slid his hand gently along her neck and down one foreleg. Never having been able to see a deer, this was his first opportunity to envisage its shape and size, and he gave a vivid running commentary of his impressions as he did so. Her neck was longer and more tapering than he had imagined—and her muzzle unbelievably smooth. But it was her legs that really caught his imagination. Below the knee joint, they were not much thicker than the base of his thumb and the idea of anything so delicate being able to survive a mad dash through woodland that would have tripped him up within five yards left him spellbound.

His enthusiasm spilled out of all the descriptions and infected me as well. The previous evening I had picked up a young heron that had fallen out of the nest and fed it with a few slugs of raw meat till I had time to rehabilitate it. 'Half a minute,' I said. 'I've got another surprise,' and I went to fetch it.

This was a bit more tricky. Herons, even young herons, have bills as sharp as spears and they can stab viciously at anything that alarms them. Or at anything bright, like eyes. So I tucked the great bird under one arm and held the bill securely with my other hand. I told him that I'd got a heron and explained how I'd rescued it when it had fallen out of the nest because its parents would almost certainly have deserted it in an unnatural situation on the ground. Or they might have been shot, so that the starving fledgling could have stepped into space from his platform nest in sheer desperation for food.

Peter stretched out his hand and I guided it to the tip of the bird's lethal bill, which I still kept safely closed between my finger and thumb. From there he was on his own, chattering his running commentary of discovery as his questing hands explored the shapes he'd never seen. Descriptions of herons impaling slippery fish with bills as sharp as needles or standing for hours at the edge of ponds and rivers on legs like bulrush stems, were now doubly exciting because his sensitive fingers confirmed the story in his mind. I decided it was time to give the lad another treat.

I happened to know of a brood of pied woodpeckers in an oak at the far end of the wood. When they are close to flying, they are rowdy birds and I had found the nest by the simple expedient of homing-in on their incessant hungry cries for food. I would repeat the experiment with Peter—without telling him—though, this time, the direction I took would have no element of chance.

We wandered casually along a woodland ride, stopping occasionally for him to make recordings of the birds he heard. When we were about fifty yards from the woodpecker tree, I suggested we stop for a breather.

'Listen,' he said, 'I can hear young birds. Over there!' and he switched on his tape recorder. 'They're not loud enough', he said. 'I shan't get a decent signal. Can we get a bit closer?' We moved closer and we could hear the harsh chatter for food quite clearly. 'What are they?' he asked. 'I thought they were starlings, at first. We've got a nest of starlings at school. But they're not starlings.' He paused a long time, listening intently. 'Are they woodpeckers? I've never heard woodpeckers.'

I told him I thought they were and that I could see the hole in the tree the nest was in. We crept right up to it without disturbing the young fledglings. By that time, it was obvious that the nest was right above our heads and Peter asked how high up it was. 'About a yard above your head,' I said, and he held up his mike within a few inches of the nest.

'How big is the hole?' he asked. 'And how far has the bird bored into the tree?' So I lifted him up to discover for himself. He measured the diameter with finger and thumb and marvelled that anything less than a steel chisel could chip a way through an inch of hard wood to the softer heart, where the tree had started to decay.

'What happens if I poke my finger right into the hole? Will they bite it?' I told him he'd got nine more fingers and wouldn't miss one so he'd better try. He gently stuck in his forefinger as far as he could and waggled it about.

A blissful smile suffused his face. 'They're sucking my finger,' he said. 'They're sucking it so see if it is good enough to eat.'

'Sucking' his finger, I thought. What an extraordinary description. All afternoon he'd been painting word pictures of his new treasure-trove, which were both sensitive and accurate. It had never occurred to me that anyone could imagine that a bird, with a sharp and bony bill, could 'suck'. Sucking implies soft, mobile lips, not the rigidity of bills powerful enough to drill through solid oak.

When I had put him down, I reached in and put my own finger into the hole—and if my mind had not been predisposed by what I'd often seen, I too would have said those birds were sucking my finger. They took it so gently, and sampled it with tongues long and sinuous enough to winkle woodlice from deep crevices or ants from their tunnels. Those tongues can caress as gently and daintily as a fairy kiss—and they certainly gave me the impression that they were sampling me to see if I was fit to eat.

It was a humbling experience to be so innocently cut down to size, for it hadn't occurred to me that a lad of twelve would teach me much about the creatures in my own wood, least of all a lad who had never had the luck to see them. All that was necessary to convert a delightfully memorable day into the experience of a lifetime was to be able to introduce him to a badger. That, alas, was no longer possible.

While there were no badgers in the wood, I used the time to improve the prospects when—or if—the setts I had made should ever be colonised again. My hand-reared Bill and his two sows had lived in a couple of setts I had made after the fashion of artificial earths, or 'drains', constructed by fox-hunters for foxes. Because these earths are made by man, the anti-hunting lobby claim that the foxes are bred for hunting.

The fact is that, if the drains are well-designed, foxes (and badgers) will take up residence there from choice. And the cubs are no more artificially bred than fledglings of the blue tits in the garden.

Nevertheless, members of the sporting fraternity are extremely careful how they build a drain. Its purpose is to ensure a supply of foxes in the area where they are wanted, to enhance the chances of good sport when the hunt arrives. The night before the meet an earth-stopper goes round with his terrier to bolt any foxes which are lying in artificial earths, after which he 'stops' the mouth of the drain with a bundle of faggots or a clod of turf. This is enough to prevent the fox returning before the hunt arrives, so that there is every chance of hounds finding him lying above ground in a thicket. They bustle him out to give a run, and 'stopped' earths in the area prevent him evading his pursuers by going to ground so that a good time can be had by all. Except, perhaps, the fox.

To help the earth-stopper's terrier bolt him easily, the drain is constructed very simply. An underground brick-built chamber, like the manhole of a drain, has two nine-inch diameter drainpipe tunnels, in the form of a horse shoe, connecting the den to the surface of the ground. One tunnel enters each side of the den so that, when a terrier crawls along one, the fox is not cornered, but can take the least line of resistance and bolt from the other tunnel. Because the pipes are cemented into the brick den, it is impossible for foxes or badgers to enlarge the tunnel system so that the tenancy can be strictly controlled.

However, not all my attempts at encouraging visitors to take up residence were as successful as the work with foxes and herons.

When we had arrived a dozen or so years before, the parkland at the end of the wood had been dotted by dozens of ancient oaks. Their branches had been lopped and pollarded in centuries gone by as fodder for the goats and fuel for ancient glass furnaces. Time had hollowed them so that hundreds of jackdaws and quite a thriving population of tawny and little owls nested in them every spring and summer.

These birds were dispossessed when the oaks were grubbed up to make way for the plough, so I thought I would see if some of the owls could be persuaded to lodge with me.

Modern beer is concocted by chemists and served under pressure that guarantees flatulence, from metal tubs. Proper wooden barrels, created by craftsmen, are almost as rare as dodos. After a long search, I ran a retired beer baron to ground who was kind enough to exert influence to procure a couple of genuine old-fashioned oaken barrels. They had been designed to hold about four and a half gallons of the proper stuff, and I felt that the cooper who created them would have preferred them to be used as nest boxes than ending as receptacles for the chemical swill that passes as modern beer.

So I bored holes about eight inches in diameter at one end and mounted the barrels horizontally in the fork of trees about twenty-five feet from the ground. I hoped, with luck, that the kestrels would take them, failing which I would have settled for a pair of tawny owls.

To my surprise, both barrels were taken by stock doves, closely followed by jackdaws. Stock doves are smaller than wood pigeons, have no white neck ring and have a somewhat dowdy, frumpish appearance. We call them blue rocks in my part of the world, though they have slight differences from rock doves, which are believed to be the progenitors of domestic pigeons. Certainly when domestic pigeons are allowed to interbreed indiscriminately, as happens with flocks of city pigeons, the predominant colour is slatey-blue and the progeny are very like rock doves or our stock doves.

The major difference is that stock doves are as shy and cagey as wood pigeons. They have to be because the trigger-happy fraternity who guard farmers' crops from wood pigeons, also let fly at stock doves if they see them.

I never expected stock doves to stand up to the aggressive, extrovert jackdaws for five minutes, partly because their puny bills seemed such ineffective armament compared to the jackdaws' stilettoes, and partly because I had always found them to be such timid birds. Not a bit of it.

One of the barrels was in the fork of an oak in front of my study window, so I got a grandstand view of the fracas. The stock doves were already sitting on two pure white eggs when the urge to love took hold of a pair of jackdaws. I thought, at first, that it was simply a grab and smash raid; that the black thugs were intent only on stealing the eggs and eating them as they do to so many small birds. They both settled on the top of the barrel and took it in turns to fly round to the entrance hole to survey the prospects.

The stock dove came to meet them wings outstretched and waving feebly while she huffed and puffed to make them go away. The defence looked about as effective as a spinster threatening a burglar with her handbag. Like most bullies, the jackdaws were not keen to mix it if there seemed much prospect of getting a bloody nose themselves. They retreated to a safe distance to wait for their victim to leave the nest.

It was a miscalculation. The direction they took may have withdrawn them to a safe distance from the stock doves, but it brought them nearer to me. I am tough on carrion crows and magpies and jays in the wood because, if they are allowed to proliferate, the chances of the survival of small birds dwindle in proportion. Jackdaws are not so bad and I normally leave them alone.

Having just been surprised by, and admired, the stock dove's defence of her eggs against odds, I was less well-disposed to jackdaws. When they settled within fifty yards of my window, they stuck their necks out too far. I took the rifle from the rack and knocked one off. They were like dragons' teeth. As soon as one was disposed of, twelve appeared to replace it and, in no time at all, the second act of the drama at the barrel was rehearsed again.

The result was a foregone conclusion. The eggs were inevitably grabbed, smashed and eaten, and the stock doves departed until the hen recovered from her broodiness and came into laying condition again. By that time, however the jackdaws had appreciated just how attractive was the dwelling where they'd squatted. Having eaten the contents of the eggs, they almost filled the barrel with an untidy mass of twigs, lined the nest with sheep's wool and hair, and laid a clutch of eggs.

The returning stock doves were predictably nonplussed but they proved to be less wet than I'd expected. They landed on the barrel and buffetted the jackdaws when they came to see them off, and even tried to get into the hole to repossess their home.

Whatever our stupid laws decree, I shall break-in through the window of my house in a trice, with a pick-axe handle, if I ever return to find squatters in possession and I trust I shall score a broken head or two, whatever the final outcome. So my sympathy was completely with the stock doves.

But I was backing a lost cause. They surprised and delighted me by the guts they showed, but they were forced to admit defeat in the end. I have no idea where they went for the next few weeks but, when the jackdaws fledged, the stock doves reappeared like magic, repossessed their barrel and reared a pair of youngsters.

*   *   *

Meanwhile the pigs had been doing their stuff in the clearing. All edible greenery had long since disappeared and they had turned over the roots and surface soil till it resembled a plough field. Apart from the odd bout of sunburn, to which white pigs are as susceptible as human blondes, they hadn't been a moment's trouble. Even that was easy enough to cope with because all that was necessary was to leave the hose that filled their water trough running till it overflowed and formed a little pool. The pigs adored it, rooting beneath the surface of the water till they created the treacly consistency for a perfect mud bath. When they had wallowed in it for an hour or so, they were not only cool but coated with a mud pack that guarded them from further sunburn.

Feeding them was little trouble. I kept a tank of pig nuts outside the enclosure and, although they were two or three hundred yards from the house, I had equipped myself with enough plastic pipe to reach almost anywhere in the wood so that all I had to do to fill their trough—and mudbath—was merely to turn on a tap.

When I went to give them their ration of pig nuts one evening, I noticed that one didn't bother to join the rest in the mad meal scrabble.

This was not particularly unusual, because they do find acorns and fruits and worms and beetles, and a great deal of other food when allowed to forage in woodland which is their natural habitat. That is what makes the meat of free-range pigs so good and, when they happen to have had a bonanza, they often spurn the processed tack their factory farm relatives have to subsist on. So I merely noted the absentee and decided to check that she was her normal healthy self next day.

When I visited them before breakfast next morning, she lay stiff and dead. What was worse, another was off her food. There was nothing the vet could do about the dead animal but take her away for a post mortem. That night, another looked poorly, and, by morning, she too was dead.

The vet checked the rest for symptoms and, not only could he find nothing wrong with them, but they confirmed his opinion with appetites as sharp as ever.

I suspected poison. About five years before, my alsation Tough had been sunbathing in the yard when I went down the village to the post. When I returned, twenty minutes later, she was dead and already as stiff as a poker. The post mortem indicated death by strychnine poisoning.

The symptoms of strychnine poisoning include convulsions and extreme agony, followed by death. Rigor mortis sets in abnormally quickly. It is one of the diabolical and cruel poisons, so powerful that it is said to kill five times. First the original victim, then the fox or crow that feeds from it and whatever eats the fox or crow and so on almost ad infinitum. It is so persistent that it can lie in the ground for years and still retain its potency. It is impossible for ordinary citizens to purchase it, but the Ministry of Agriculture issue permits for it to be obtained for killing moles. Apparently a humane death for moles is of no importance. They die underground and what the eye doesn't see, the voting public doesn't grieve about.

I never discovered where my alsatian picked up her strychnine, for the yard is fenced-in and she hadn't been out while I was away. Perhaps a mole had got to the surface and been carried by a crow that dropped it in the yard. As moles are unpalatable creatures, I doubt if Tough would have eaten mole carrion if she had found it. The more likely explanation was that the poison had been obtained by permit, for killing moles, but put into eggs or carrion for catching crows. Crows will often carry eggs before eating them as thrushes crack snails on a 'thrushes' anvil', or big stone. She might have eaten spilled egg.

I reported my suspicions to the Ministry and they said they would check people holding permits in my area but, if they found anything out, they did not tell me.

Such an experience with a favourite dog rankles in my mind as vividly today as when I found her dead. It sharpened my concentration on the problem of my pigs. If, as I feared, they had died from poison, it was vital to discover what it was and where they got it so that I could prevent the dogs picking up the same stuff. The lack of stiffness seemed to rule out strychnine, but it could have been something in their food or pesticides or one of a thousand things.

To limit the risks with the pigs, I moved their enclosure at once to another part of the wood, opened a fresh bag of pig nuts—and waited for the vet's verdict. He passed on the pigs' suspected organs to ADAS, Agricultural Development and Advisory Service, of the Ministry of Agriculture, Fisheries and Food. They thought that 'a toxic agent rather than an infection' was the cause of death. As they didn't even hazard a guess what the toxic agent might be, we weren't much the wiser, so I never risked bringing the pigs back to that enclosure, nor allowed the dogs to wander freely in the area.

Apart from this worrying episode and the continued absence of badgers in my wood, everything was going fine. Harvest mice and grass snakes were hopefully established wild in the wood and the fallow deer were steadily growing tamer because there was now nothing to frighten them. A succession of mild winters combined with complete privacy in their heronry, had enabled the number of successful nests to increase annually till it levelled out at around fifty-five, which is presumably the number of pairs the surrounding area will support. For the moment, things were looking up.

CHAPTER 6

The Men from the Ministry

Within three months of finding the pigs poisoned, I got another nasty shock. I was wandering down a woodland ride when Tick froze, rigid in a point. Constant companionship unravels tiny clues and I can usually tell at a glance from her attitude what quarry lies hidden in the heart of a bramble patch or reed tussock. The degree of her excitement implies whether she had been transformed by the heady scent of pheasant, or the challenge of grey squirrel, which she is allowed to chase, or rabbit, which she would like to catch.

This was none of them. Moving quietly up to peer over her shoulder, I was surprised to see a fox. It was neither facing her, in snarling defiance, nor curled asleep, though I did once catch a fox napping, in summer sun on a southern bank. This fox was past doing either. It lay stretched, rigid in death, in full view at the edge of the ride.

Most creatures creep away to die in privacy—if they can. They do not willingly lie down and give up the ghost where all the world can see them. The most obvious explanation was that this fox had been shot and lay where it dropped in its tracks.

If that had happened, one thing was certain. It was not I who had been the executioner and, since our wood is not hospitable to poachers, the inference was that it had been shot elsewhere and tried to crawl home to die while it still had breath. I turned it gently over with my foot but could find no trace of blood. Bending down, to examine it more closely, I eased back an eyelid and concluded, from the fact that the eye still shone bright and had not yet glazed, that it had not been dead for long. The fact that Tick had winded it from so far away lent colour to the theory.

I had been worried enough by the loss of the pigs, not so much by financial considerations as by the fact that the dogs might find a dose of whatever had killed them. The Man from the Ministry had said that they seemed to have been poisoned, though he'd ducked the issue when it came to submitting a more precise diagnosis.

Few things are more worrying than not to be able to take your own well-trained dogs in your own wood for fear that they may be poisoned by something they might find hidden behind any bush or clump of cover. The fox seemed to offer the opportunity of settling, for better or for worse, whether my fears were groundless.

Was there a genuine danger of accidental poisoning, perhaps by legally used chemical pesticides, or worse, from illegally doped baits put down for vermin?

Deciding to call in the help of the Ministry of Agriculture, who tell farmers how to control their pests, I returned home to fetch a plastic bag as a shroud in which to take it to ADAS, the Ministry's Advisory Service.

I suggested to them that I feared the fox might have picked up a dose of the same potion that had killed the pig they had examined *post mortem*, three months before in August. I asked them to check particularly for poisonous pesticides as I had heard that a farmer, who did not live far away, had found several dead crows and two dead foxes lying within a few yards of the carcass of a hare stained suspiciously green.

I realised that the fox might not have been poisoned at all, but could have died from shot gun wounds, injuries from a road accident or even old age or other natural causes. But I should have been surprised if it had only been taken ill because I have never found a dead fox in the wild that had not come to a sudden or violent end. The instinct to creep away to die in dignified seclusion is too strong.

So I left my fox in his bag at ADAS regional headquarters and, since the findings about the pig were inconclusive, asked them to treat this problem with great urgency so that, if poison was the cause of death, I could take effective steps to guard my dogs and domestic stock from its source.

Ten weeks later I had not heard a word so I wrote, at the beginning of February, to remind them that I had submitted a fox carcass for analysis and repeated my request that they should take some urgent and efficient action. I complained that the only communication I had so far received was the usual formal bureaucratic bumph acknowledging receipt of the fox on the previous November 25th.

I mentioned, in passing, that I had subsequently found another dead fox but that there had seemed to be no point in adding it to a load they couldn't carry. So I had asked a personal friend in the medical profession for an independent opinion.

Within three days the Regional Pest Officer sent a long reply. He said that a *post mortem* had been carried out on November 26th which had revealed subcutaneous and brain haemorrhaging '. . . and although no shot gun pellets were found, it was thought that the animal could have been shot. (Possibly with a .22 rifle).'

He added that no proof of poisoning had been found, but that the stomach contents had been retained for later examination.

He said that ADAS could not undertake to investigate every case of alleged misuse of poison and that, if the Ministry Pest Infestation Control Laboratory (PICL) could not undertake an analysis, I should get a *post mortem* done by a vet and 'send appropriate tissues and organs for analysis by an independent analyst'.

If the *post mortem* had been carried out on November 26th, as was alleged, I could not understand why it had taken till February 5th (and only then after my prodding) to communicate the result, especially since I had asked that the case should be dealt with urgently.

So I replied that the subcutaneous and brain haemorrhaging, to which he referred, was unlikely to have been caused by bullets or shot gun pellets since the underside of the skin would have been marked or punctured, which would have been obvious as soon as the animal was skinned. I asked, in view of this observation, if his pathologist had any theories about what disease or specific poison might be responsible for the haemorrhages he described.

This letter was passed to the Chief Chemist at PICL who wrote to say that he was responsible for the staff who investigate the causes of death of about a hundred and fifty specimens of wildlife each year, when the creatures have been found on or near agricultural land. He said that my fox had arrived at a time when the staff were heavily committed to another research project, and he confirmed that an immediate *post mortem*, on November 26th, had included skinning the carcass. (So my assumption that the possibility of shooting could be excluded was correct.)

He also confirmed my belief that brain haemorrhaging *is* a symptom of certain acute poisons—though his pathologist had eliminated some possible causes of death. He promised to have the analysis completed in due course and to let me know the result.

That was more than three years ago, but I have heard nothing yet!

Although the recommendation of the Advisory Service had been to approach an independent analyst, PICL contradicted it flatly. The Chief Chemist admitted that he 'was not too surprised that I was unable to obtain satisfaction from an independent analyst, since the expertise in this area lies almost solely in this laboratory.'

When one 'expert' proclaimed that it had probably been shot and the other poisoned, but neither bothered to follow up with a conclusion, the credibility of both is open to question. Neither inspired either my confidence or respect.

Familiarity with poisonous agricultural chemicals seems to breed complaisance if not contempt in such minds.

The Ministry publication *Approved Products for Farmers and Growers* (revised annually), which first disturbed me when the potato-picker suffered from arsenic-poisoning, is a catalogue of chemicals spread about the countryside to control various insect pests and plant diseases. The potential side-effects, which can destroy harmless plants and threatened species of wildlife by accident, make truly horrific reading. It is easy to see why the Ministry of Agriculture begins by covering itself by disclaiming all liability for damage as a consequence of the use of the products it *approves*.

This seems a wise precaution, because many of these approved chemicals are diabolically dangerous, not only to the agricultural pests they are designed to eliminate, but also to wildlife and to man himself. The list includes over thirty 'poisonous substances' requiring special precautions. They appear in the official *Poisons List* and come under the provisions laid down in the *Poisons Rules* under the Pharmacy and Poisons Act 1933. These 'Rules' and the Act and the Poisons List can be purchased from Her Majesty's Stationery Office. I simply don't understand why they don't summarise the relevant extracts alongside each of the Approved Products in the Ministry guide, since some of them are so dangerously toxic that there seems no possible excuse for not drawing attention to the specific hazards implicit in following the Ministry's advice.

There is also an entirely separate booklet entitled *The Safe Use of Poisonous Chemicals on the Farm* which does highlight some of the consequences of assuming that the Approved List is even reasonably safe to use. It seems incomprehensible to take the risk of these sensible precautions being omitted through ignorance, when it would have been quite practical to combine all the publications in one booklet.

Some assessment of the scale of the hazards involved can be made when it is realised that over thirty of the specified substances cannot even be applied legally without special protective clothing for the operator. This recommended gear includes rubber coat, rubber boots, rubber gloves, sou'wester hat, face shield, dust mask and respirator. The most unimaginative would not assume that agricultural workers would be ordered to kit themselves out like spacemen without good cause.

A glance at the symptoms caused by neglecting to take precautions, not even described in detail in the guide, will confirm that such scepticism is far from scaremongering.

There are compounds which produce such headaches, fatigue and heavy sweating that it is vital to keep the patient absolutely flat and at rest. Until he gets to hospital, he must not be allowed to walk or take any physical exercise whatever, and he must be kept cool by fanning, sponging with cold water or removing his clothes entirely.

The Approved List is littered with systemic organophosphorus poisons, commonly used as insecticides, which produce nausea, giddiness and general weakness, while the organomercury products are even more insidious. Their effects may not manifest themselves for several weeks; then the whole central nervous system may be afflicted until muscle coordination deteriorates so badly that the patient cannot so much as fasten his buttons.

Most terrifying of all is the fact that some of these 'approved' products produce damage which is cumulative and irreversible. Very small doses of the chlorinated hydrocarbons, for example, can be stored in the fat until the cumulative result is lethal. Some of these, and similar approved products, are recommended to be broadcast as vapour from aeroplanes over our fields.

The law requires employers using such substances to keep a register of every worker, with his name and address, and to record the hours he works and the poisons he uses. If he is ill or absent without explanation within fourteen days of using substances to which the *Poisons Rules* apply, the Inspector must be notified by his employer.

I believe that the dangers of such chemical farming should not be glossed over but given maximum publicity, because adverse public opinion is one of the most powerful weapons to produce legislation to force effective precautions to be taken.

Even when the men from the Ministry are persuaded to provide an adequate explanation of the risks involved to accompany their approval of the poisons they advise growers to use, there will still be unacceptable risks inflicted on wildlife—for wild birds cannot read the most plainly written warnings.

This has been obvious since the early 1950s when organophosphorus compounds and chlorinated hydrocarbons first came into fashion.

Reports began to filter through, mainly from the great corn growing areas of East Anglia, that large numbers of birds and animals were being found dead for no apparent cause, and that whole stocks of bees were dying. Chemical seed dressings and insecticides fell under suspicion despite the protestations of the scientists.

This man-made plague reached a climax between 1956 and 1961. Five hundred poisoned wood pigeons were picked up in one day under their roost. In less than 1500 acres of woodland, 5568 wood pigeons, 118 stock doves, 59 rooks, 89 pheasants and thousands of small birds were collected. It is likely that this was no more than the tip of the iceberg and that far more died and lay, undiscovered, in the oblivion of thick cover.

Most of these early deaths were thought to have been caused by poisonous seed dressings, which were unfortunately so stable that they remained toxic inside the inside of their victims. In two months in 1960, no fewer than 1300 poisoned foxes were found. They had died from eating the birds which had died after eating the dressed corn.

The boffins at first denied this and the rumour was spread that foxes were dying from an obscure 'fox disease', said to be caused by a virus which was specific to foxes and which was either exceptionally infectious or contagious.

Bureaucracy didn't want to know, for the answer might have turned out to be unpalatable as a vote-catcher. Then *The Field* published an article by a Capt. Crawshay which turned out to be a block-buster. The captain was a practical farmer who was also fond of his hunting and his shooting. He objected to being sold products which interfered with his pheasants and his foxes. He thought he had detected the culprit and he decided to put his theory to the test.

He took a bunch of laying hens, which were due for culling and he fed them on corn that had been dressed with new-fangled corn dressings. When they died, he obtained some foxes (by unspecified means!) and fed them on the hens. As he had predicted, the foxes also died. They had convulsions, went into comas, went blind and died with the same agonising symptoms as their relatives in the wild.

The resulting limelight aroused public wrath which forced the chemists to investigate. They came to the same conclusion, though, in the meantime, thousands more insectivorous birds had been slaughtered, as well as badgers, carnivorous birds and domestic dogs and cats.

So a scheme was adopted by manufacturers and farmers to limit sowing corn, dressed with pesticides, to the autumn months. It was claimed that pheasants and pigeons and other wildlife do not bother to dig up grains in autumn, when food is plentiful as much as they do in winter and spring, when times are harder.

But their scheme was (and still is) only voluntary and so has no effective teeth.

What was not appreciated at the time was that emotive song birds or sportsmen's game are not the only important creatures to be considered. Pesticides, designed to exterminate harmful insects, are just as dangerous to beneficial insects too. Ladybirds and other predatory beetles suffered as badly as the villains of the piece. The chemical warfare, if carried to extremes, will effectively rule out the natural, biological controls (where beneficial predatory insects are encouraged to prey upon pests) which should be the ultimate aim of the scientists.

Conservationists, who raised hell in the fifties about the havoc caused to wildlife when the menace of poison on the land was first appreciated, were disturbed that as soon as the heat was taken off, far more diabolical concoctions were brewed up. Some were so lethal that it was necessary to keep stock from treated land for specified periods ranging from a day to no less than eight weeks.

The mind boggles at the idea that chemicals dangerous enough to be lethal to stock for so long are considered fit to be 'approved' for spreading on the land where wildlife cannot be safeguarded from contamination.

Notes about resistant strains are also important. Nature is far too clever for the brainiest boffins because, almost as fast as they dream up the most horrific ways of spreading death and destruction, their victims evolve strains which are resistant and survive. There are now strains of bacteria which do not appear to be affected by antibiotics, as some strains of rabbits are immune to myxomatosis.

Scientists are trying to evolve an even more obscene and deadly strain of this rabbit pestilence—in spite of the fact that it is theoretically illegal to spread it! If they succeed and the myxomatosis virus once more produces defensively immune mutations, there is the possibility that, eventually, a strain might be evolved that not only attacks rabbits but is also lethal to man himself. If so, I trust the boffins who produce it will be the first victims.

Nevertheless, however bitterly we deplore the wholesale use of poison on the fair face of England and however revolted we may be by those who deliberately use such foul germ warfare as myxomatosis, only modern Canutes will squander their energies trying to turn back the tide. Scientific controls of pests and weeds are here to stay, so that the most profitable approach is to spotlight the methods used to minimise the dangers so the excesses may be curbed by the sheer weight of public opinion.

Although I believe that my dog and the pigs and the fox died from poison, I was never able to trace the source with enough certainty to get a conviction. It has been illegal to lay poison in the open for the last seventy years, but gamekeepers and hill farmers have waged war on predators by laying poisoned baits for generations. It is a quiet weapon and it is very hard to prove who laid the bait, which is utterly indiscriminate.

It is bad enough to lose a favourite dog or a rare wild creature because it accidentally picks up a bird or small mammal which has also been accidentally poisoned by pesticides meant for agricultural pests. To lose the same animal because some lout has been putting down poison illegally and deliberately is intolerable.

In Hannam's day the common 'dope' was strychnine. It was used for hawks and owls, dogs and cats, badgers and foxes and crows, magpies, jays and jackdaws. It comes in powder form, like white flour, and the head keeper of a noble earl once showed me how to use it.

He made a hole in one side of an egg, about the size of a silver sixpenny piece (which was about as big as a new penny in the worthless washers we now use for money). Tipping the egg over, he shook out about half the contents, so that he could shake the remainder round within the shell, and picked a hollow stem of dry grass which he sharpened like a toothpick. Then he opened his tin of strychnine and thrust the sharpened point of his grass stem (about as thick as a darning needle) into the white powder. When he withdrew the stem, bearing a tiny pinch of the poison in the hollow point, he gently tipped it through the hole in the eggshell. He swirled the contents round, to mix his witches' brew, and pressed the egg deep into a patch of sticky mud so that it would be held as firmly as by an egg cup while the victim pecked or bit it.

Throughout the operation, he kept the tainted grass stem safe between his thumb and finger and, as soon as he had put the egg down, he reached in his pocket with his free hand for matches, struck one and burned the grass stem without ever allowing it to touch anything else. 'That's all you need,' he said, 'and *never* throw down anything that has touched strychnine until it has been burned. You can't be too careful,' he added. 'If you got a few grains under your nail, they'd do you in when you sucked your thumb.'

I resolved to be careful to the point of doing all in my power to make it a criminal offence to use the stuff for any purpose at all.

Strychnine is still in common use. Apart from being illegally smuggled into the country, it is regularly used by the Ministry of Agriculture Pest Officers and accredited professional mole catchers. They dip earthworms in the powder, or in a solution of the powder and water, and drop them into the underground runs of moles.

Moles do not pursue earthworms by digging for them, as is popularly supposed. They dig a network of underground burrows into which worms and insects tumble as they are moving underground. All the mole then has to do is to patrol his network of tunnels and eat the prey which has conveniently fallen into the trap. When times are good, and worms are plentiful, the mole nips them and disables them so that they will still be there when he

returns more hungry than at that particular moment. So the odd worm dropped in among those he has caught does not alarm him. He scoffs it down, strychnine and all, and dies in agonising convulsions.

Moles are also exceptionally pugnacious animals, fighting any rival mole that ventures into their territory, so it will not be long before another mole notices the lack of activity and explores the vacant area and, finding the neighbouring mole, he challenges him to fight. Dead moles don't fight, but live moles are cannibals, so he eats him. Strychnine and all. So the second mole dies and a third and a fourth. It is a devastating way of catching them, well within the capability of unskilled operators.

Not everyone wants a Ministry Pest Officer on his ground, or a professional mole catcher, so it is possible to apply for a permit to obtain strychnine and do the job yourself. Assuming that none of your friends travel to Ireland and will smuggle some in to save the paperwork, it is perfectly possible to obtain strychnine, ostensibly for killing moles (its only *legal* use). Unfortunately, it is too often misused because keepers have prized it for generations to poison anything that they class as 'vermin'.

In any case, it is no longer necessary to risk being caught smuggling a dangerous poison into the country or receiving the stuff from someone who has some for illegal sale.

There are other substances in the *Approved Products for Farmers and Growers* which are as dangerous as strychnine but can be bought from agricultural merchants in five-gallon drums. Accidental damage from this source is bad enough, but the men from the Ministry, who approved them, do not accept responsibility for providing active help, *even when blatant misuse is suspected*.

This was made perfectly clear to me in correspondence resulting from the fox I found so that there seemed little point in pursuing the matter when the body of a badger was found within a few yards of the enclosure where the pigs had died.

The victim was discovered the following spring by a distinguished ornithologist, who was looking for the woodcock which occasionally breed here. He remarked, when he came out of the wood, that he'd found a 'pretty crummy badger'. When I heard where he'd found it and went to examine it, I realised that even a scientist with enough enthusiasm to do a *post mortem* would have had his work cut out. All that remained was a mummified corpse, parchment skin stretched over the skeleton with a few yellowing tufts of wispy hair still adhering.

It raised the question of how the pigs died. Like foxes, it is not natural for badgers to die in the open. They nearly always have the strength and guts to struggle home to die. I examined the remains and satisfied myself that no broken snare remained around the body, no bones were broken and I could find no evidence of shot, though the remains were too far gone to be at all certain of that. But, in view of the reports on the pigs and the fox, poison was certainly a possibility. Not having had any formal training in pathology, I had no accurate idea of how long the creature had been dead.

If it had not died at about the same time as the pigs, perhaps some other victim had also died from the same cause and, being inveterate scoffers of carrion, there is little doubt that the pigs would eat any creature which happened to drop dead within their enclosure. Although the suspicion would need a great deal more hard scientific evidence to steer it towards certainty, it left niggling doubts in my mind.

The official attitude to the poisons used in the countryside seems far too complaisant and slack. Some years ago, when wood pigeons were causing serious damage to crops, a series of experiments was conducted to establish whether they could be controlled by the use of alfachloralose.

The idea was to treat tic beans with alfachloralose and scatter them on the fields as bait for wood pigeons. In theory, tic beans are too large for smaller birds to eat but wood pigeons have enormous gapes and cram large quantities of anything up to the size of acorns into their crops. So, unfortunately, do pheasants, and the boffins who dreamed up the theory did not leave their lab stools often enough to know that, in practice, other smaller birds, like great tits, are perfectly capable of demolishing the husks of quite large grains—and ingesting a dose of the dope in the process.

Not to bother, the men from the Ministry said. Alfachloralose is not a poison, it is a narcotic. It will simply drug the victims and they will recover if an operator does not go round soon after they have taken it and pick them up before they come round. It was soon obvious that a surfeit of alfachloralose is not as simple as having one over the eight. It does not only make the victim drunk; a hefty overdose will kill him.

Simple conservationists could not see the difference between ingesting a fatal dose of poison or an overdose of a narcotic which had an equally fatal effect. The distinction seemed merely splitting bureaucratic hairs because whatever eats either will stay dead just as long. There was soon an outcry about people who claimed it as their right to poison the innocent along with the guilty—so long as the theoretical aim was the control of pests.

The experiment would have done less harm if it had not been conducted in such a glare of publicity, but the Ministry issued licences for farmers to conduct experiments where the pigeon damage was worst and, the rural grapevine being what it is, eyes were skinned and ears pricked the length and breadth of the land.

Gamekeepers who had never heard of alfachloralose jumped on the wagon to catch foxes, under the deliberate illusion that it was 'only to drug' them, instead of running the risk of prosecution for putting poison in the open. Eggs were laced with the stuff for magpies and crows, and rabbit carcasses pegged out because, in keepers' eyes, anything that will eat a pegged-out rabbit *must* be vermin. The hard fact that it is illegal to use the stuff without a Ministry licence was conveniently overlooked because there are none as thick as those who don't want to understand. After all, if it was 'only a narcotic and not a poison' why should it be as illegal to use it as if it were a poison? The men from the Ministry ducked the issue. All they will say is that it can't be obtained on the open market.

But it can be obtained quite easily. The Royal Society for the Protection of Birds proved the point by answering an advertisement in the sporting press and forking out twelve pounds fifty. They received, in return, through the Christmas post, half a kilo of alfachloralose, which would have been enough to poison five thousand birds, not just to give them a hangover.

It is impossible to assess how many people, who had never heard of the stuff before, are now using it to kill vermin which attacks game, foxes which threaten lambs—and anything else that gets to the bait first. The experiment was dangerous and inept. It left the perpetrators looking very irresponsible.

Some of the other poisons which are deliberately and illegally misused are far worse, especially those which say stock may return in a short while.

The Royal Society for the Protection of Birds issued a report early in 1979 which indicates that either a lot of birds return during the forbidden time—or that deliberate misuse, by doping bait with greater concentration than would be used to spray crops, produces very different results. They find that acute poisons including strychnine and so-called narcotics, like alfachloralose are being used, illegally, to kill protected birds; that they are used without licence to kill birds which could be destroyed legally by less dangerous methods—crows and other birds not covered by protective laws could be shot or cage-trapped, for instance—and that the poisons are used, also illegally, to kill foxes and other mammals in such a way that many birds are also killed by accident.

Far from getting better, the problems of illegal use of poisons are getting worse. During the past few years the RSPB investigation staff have examined over a thousand victims including buzzards, ravens, kites and eagles, all of which died from poison.

In hill country, the poison is usually put on bait for foxes, wildcats, ravens and crows, but eagles, kites and buzzards also fancy the rabbits and hares that are laid out. So do badgers and sheep dogs, which are common victims too.

In farming country, where shooting is either considered as a sacred cow or a lucrative crop, foxes and badgers, hawks and owls are all 'vermin' which interfere with sport or profit. Eggs are among the favourite baits in these areas and, in one incident that has already been spotlighted by publicity, a JP's wife found some pheasant eggs strewn about a field and collected them for a local animal sanctuary. Despite the fact that it is supposed soon to lose its potency, the approved pesticide with which the eggs had been

laced, persisted when they were boiled. The birds which were fed on the hard-boiled eggs died as surely as the 'vermin' would have done if they had picked up the eggs instead. Sooner or later, a finder of such delicacies will boil them for himself.

Scotland appears to be one of the worst areas for the use of poisoned baits, which may not be surprising since they were years behind England and Wales in banning the gin-trap. Scottish sporting estates are so large—and often so remote—that it is difficult to get an objective assessment of the problem. At least six golden eagles died from eating poisoned bait in 1972 and seven buzzards from dining on doped rabbit, but such cases go mostly undetected.

It may be significant that there is a sharp annual rise in the number of reports of poison during the tourist season in Scotland when many knowledgeable naturalists take their holidays there. So the thousand or so poisoned birds which the RSPB have examined can only be an insignificant proportion of the real scale of casualties.

Now that our present economic mess allows rich foreigners from the Middle East and Europe to pay more for our sporting facilities than we can afford ourselves, matters are likely to get worse, since they insist on getting value for their money and our threatened species mean nothing to them.

Perhaps it is unfair to pick at the motes in foreigners' eyes before we have curbed our own arrogance in assuming that we have the right to annihilate whole species either because they interfere with sporting interests or agricultural convenience. The case of badgers in the West Country is a good example.

Up to the end of the last war, Bovine Tuberculosis was common in both cattle and human beings. Our TB sanatoria were full to overflowing, although Bovine TB was not the only form to be treated. The disease was largely eradicated in man by modern drugs and a 'clean milk' policy, where milk was either sterilised, pasteurised or produced from herds that were accredited to be free from the disease.

For generations, cattle had been selectively bred to produce high yields of milk or rapid growth of beef. Nature concedes nothing without exacting her price, so that selective breeding can only be a compromise. If particular characteristics are desired, they must be obtained at the expense of something else. 'Natural' selection produces survival of the fittest but usually at the expense of the unnaturally high production selective breeders strive for. The converse is too often true.

By the end of the last war, our cattle were making farming millionaires from the milk and meat they produced—but they were abnormally susceptible to disease as the penalty. About twenty-five per cent of them showed symptoms of TB.

The Ministry vets set out to remedy the defects by testing all cattle for TB, by law, and slaughtering any reactors that they found. By exterminating the weak, they argued, they would eradicate the disease entirely and produce a 'clean' national herd. Initial results were hailed as a huge success because the incidence of Bovine TB declined dramatically from about one in four to a tenth of that figure.

Although this was true as a generalisation over most of the country, there was a major black spot in the West Country, notably in southern Gloucestershire/northern Wiltshire/Avon and certain parts of Cornwall. By the end of the 1960s, more herd breakdowns were occurring in this region of the south-west than in the rest of the country put together.

Great pressure was applied to the Ministry to do something about it, till it became politically expedient at least to be seen to be trying.

The vectors known to have transmitted TB in the past were commonly cat, pig and people. An infected cowman could be lethal but Ministry reports are remarkably reticent about explaining just what steps they took to eliminate the obvious.

In June 1971 luck came to their aid. A badger carcass, said to have been a road casualty, was collected from a farm in Gloucestershire where Bovine TB existed in cattle. *Mycobacterium bovis* (Bovine TB) was diagnosed in the badger and the Ministry, grasping at the straw, started a witch hunt in the area.

Badgers excrete in latrine pits, as cats do, but, unlike cats, they do not cover up their dung. Badger droppings were therefore easy enough to find, and examination in the Ministry laboratories disclosed the presence of Bovine TB.

This was not surprising since, at some periods of the year, badgers' diet consists of up to sixty per cent of earthworms. Earthworms come out onto the surface to mate and are likely to become coated with bacilli if tubercular cows are grazing and excreting in the meadow. Badgers also feed on dung beetles, found under cowpats, so that there is a real possibility that infected cows might, in turn, infect the badgers in their pasture.

Whether the badgers originally caught TB from cattle is now irrelevant. The harsh fact is that samples of badger droppings were shown to carry TB bacilli and subsequent *post mortems* of badgers from the farms where cattle were infected confirmed that up to twenty per cent of badgers in the same area were infected also.

The fact that such a high proportion of cattle had TB may have been partly due to the weakening effect of selective breeding specifically for high output of milk and meat at the expense of everything else. The ruthless culling of all reactors to the TB test may have had a spectacular effect short term—but in the long run, the advantages it produced have proved illusory. Natural immunity and inherent resistance to disease have been among the factors bred-out by using generation after generation of animals which have never been subjected to the slightest whiff of infection, and have even had to be kept on their legs by including preventative medicines in their diet. The one hope of diverting attention from the scientists' and geneticists' blunders seemed to be to find a scapegoat which could take the blame for the apparently inexplicable high incidence of TB in the West Country.

The last straw of hope was grasped, and live badgers were sent to the laboratory, infected with TB and confined with 'clean' calves to see if they passed on their malady. The Ministry vets are reticent about the value of experiments under such unnatural conditions because proof of the ability to transmit disease in the laboratory is a far cry from demonstrating that the theory is likely to be converted to practice under quite different conditions in the field. The integrity of such work is open to question.

The men from the Ministry were prosecuting counsel, judge and jury and they condemned badgers over a wide area in the West Country to death. The 1973 Badgers Act, although a protective measure in theory, had left a loophole for the Minister of Agriculture to authorise the destruction of badgers 'to prevent the spread of disease'.

Poison was out of the question because the Protection of Animals Act 1911 outlawed the use of poison except for a very few exceptions, including rats, mice and moles but *not* badgers. The same Act prohibited the use of poison gas.

To find a few badger dung pits in heavily populated badger country is simple enough. To kill the badgers that made them, without the use of gas or poison, requires skills of a different calibre, and the men from the Ministry soon began to flounder.

They decided to snare their quarry and to use the latest thing which is the self-lock snare. I explained earlier that badgers have exceptionally small heads in proportion to their bodies and even skilled gamekeepers find them difficult to kill comparatively cleanly by strangulation. The toggle of self-lock snares ensures that, when once the noose tautens, it does not slack off again, but bites deeper and deeper into the flesh until it buries itself from sight. To my simple mind—and I have had ample personal experience of trying to liberate badgers from these snares—the self-lock snare can be as diabolical an instrument of torture as the illegal gin-trap.

Members of the Gamekeepers' Association, a body not famous

for fuddy-duddy sentimentalism, probably know more about snaring than the rest of the population put together. Their job entails the efficient control of the enemies of game but they value their good name and are unwilling to cause unnecessary suffering. They have drawn up a strict Code of Conduct for snaring because they are too well aware that, unskilfully used, snares can cause great cruelty. They specify such technicalities as the breaking strain of the wire to be used, the swivels and the way the snare is to be tethered. They insist that *all* snares must be visited regularly and daily between sunrise and sunset. And, most important of all, they are quite specific that the 'free-running snare', with a running noose that is not jammed by a toggle, causes least distress. They do not like 'stop snares' which damage the skin of the neck because the animal continues to struggle while it is in the snare.

Their Code of Conduct contains the unequivocal statement that 'the self-locking snare is undoubtedly the most inhumane of the three. Its purpose is to kill any animal caught by the neck and *extreme suffering* [my italics] is caused to any animal which is miscaught, i.e. round the body or by a leg.' Under no circumstances, they conclude, should their members use a self-lock snare.

The men from the Ministry did not, apparently, have the practical experience to know about this and they made the astonishing decision to start their campaign by a public demonstration of snaring badgers in May 1974. The gallery that turned up to watch predictably included members of the public who took pity on badgers which had been convicted on such circumstancial evidence.

Because it requires specialist skills to snare a badger round the neck, the loops had been set large enough for a badger to step into so that it was quite deliberately caught round the belly.

I have before me, as I write, a photograph of a lactating sow badger that was caught in this fashion at the Ministry's own demonstration of how to 'control' them. The wire had bitten into her udder, expelling milk that should have fed her orphaned cubs. As a result, a private prosecution was brought against the Minister of Agriculture and his officers for transgressing the Badgers Act

1973, which makes it an offence to cause 'cruel ill-treatment' to a badger.

Amongst others, I was asked by the Gloucestershire police to give my views, as an expert witness, in a written statement and I had no hestiation in testifying that such a slow and painful death was cruel in the extreme. The Code of Conduct drawn up by the Gamekeepers' Association endorses the view by men whose profession entails the control of predators.

The private prosecution, brought by Mrs Ruth Murray, lasted for two days and, although I was unable to attend personally, the transcript of the evidence indicates that the Ministry claimed that it had an unpleasant job to do, and that the pest officers knew of no more humane way of destroying badgers.

The outcome was inconclusive in that the Minister was not convicted—though he was refused costs—but it was made clear that snaring in this fashion was *not* humane and the defence would not be accepted again.

My own opinion is that it was a tactical error to prosecute the Minister himself since the State was bound to pull out every stop to evade such a humiliating conviction and that, however much of an ass the law may be, no court will pillory a Minister of the Crown if there is a loophole to avoid it. There is no shadow of doubt that cruel ill-treatment was inflicted and I believe there would have been a better chance of obtaining a conviction, that might also have outlawed self-lock snares for other animals as well, if only the anonymous pest officer who actually set the snares had been prosecuted without his boss.

Be that as it may, the Ministry officials retired, discredited in the public mind, to wipe the egg off their faces.

Self-lock snares were not used publicly again, though in the Ministry report two years later, when indignation had subsided, it is admitted that only snares are used (type unspecified) for catching badgers for radio tagging,★ 'because of the obvious advantage of snares over traps in catching badgers and the disproportionately large amount of time required pre-baiting and setting traps'. Since the animals are required alive, the snares are visited hourly, which must at least reduce the period of their agony.

It is worth examining the evidence on which this mammoth campaign against badgers is based, to assess whether they are the real culprits or merely the scapegoats to divert attention from the Ministry vets who do not yet know the real cause for cattle in the West Country having a far higher incidence of Bovine TB than cattle anywhere else.

There is no doubt that in the area under consideration badgers *do* have an incidence of up to twenty per cent of their numbers infected.

The published experimental evidence for transmission between badgers and cattle is interesting and shows just how artificial the lab conditions were. The *Veterinary Record* published an account which stated that nine castrated Jersey calves, aged two and a half months, were allocated to three equal groups, each sharing one pen. The calves were clinically healthy.

One group was injected, intravenously, with TB isolated from cattle, one calf being given 0.1 mg, one calf 0.001 mg, and the third calf 0.0001 mg. The second group was injected with same doses of TB, isolated from one badger, and the third group was injected with the same doses of TB from a different badger. All the

---

★ Badgers are caught by the scientists working for the Ministry and fitted with miniature radio transmitters, sometimes fastened to their backs with straps similar to dog-harness. The scientists can then monitor an animal's movements by tuning in to the wave-length of the transmitter it is forced to carry.

calves were fed on a normal diet, inspected for TB regularly and examined *post mortem*.

The calves infected with TB from cattle and from one badger showed similar symptoms. They developed fever, anorexia, lassitude and 'respiratory distress leading to fatal termination', which is the scientific jargon for a pretty nasty death.

But the group infected from the other badger 'developed no clinical symptoms and only small and less extensive lesions were found at autopsy although the calves of this group reacted to the TB test approximately to the same degree as the other groups.'

Why the difference? Is there *any* possibility that badgers, exhibiting signs of TB, are not *necessarily* infective to cattle?

The report goes on to state that 'the organism recovered from lesions of this third group was *shown to be fully virulent to guinea pigs*'. And cultures prepared from infected guinea pigs induced disease in a further calf.

You don't often find guinea pigs wandering around in badger-infected cow pastures, so the chance of a badger infecting a guinea pig which infected a cow seem pretty slight! Or if the men from the Ministry are not really so desperate to drum up proof that the badger is the scapegoat, why did they not simply cross-infect direct to another calf?

They say that badgers are normally infected by inhaling TB bacilli—but they are happy to inject them intravenously and *assume* the experimental data which forms the cornerstone of their campaign would be the same.

Nor is the question of possible alternative sources of infection dealt with very satisfactorily. TB bacilli were also found in fox, brown rat, mole and earthworm, all of which are given a verdict of 'innocent' by the Ministry vets. They say that the body temperature of the earthworm is too low for the bacilli to multiply. But if a worm crawled through an area of concentrated infection, could it not in turn transmit the disease? Malaria does not breed in mosquitoes, nor the virus of Dutch elm disease in elm bark beetles, yet both are guilty of spreading their specific plagues.

Rats, moles and foxes are reputed to be *infected* by Bovine TB but not to be *infective*. If this is really so, why do the Ministry vets refuse to duplicate the experiments on which they based their theory that badgers are the only culprits. Why do they not put three bunches of calves in three pens and inject rats, foxes and moles with the same doses of infection that they used on badgers? At least it would show they had the courage of their convictions.

If the disease really is as transmissable between cattle and badgers as they pretend, why did not badgers *all over the country* contract the disease before 1960 when it is claimed that twenty-five to thirty per cent of cattle all over the country were infected? And if badgers all over the country *did* have TB in those days, how did they get rid of it without an eradication campaign? Why is it found now *only* in the same limited areas of the West Country from which it has never been eradicated in cattle?

Is there no possibility that there is some factor about the stricken area which has not yet been spotted either by the Ministry men or those who doubt their word?

Surely, if cattle *and* badgers *and* foxes *and* rats *and* moles are infected, it may well be that they have a common infective source which would be more likely to be discovered if the scientists would approach the problem with an open mind instead of being so worried about justifying the conclusion to which they first jumped.

Gloucestershire is more densely populated by badgers than anywhere else in the country so that the Ministry argument that this or that infected herd was found to be within a short distance of a badger sett is meaningless. It would be difficult to find a herd, infected or not, in many wooded areas of the county that is not within a short distance of a badger sett.

I was associated with the television programme *Badger Watch*, in which badgers were observed in darkness by infra-red sensitive cameras in the area where the Ministry experiments are taking place.

My experience of badgers is such that I was at first astonished that the badgers we were observing tolerated BBC engineers disturbing the sett by poking microphones down the holes and tramping close to the sett to service the remotely-controlled cameras within a few hours of live transmission. The badgers that I know would have deserted the sett and gone somewhere else or, at best, have stayed below ground for most of the night.

The only theory I can postulate for their toleration of us is that they had nowhere else to go; that the whole area is indeed so densely populated that they would have run into intolerable territorial aggression if they had tried to move elsewhere.

When the television programmes were over, a dead badger, which was found to be tubercular, was discovered in the area so the whole colony was killed. *Post mortem* examination indicated that, out of thirteen badgers killed, six were infected. The Ministry, in their published report, justified the death of the other seven on the assumption that they 'would probably have contracted the disease'.

I do not believe that it is reasonable to take such a case as being typical, or to base a management policy on such abnormal conditions. TB is a disease notorious for thriving on over-population so that the local badgers could be expected to be abnormally liable to suffer from TB, and data derived from experiments with them may not be typical of other parts of the country.

Whatever doubts they may have about the competence of the men conducting the experiment, few naturalists or countrymen would quarrel with the necessity of culling infected animals. The Ministry of Agriculture assures us that its officials only intend to destroy badgers which are infected or using setts used by infected badgers; they also say that 'no satisfactory method has been found for testing live badgers for the presence of the disease'!

It would not seem unreasonable to suggest that some priority should be given to what must surely be a fairly simple procedure, since the men from the Ministry certainly do not destroy a herd of cattle in order to find the reactors!

There are now satisfactory cage-traps available which may take more skill than operating a gas pump, but they could surely be used for 'sampling' the condition of a colony before wholesale destruction is embarked on, if the land owner happens to wish to retain his badgers unless they are actually infected.

In order to test the theory that badgers are indeed responsible for the transmission of Bovine TB, the men from the Ministry have decided to obliterate the badgers in the Thornbury area of Gloucestershire and to monitor the subsequent incidence of TB among cattle.

Nature abhors a vacuum and, in normal circumstances, it is virtually impossible to clear a large area of any species for the simple reason that it immediately refills from the periphery. Animals in adjacent territory soon discover that, just over their doorstep, there is territory containing good food and habitat—and no competition—so they immediately move in to replace the animals which have been artificially removed.

The Ministry had an unpleasant demonstration of this phenomenon a few years after the last war with rats in the Craven Arms district of Shropshire.

The rat poison Warfarin, which kills by preventing blood clotting, had proved so effective that there seemed hope, at last, of getting rats under control, if not eradicating them. A pocket of rats appeared near Glasgow which had developed a resistance to Warfarin, and another near Craven Arms. It was vital to prevent them breeding and spreading the immunity, so a *cordon sanitaire* was thrown around Craven Arms and Ministry rat catchers flooded in to wipe the whole rat population out in the area.

The rats won. No sooner did the rat catchers poison and gas and catch most of them, than interlopers recolonised the vacant space, interbred with the resistant survivors and reproduced their invincible kind.

A far more curious reason for the inability of the men from the Ministry to control wildlife emerged in East Anglia, where coypu had escaped and were colonising the Norfolk Broads. Coypu are large mammals, orginally imported into the country by fur farmers—coypu fur is known in the trade as nutria. They are aquatic, weigh about 15 lbs (about two-thirds as large as a badger) and dig obvious burrows with holes up to twenty inches in diameter. By 1962, there was an estimated population of 200,000 and the Ministry moved in with all guns blazing, just as it has now done with badgers in the West Country.

They were lucky to start with because the hard winter of 1962/63 killed ninety per cent of their quarry for them. The area of

colonisation was so restricted, the holes so obvious and the quarry so slow that success seemed to be in sight by 1965. Ten years later they were still at it and the population in the spring of 1978 was estimated at 8000 in the Coypu Control Area. The Coypu Strategy Group was set up in 1977 to assess the prospects of eradicating coypu in Great Britain, and it came to the conclusion that they were pretty poor.

High on the list of reasons why complete eradication is impracticable is the statement that 'there would be lack of motivation in the trapping force in the face of imminent loss of employment'. The trappers will not trap themselves out of a job!

So similar experiments with badgers in the West Country may face similar difficulties. The areas they clear may be quickly re-colonised and, just when success seems to be around the corner, the tail may wag the dog again.

The experiment near Thornbury in Gloucestershire has unusual advantages on its side. The area involved is bounded on one side by the river Severn and on another by the Little Avon. The other two sides are along the M4 and M5. So, although it is not an island entirely surrounded by water, the two motorways are the next best thing. Serious re-colonisation from the periphery must be a smaller hazard than most places the Ministry might have chosen. Since there is no immediate prospect of total success in the whole West Country area, it may be possible to instil the trappers with the motivation to continue effectively.

The Ministry did not know how many badgers they had killed by 1978 because it was impossible to count corpses which had been gassed in tunnels far below the ground. But between *three and four thousand* setts have been gassed—and the numbers are rising monthly. A yardstick of the unstoppable drive to re-colonise setts where the animals have been exterminated is that one sett has had to be re-gassed no fewer than *twenty-four* times. The mind boggles at the scale of the slaughter.

Perhaps the carnage is unavoidable, if not justified by everyone's standards. TB infection is one of the natural ways of guarding against over-population, and perhaps it makes little difference, in practice, whether over-populated badgers in the West Country are decimated by disease or by Pest Officers' gas. The evidence against badgers passing TB on to cattle is overwhelming in the laboratory, but still quite unproven in the field. Perhaps when the Thornbury experiment is complete and the badgers there are no more, then maybe the incidence of the disease in cattle may shrink to average national levels.

Or, perhaps—supposing that the men from the Ministry are honest enough to admit it—cattle may still be infected when the badgers are gone so that their innocence will be proved posthumously. In that case, the scientists would have to think again and start a search for the real source of the infection.

Meanwhile badgers all over the country—where there is no sign of Bovine TB—are suffering from the publicity the West Country campaign has sparked off. Farmers who have invested all their capital in dairy cows will take no risks. Hearing the officials say that TB *is* spread by badgers in the West Country (not *may be* spread), they are annihilating whole colonies of badgers all over the country. It is no good bleating that this is against the law because farmers are a law unto themselves on their own land, and who can blame them? Badger-digging, which had been virtually stopped by the 1973 Act, has started again and there are persistent reports that badger-baiting with bull terriers, which must be the cruellest 'sport' (*sic*) of all, has started again in the West Country, where anti-badger feelings have been whipped-up to the point where nothing is considered too bad for them.

There are still those who believe that the badger may be more sinned against than sinning; that he may be just as much a victim as cattle are of an as yet undisclosed source of infection, though most would also agree that any badgers that do contract the disease are best killed before they spread it either to other badgers or cattle.

But those who resent and are sceptical about the Ministry of Agriculture campaign will be somewhat mollified to know that the Nature Conservancy Council has commissioned an independent programme of research to examine the whole implications of the effects of TB on other species of wildlife as well as badgers.

The study is being undertaken by the Department of Medical Microbiology at the London School of Tropical Medicine. The Nature Conservancy Council does recognise that it is necessary, *on present evidence* (my italics) to control TB in both badgers and cattle. But I trust that the assurance that 'there will be close liaison with the Ministry of Fisheries, Food & Agriculture' does not imply that the 'independence' of the study is to be purely a nominal cover for a whitewash operation.

Perhaps the NCC study will come up with an alternative to culling all cattle that react to the test which is always liable, by selectively breeding out all traces of the infection, to produce a strain with no inherent resistance.

One alternative might be immunisation by vaccination (as is practised with human beings). The idea isn't new and I gather that one objection to it might be that the Common Market wouldn't like it. That should be the least of our worries.

Another objection would be that immunisation is never one hundred per cent effective. It could well be more effective than having to slaughter reactors which turn out at *post mortem* examination not to have been infected. In 1976, for example, of 1058 cattle that reacted to the TB test, the Ministry said that 'half may not have been infected at all'. Of those that *were* confirmed *post mortem*, some were old and had broken-down lesions. Some had been introduced from Ireland. 'The majority had been passed on by an infected badger or badgers which had access to the farm where the cattle were kept'. Not 'might' have been passed on, be it noted, 'passed on'—without a shred of hard evidence. Perhaps the independent NCC enquiry will be more objective.

It can also be said that, when a beast had once been immunised, its reaction to the standard TB test would be affected, which might cause the threat of redundancy among the inspectors. If they could be trained to do the vaccinations instead, it might soften resistance because, unlike successful coypu trappers, they would not then necessarily work themselves out of a job.

While the badgers in the West Country are being buried under a cloud of suspicion, an infintely more serious danger has been creeping up on us at the rate of about twenty miles a year.

Rabies has been inching westwards across Europe from Poland since 1939. It is now approaching the channel coast in France and it should be of some comfort to know that the English Channel is deep enough and wide enough to prevent it getting to our shores by natural means. We are fairly safe—unless it is carried here by an animal or person who has already contracted it so that the disease is in a state of incubation when it arrives.

The symptoms and effects are horrific. The victim is normally bitten by an animal which already has the disease and it usually takes an incubation period of between two weeks and two months of suspense before the symptoms appear. The disease is about seven times as common in males as females, both human and animal.

First symptoms are a minor degree of headache, tiredness and weakness, similar to influenza. The disease escalates through the central nervous system, the patient goes mad with thirst, accompanied by an insane fear of the water he craves (hydrophobia) and extreme terror, muscular spasms and agony are eventually followed by the merciful relief of death, usually within a week. There is, as yet, no cure.

The most likely way for the disease to enter the country is on a dog or cat or other infected animal which is smuggled in. It would be a social crime as bad—or worse—than tossing a bomb into a crowded bar. The Ministry of Agriculture wages a publicity campaign against it and heavy fines and occasional imprisonment are usually imposed when transgressors are caught.

Such pussy-footing is utterly inadequate. Everyone who smuggles an animal past the customs officials, whether by design or in ignorance, should automatically be put in jail for the maximum sentence. And no smuggled animal should be put in quarantine kennels: it should be destroyed without any possibility of appeal.

But even if the authorities can be persuaded to take such reasonably tough (though possibly unpopular) action, there is still the chance that rabies will be introduced, perhaps by a cat or rat 'jumping ship' or some other unfortunate accident and, apart from the chance of it infecting a human being, there will be the risk of the disease infecting wildlife.

On the continent, the commonest vector is the red fox which is liable to infect other wildlife and domestic dogs and cats because, when the disease reaches the 'furious' stage, even timid creatures lose their fear and will attack almost anything that moves. The virus is carried in the saliva and the disease is usually transmitted by innoculation, when the fangs puncture a victim's skin.

It has been found, on the continent, that when foxes are culled effectively enough, the disease diminishes and sometimes actually dies out, because about eighty-five per cent of all rabies cases in certain continental countries occur in the common fox.

Some countries, therefore, have waged all-out war on foxes by poison, gassing, shooting, snaring and trapping in order to contain the plague. But all carnivores can contract it, including badgers, pine martens etc., and it is also common among deer in some countries. (Any warm blooded mammal can catch it.)

As a result, the attitude to wildlife in any country where rabies gets a hold is drastically changed—for the worse. *Any* animal, wild or domestic, which shows suspicious symptoms is shot first and examined later. Only fools will take risks with such a scourge.

Nevertheless, rabies is no novelty to our shores. Throughout the Middle Ages, English literature is studded with unfortunates who were bitten by mad dogs or scratched by rabid cats, but references to cases of wildlife having rabies are few and far between.

Perhaps this is due to the fact that foxes were very scarce. The countryside was clothed in woodland through which hounds could follow their fox far faster than the horseman. Nobody was interested in seeing hounds start the hunt, and then disappear into the first thicket so that huntsmen had to spend the rest of the day finding them. . . . The obvious answer was not to hunt fox but hare which, having a smaller territory, tended to show better sport running round in circles so that the huntsmen could keep in touch.

Foxes were regarded as vermin and, far from attracting social stigma by catching one, there was a bounty from the church wardens on every fox brought to book. As soon as a fox settled in the parish, the lads of the village earned their ale money by digging it out. Foxes were a scarce commodity. Probably too scarce to spread rabies.

As farming techniques improved, woodlands were cleared for agriculture and sportsmen discovered that, in open country, foxes provided far more fun than hares. So a trade sprang up which imported foxes from the continent and, in the late eighteenth century, up to two thousand foxes a year were going through Leadenhall Market alone to satisfy the demand for huntable quarry. Landowners who paid hard cash one day for foxes from Leadenhall were not prepared to see a bounty being paid the next day by the church wardens in their own parishes. So the bounties stopped and vulpicide, the killing of a fox with anything but hounds, became a social crime.

It still is in this country. Practical continentals, on the other hand, keep their foxes culled as hard as they can, the target being less than one per square kilometre, the theoretical break even point for spreading rabies.

The men from the Ministry here won't play. They say that Nature abhors a vacuum and that if they kill foxes in one area, it will refill from the periphery and that the population movement this causes may do more harm than good. Precisely the opposite of what they say about badgers, where they are trying to eradicate them completely from the area in the West Country infected by Bovine TB!

Perhaps another reason is that vulpicide is still socially unacceptable in some quarters and might be a mammoth vote loser until the panic that will undoubtedly ensue if rabies does arrive, gives priority to a more realistic approach. The need for effective action, in that event, will be greater than it has ever been before because foxes have become so urbanised in recent years, that some people assess that there are more town and suburban foxes than there are out in the countryside. Such density would pose unprecedented risks to domestic dogs and cats, which in turn, could threaten humans.

The alternative that the men from the Ministry propose is horrifying. Instead of trying to limit the risk while there is still time, they propose to wait till rabies arrives. They would then take an area 24 miles × 24 miles and lay poisoned bait at 100-yard intervals in lines a mile apart. It is calculated that about nine thousand baiting stations would be required for each infected area. The poison proposed at present is strychnine! Nearly nine thousand dollops of the foullest and most persistent poison round each focal point where rabies is reported! The exercise would be repeated, at intervals, three times. The prospect does not bear thinking about.

Each dose of poison would be placed in a fowl's head, which is bait that can readily be procured in quantity from processed chicken factories. And each bait is to be buried, theoretically to be recovered like buried treasure after two days if Charlie fox prefers his own *à la carte* menu elsewhere.

How many dogs or cats or other wildlife would also be killed is anybody's guess. How many children even.

Everyone agrees that poison is indiscriminate and highly dangerous—but almost any risk will be acceptable to wipe out rabies if it ever does arise. The alternative possibilities with foxes are not encouraging.

Hunting with hounds as a control is worse than useless. They *may* catch the fox they are hunting but they will certainly disturb and disperse any others in the area, spreading the risk of infection.

Shooting is almost as bad for causing dispersal, as the Ministry found out to its cost during its attempts to wipe out wildlife at

Camberley, in 1969, when a dog contracted rabies shortly after leaving quarantine, and escaped temporarily. In densely wooded country, it is virtually impossible to drive foxes to guns and they simply seek less disturbed quarters.

Gassing earths is ineffective except during the two months or so a year when vixens stay below the ground with cubs. Contrary to popular belief, foxes spend a very high proportion of their lives above ground in suitable cover. Snaring on a wide enough scale needs great skill and would do untold damge to other wildlife. Trapping with 'leg-hold' traps (the bureaucratic jargon for more emotive, illegal gin-traps) is also written-off on the grounds of skill required in trapping and damage to other wildlife.

Unpalatable as the solution may be, poison seems inevitable as a last resource, but even the Ministry admit that 'it will be preferable to use a more humane and transiently persistent poison'—than strychnine! So what are they waiting for? Surely top priority should be given to the task of finding not only a 'less persistent' dope than strychnine, but a less universally palatable bait than fowl heads.

The men from the Ministry's track record for their activities concerned with wildlife is not inspiring. They are still dissipating energy on badger control when the urgency for effective plans to deal with rabies is obvious. Drugging wood pigeons (or poisoning them?) simply resulted in local knowledge of alfachloralose becoming universal. Nothing apparently was learned from the failure to eradicate Warfarin-resistant rats from Shropshire or coypu from East Anglia—except that they are still, like Canute, intending to repeat the exercise with foxes, if rabies arrives. In spite of this, they refuse to try to limit the task by reducing their population nationally before the necessity to exterminate them locally ever arises.

If they think this is impractical, I would point out that, certainly in my area, more than a dent in the fox population has been caused by the current market price of pelts. Good winter skins have been fetching more than £25 each and our local tannery will pay £15 for a good, clean fox, unskinned and just as he is when he is caught. Perhaps the church warden's bounty was not such a bad idea after all. Perhaps some of the taxpayers' money spent on the Ministry would get better results put into the pockets of more practical countrymen, catching foxes for reward?

The best non-technical assessment on the subject does not originate from the Ministry of Agriculture, but from the Nature Conservancy Council, under the title *Rabies & Wildlife*, 1978.

Some measure of their misgivings can be gathered from the fact that the NCC is itself initiating two independent three-year research contracts on topics related to a rabies outbreak. The first is concerned with possible transmission routes between domestic animals and wildlife. A study will be made of contacts between feral cats, foxes and badgers in a port and in neighbouring urban and rural areas, to assess how rabies might pass from domestic animals in a town to wildlife in the countryside. The second study will be of the social structure of fox populations and the anticipated effect on the spread of disease that would follow various control measures.

Perhaps, while they are at it, the Conservancy workers should do some work on baits which would be attractive to foxes but not to other animals, and on poisons that would be degraded and become harmless if not quickly eaten.

My own experience is that foxes are very fond of dead rats which do not seem palatable to many other mammals, although birds like crows will eat them. But if my dogs find a dead rat, they ignore if it is fresh, and do nothing worse than roll on it if it has gone 'high'. Many animals, including dogs and cats, would eat the poultry heads the Ministry propose to use but if the Nature Conservancy could find a bait, specifically attractive to foxes, some of the risks of the proposed Ministry plan might be alleviated.

Strychnine, of course, is unacceptable in every possible way— persistence and inhumanity in particular. Surely the boffins who 'approved' the poisons for farmers and growers should not find it difficult to prescribe a poison that neither smells nor tastes objectionable, would kill painlessly and quickly and would soon be degraded into harmless substance if nothing took the bait? And, if they do know one, I beg of them to cloak it in the anonymity of a secret number so that evilly disposed persons can never obtain and use it illegally against rarities, as they have done with alfachloralose.

Long-term, more sophisticated measures may be proved to be practicable. The Americans, for example, are working on methods of reducing fox populations, not by poisoning them—and causing an influx from the surrounding country—but feeding baits that impair their reproductive capacity. This would have the effect of reducing the population without causing the vacuum effect that the Ministry fear would cause dangerous movements from one area to another.

The other long-term possibility is the production of a vaccine which could be inserted in bait that foxes would eat to produce immune foxes. At present this is pie-in-the-sky, if only for the reason that a bait containing sufficient vaccine to immunise a fox might actually infect a smaller animal that took it by mistake.

It is obvious that, although the threat of rabies has been hanging over us for years, scientists have scarcely trodden on the threshold of discovering a remedy so that a sensible programme of research priorities might be no bad thing.

CHAPTER 7

Compromise

Just two years after an invasion of pantechnicons brought a glut of gamekeeping gear next door, another squadron arrived to take it away again. Huge lorries rumbled past the house, stuffed to the gullet with all the paraphernalia required for mass-producing pheasants. There seemed to be enough wire netting and moveable pens, dog kennels and incubators and gas-heated brooders to provide the capital equipment for a game farm. The shooting syndicate had evidently decided to strike camp and sally forth in search of better coverts.

I confess that it didn't bring many tears to my eyes because the lease had still twelve months to run and the prospect of our rural peace being undisturbed by keepers or shooters gave me peace of mind.

In order to assess the prospects, I trespassed round the woods beyond my boundary to see how many badgers were still in residence. An ancient traditional sett under a yew tree near the road had not been used for months. The main holes were choked with nettles instead of being polished with use, the tracks from the sett to the wood were overgrown with weeds and there were neither piles of fresh dug earth nor bedding outside the entrances. The same thing had happened to other setts I knew. The badgers had either moved off of their own accord or been struck, like mine, by some catastrophe when they had strayed away. Or they could have met their fate on their home territory.

There was no means of knowing what had happened to them, or by whose hand they had died. All that was certain was that a number of former badger strongholds were sadly deserted and vacant.

No Badgers in my Wood

Nor was there any way of assessing the extent of the catastrophe because the country beyond my neighbour's land was unfamiliar to me and I had no idea what the normal complement of setts should be. But, since the whole area is well-wooded, banky land I was fairly optimistic that any void would soon be filled because Nature is never wasteful enough to allow good food and habitat to remain vacant for long.

Sure enough, within a month or so, the artificial drain I had built in Primrose Dell showed signs of occupation. When I first made it, I was keeping the rides in the wood trimmed and open the hard way. I was mowing them with a motorised scythe, similar to the ones used to keep the verges in parks in order. It has two wheels and the operator walks behind it, steering it by long handles. It is a powerful tool that can slice off sapling trees at ground level so long as their stems are less than about an inch in diameter. The clutch is either 'in' or 'out'. There are no half measures and, when it is 'in' and pushing through stiff undergrowth, it is almost impossible to free, so that there is no way I know of stopping it quickly, save shorting out the plug.

For the level swathes of public parks, it is doubtless a delightful implement. All that is necessary is an operator who can stroll behind it at a gentle three miles an hour and be unimaginative enough not to be easily bored.

In our wood, it is a different matter. The cover is thick and full of hidden pitfalls so that it leaps and lurches and slews around unpredictably. It would be easier to tie a heavyweight all-in wrestler in knots than it is to keep my diabolical machine on course. A couple of hours' work mowing rides with it leaves me as limp as a soggy floor cloth.

Because of the concentration it required, I had almost mowed the path past the artificial sett in Primrose Dell before I noticed badger-work out of the corner of my eye. I had passed by so often during the last couple of years that I had got used to the unkempt deserted aspect of the place. As my scythe spluttered by, a wisp of grassy hay at the mouth of the pipe caught my attention.

It took less than a split second to dawn on me that the debris outside the sett was badger bedding—and that badger bedding does not appear outside badger holes unless there is a badger in residence to drag it there.

My guts twinged with panic lest the nasty, noisy, smelly machine had been heard or smelt by Brock underground. Or that my footfalls and the pong of human sweat might have disturbed him. My unconscious reflex flicked off the throttle as quickly as I would have stamped on the brakes if someone stepped in front of the car. Stopping the engine, I let the machine free-wheel silently downhill. Crossing my fingers that I had caused no irreparable harm, I man-handled my monster out of ear-shot, started the engine again and took it back to the yard.

Next morning, I went with a pair of binoculars to examine the sett in detail without getting near enough to disturb the occupants. When I was within fifty yards, the dogs 'dropped' with no command from me. They know the whereabouts of every sett in the wood—and they also know that the vicinity of badger setts is forbidden territory. At first, of course, I used to drop them and make them wait until I had completed my examination and left the sett fifty yards or so away. Then I called them to me and fussed them for their impeccable behaviour. They soon cottoned-on to the routine until now I can walk up to a sett in the full confidence that the dogs will be lying down, waiting quietly for my command to 'Come'. But I took my hat off to them for remembering the routine. There hadn't been a badger there for so long that there had been no cause to treat the area with more respect than if it had only been a rabbit bury, and I hadn't made them drop for months.

When I noticed the signs of occupation that fresh bedding implied, I suppose my elation was telepathic for the dogs sensed my excitement and fell naturally into their old habit although I was quite unaware how they realised what I wanted. Our relationship is so close that I sometimes think that they can almost steal thoughts from the back of my mind.

When I gazed through my glasses that day, I saw that the bedding I had noticed was gone, but that there was a fresh pile by the other entrance. So there was a badger there and he, or she, was still in residence. Illogical though it may seem—for I could only surmise what had happened to the others—the rumble of those departing pantechnicons echoes through my memory as a song of thanksgiving. Whatever the hazards I didn't know about might be, *this* badger seemed less likely to be strangled in a snare. I speculated whether it was a cub, turned out of the home sett to fend for itself and avoid overcrowding. Or an old boar, turned out by a nursing sow lest he develop an unnatural appetite for the cubs he had sired. Or, most extravagant hope of all, that it was another sow which might delight our eyes once more with badger cubs playing in our wood.

I shall never know which guess was nearest right because I did not tempt providence by risking further disturbance. A week later, the bedding was battered and flat, the earth outside the holes was pock-marked by rain, and no animal feet had repaired the damage by padding the tiny craters flat again. To add insult to injury, there was a pile of fresh rabbit droppings in the entrance to the pipe, expressive of contempt for absent brocks. No rabbit would have dared do this while badgers were in residence because the earthenware pipes were so large that they provided no security from pursuit.

Not knowing whether I was the cause of the brevity of the flying visit, I took no more risks of shattering the stillness with my mechanical scythe or even by my footfalls. While the badgers were still absent, I returned and cut a swath to make a new path in a wide detour so that we could go down that end of the wood without risk of getting too close to the sett. The closest the new path approached was at the far side of the pool, where the holes could be examined through field glasses from a safe vantage point.

Although there were still no badgers in my wood, the fact that there were still some in the area prospecting for habitat held high hopes for the future. If, as seemed likely from my search of the adjacent wood, a large area had been cleared of badgers, any that repopulated it from the periphery would fill the ancient traditional earths first. The fact that the Ministry of Agriculture had gassed a single, favoured sett in Gloucestershire twenty-four times was proof enough of that. My home-made, artificial drains must seem second rate residences by comparison to setts they had dug for

themselves in the big wood, precisely how and where they wanted them. They were only likely to take up permanent residence in mine when the natural ones showed signs of over-population and overspill accommodation was a necessity.

By the same token, the future held great peril. There was not likely to be any disturbance in the big wood for the next year, until the current shooting lease ran out. What happened then was anybody's guess. My neighbour is a business man who has achieved success by making his assets breed. If he let the shoot again, it was perfectly possible that the new tenants might install a keeper who didn't like badgers any more than Hannam had. If he removed the badgers from the setts on his beat, any that settled with me in the meantime would be likely to replace them under the illusion that setts dug by their ancestors must be better than anything I could do. But that lay in the future.

About this time, I decided to have a go with muntjac, which are the smallest species of deer found wild in England. Their ancestors were imported in the last century from China by the Duke of Bedford to his family seat at Woburn, where he also found sanctuary for Père David's deer, which would now otherwise be extinct. He is also credited (or debited!) with importing the first grey squirrels to be liberated in this country—which were not among the benefits the Duke bestowed upon mankind.

The descendants of 'his' muntjac deer, however, are quite delightful. No bigger than a fox, with summer coats almost as red, they are secretive lovers of deep cover. The bucks have small, spiky antlers and, surprisingly for deer, they carry canine teeth, in the male about as large as terrier dogs' and smaller in the females.

Some of these curious little deer escaped from Woburn Park during the last war, and they are gradually colonising the country. They pose no serious threat to agriculture or forestry because they love to skulk in thick cover and often travel for miles unseen in summer. They creep through standing corn and hay or along thick hedgerows, and have already spread in some numbers as far north as Warwickshire. Such is their urge to colonise fresh ground, that they are sometimes found deep in the hinterland of Midland towns and cities where they are hunted by town dogs or run over by motor cars.

A doe that had been rescued in the nick of time from dogs was sent to me some years ago for rehabilitation. The horn on her hooves had been worn to the quick on hard pavements and she had been badly mauled before the dogs were driven off. About the same time, a buck arrived which had been cornered on a factory estate and had panicked through the office door for cover. Not liking what he saw, he dived through the plate-glass window, knocking himself out in the process! He was picked up and put safely in a box before he came round again.

I kept both of them for a time in an enclosure, until the doe's lameness had worn off and the buck had steadied down and did not panic when he saw the dogs or me. Then I opened the gate and allowed them to wander off into the wood.

They stayed around for months and we often saw them when we were out at dusk or dawn, but gradually wanderlust gripped them and their appearances dwindled until they ceased. We have since seen several within a two-mile radius, but have no means of knowing if they are 'ours' or if they are southerners, prospecting for new territory.

I had often thought of rearing one, so that it could grow up in the belief that our wood was its home territory, but I find it impossible to bottle-rear any young animal without getting, to some extent, personally involved. The responsibility of accepting its total dependence and the familiarity bred of such close contact sparks off an affection deep enough to cause a great distress if it comes to a sticky end. The prospect of some lout snaring or gassing or poisoning a badger that has lost its fear of man because of its confidence in me, sets my fingers itching for a pickaxe handle. If I reared anything as gentle and inoffensive as a muntjac deer and it was shot by some spiv, too ignorant to distinguish it from a fox, I could not rest until I had exacted retribution.

The wood was now surrounded by deer-proof fencing and the mesh was small enough to keep foxhounds out but not to keep a muntjac in. As foxhounds are one of the greatest dangers to these delightful little deer, that, at least, was a start. Temporarily, at least, there was neither a keeper nor shooters over my boundary and all my farmer neighbours are kind and helpful to such experiments. When a friend telephoned to say an orphan fawn had been brought to her, which she was bottle-rearing in her bathroom, I gladly took him off her hands.

I kept him in the study during the daytime and in a well-strawed outhouse at night. When he got a little stronger, I fixed a wire-net fence in front of my study window so that he could come and go between the house and a large paddock which also included the shelter he used at night.

He wasn't a moment's trouble to rear—apart from the fact that he took about a quarter of an hour to bottle-feed, four times a day. With such regular companionship, it is not surprising that we got to know each other pretty well.

There was, however, one snag. If I loosed him when he was weaned, the chances were that he would not be content to hang around as a solitary bachelor, since muntjac prefer small family parties. He would probably stray in search of fresh pastures and a mate. So I gave up the immediate idea of letting him go and managed to obtain a young wild female which I put into his large enclosure. By that time he was about eighteen months old, a model

of handsome virility, and he was obviously delighted with his bride. My immediate plans are to allow them to breed, when I shall make a hole in the enclosure fence large enough for an immature youngster to use as a 'creep' but too small for escape by adults. Then, with luck, the youngster will establish territory in the wood outside, coming and going to the enclosure so that, in time, we can loose the old pair to join it with less chance of them wandering right away.

I stopped handling the buck after he was weaned because I didn't want him to grow up too tame. All male deer can be extremely dangerous when they are adult if they have lost their respect or fear of man. I am not suggesting that a creature as small as a muntjac buck would pose a serious danger to my friends or me, but he might have been extremely vicious with dogs.

One day, with luck, a female only a few days old will arrive on my doorstep, and I shall not hesitate to bring her up on the bottle to be as tame and affectionate as possible. Previous experience with my Miss Roe-Doe who I bottle-reared, which stayed around to delight us for ten years, was very encouraging; Honey, my white fallow doe, has had a string of fawns by wild bucks and is still as tame and confiding as ever. So a really tame muntjac, which could mate with the buck I have already reared, would be worth every second of the time it would take to rear her.

Meanwhile, our fallow deer had done too well. When they could come and go as they pleased to the miles of woodland that comes up to my boundary, they simply went away when food was short in our wood. In October they returned for the acorn harvest and to make rumbustious love during their season of rut. My tame doe, Honey, and her retinue of about fourteen were too fond of soft living to stray far away. They turned up each evening to feast on the corn and flaked maize and dog biscuits I put out for them on the bird table I'd fashioned from the grindstone of a corn mill.

When I heightened the boundary fence to keep out foxhounds, the deer could stray no more. The adult does had a regular annual fawn so that the population increased by about fifteen per cent a year. The Forestry Commission manage the deer on their side of the fence by a carefully formulated management policy.

Not so long ago, they treated deer as vermin and drove them to waiting men with shot guns, who slaughtered them indiscriminately. This got the Commission such a vandal reputation that they appointed a competent naturalist to restore their public image. He made careful surveys of the forests to establish how many deer the available herbage could support without unacceptable damage either to trees in the forst or to crops around the edges. Then he did a census of the deer to establish what surplus must be culled to leave the optimum size herd.

The culling was done selectively, by skilled marksmen with rifles. They were instructed to take out all the weak, diseased or bad specimens first, after which they were to 'adjust' the sexes to give the correct ratio for a viable herd. The bucks with the best heads were left as stockgetters instead of being shot as specimens, which is the normal practice in stalking circles. So deer are now regarded as a forest crop which can be sold to cover the wardens' wages and usually to cover the derisory rent that most landowners recoup when the Forestry Commission takes over their land. The thousand acres next to me, for example, brings in a princely half a crown an acre per annum. Or twelve and a half new pence in modern jargon. Cleared and reclaimed for agriculture, it would be worth two hundred times as much.

Many of my deer are so tame that I was very loath to shoot them

and their population began to increase when I prevented them straying to land where they would have been shot. I realised that I would have to face up to it sooner or later—as indeed I have—but I put off the evil day as long as possible by extending the area they could graze to cope with their rising population.

One way of doing this was to widen the woodland rides. By taking out a row or two of the miserable little pine trees which are a legacy of the days before the Commission regurgitated the lease they enjoyed when I arrived, I was able to hire a bulldozer to grub out the roots. I harrowed the land it cleared and sowed it with grass and clover seed so that the three miles of rides, ten yards wide, provide around ten acres of grazing.

Even this was not enough, but behind the pool, opposite my study window, there was a large patch of bracken where the trees had never taken well. I costed it out and found I should be able to afford to clear, lime and seed it for what I should get by flogging the Christmas trees.

It has made a glade, about four acres in extent, which is as

interesting and attractive as a miniature deer park. The sombre
pines that border it form ideal cover for the deer to lie-up and it
keeps the pasture warm and undisturbed. We bulldozed the roots
from the trees we took out into a huge pile and covered it with soil,
on which grew a dense blanket of bracken.

There are a few rabbits amongst the roots and a litter of fox cubs
might be reared there in spring, if I leave them. One day, perhaps,
the holes will be opened out and it will be colonised by badgers—
which would be exceptionally difficult to gas, because the roots
will never consolidate enough to make it easy for pest officers to
exclude air or to pump gas into the secret recesses. So if ever the
men from the Ministry decide to wreak their havoc here, they'll
find the task will test their ingenuity.

Pest officers have joined the VAT men and the army of other
bureaucrats who can legally enter our homes and our land
however bitterly we resent them. Being territorially-minded
myself, I keep a sharp alsatian loose about the place, which
encourages the civility of calling at the door before embarking on

such legal trespass, and I always sally forth to talk to such officials carrying my tape recorder with microphone switched on as a polite warning against bureaucratic bluster. The prospect of a transcript of the dialogue landing on the Minister's desk usually steers discussion into reasonable channels. It is a prudent precaution because the legal powers of entry are not limited to entry for the purpose of destroying badgers. They include entry for the purpose of surveillance, which might well be interpreted as a licence to snoop where and when they pleased. Big Brother is watching us too often.

Apart from the potential hospitality to badgers in my wood, Hannam would have approved of the changes I am making. When we came, there were about forty acres of mixed woodland, mainly oak and birch, ash and hornbeam and alder on the side of the wood nearest the house. The far side, which was then leased to the Forestry Commission, had been more or less clear-felled and planted with a stifling shroud of Corsican pines. However, I do not wish half my land sterilised by conifers too dense to tolerate a variety of habitat on the ground beneath them. My ambition is to have manageable patches of dense cover, interspersed with clearings where deer can feed, and patches of wild rose and bramble for birds to nest, augmented by any lovely native English hardwood trees and wild flowers that I can encourage.

The reason that Hannam would have approved is that the terrain he loved for game was similar, but on a large scale. He loved lots of little fields, surrounded by hedges and interspersed with spinneys and coverts. He encouraged tracts of native English woodland with an understorey of rhododendrons and dogwood and tussocky grass. If you leave a nature reserve to its own devices, it eventually grows into climax woodland with dense enough top cover to shade out the lower vegetation. By 'managing' it to produce constant variety, it is possible to persuade a wonderful variety of wildlife to thrive there too.

I have trodden the wood so often that I feel that I could be dropped blindfold in it and know precisely where I was by the feel of the ground under my feet. Actually, I know that to be a gross exaggeration because I have occasionally lost my bearings in dense fog and been unable to find my way home till I have reached the boundary fence to guide me.

Nevertheless, I do know it so intimately that it comes as a shock to find a beautiful tree I do not recognise. Therefore, when I have the luck to make such a discovery, I take immediate action. There is a wonderfully ancient wild crab apple, for example, within a hundred yards of my study window, that I only discovered by accident. It was in the middle of a thicket, mainly hawthorns, and I took it for granted that they were all the same trees, rather than battling through the prickly jungle to find out. Then I noticed the deer congregating in the area, long before the hawthorn berries fell and curiosity prodded me to go and see what they were feeding on.

I discovered a carpet of crab apples. Not the tiddly little ornamental crabs that are often used with poisonous laburnum and ornamental cherries to ponce-up suburban gardens. These were pale green belly-aching crabs, the stuff my grandmother used for proper crab apple jelly. The trunk of the tree is nearly two feet across and its crown nods on the same level as surrounding oaks that have been there for a century and a half or more. So out came the chain-saw to convert the thicket of hawthorn into toe-warming logs, and within an hour the crab stood proudly in its own little clearing where light and air could encourage a dense overcoat of leaves again. Left to run riot, the hawthorns would have crowded out all chance of it fruiting.

My optimistic dreams of the badgers' return were shattered that autumn when I realised that the golden days might soon be over. My neighbour who owns the land next door, but lives half way across the next county, wrote to say he was about to let his sporting rights again, and that he proposed to advertise the lease for tender to the highest bidder. There is nothing more unsettling than uncertainty because, although I hadn't yet got any badgers actually living on the place, I knew that they were beginning to trickle back to the area from the surrounding countryside. When they had refilled the vacant traditional setts, it was a fair bet that the overspill would take up residence with me.

I contacted all my shooting friends to try to persuade them to take up sporting rights, on the assumption that a devil you know is preferable to one you don't. And they knew me well enough to trust my word implicitly if I said that I would co-operate. Most of them had looked the shoot over three years before and decided that the farmland was too much of a prairie and the woodland was in blocks too large to drive. A local vet and his pals were quite keen to run it as a rough shoot, but the price range expected was uneconomic for anything less than first class. It was taken, eventually, by a syndicate who were total strangers to me.

Rumours down the rural grapevine were not encouraging, but I was invited to the meeting when details of the lease were to be finalised so, seizing the chance to put my case plainly, I explained that I was professionally interested in badgers and conservation. They, on the other hand, were paying hard cash for sport. We could either be mutually destructive or quite the reverse. I pointed out that I live at the far end of their keeper's beat so that an extra pair of sharp eyes, on the most difficult boundary for him to supervise, could discourage trespass and raise the alarm of poachers. My oak wood is an irresistable lure for pheasants during the acorn fall so that it could help to hold them in the area—or drain them from it, as I chose. If badgers did not occupy my setts, then foxes might and I need do nothing to discourage them. All that I asked in exchange for co-operation was that they did not lay poison in the open, which is illegal anyway; that they did not use self-lock snares; and that any badgers accidentally caught in free-running fox snares should be released unharmed. It seemed a reasonable compromise all round so we parted with protestations of mutual goodwill.

Fine words do not necessarily produce fine deeds. As soon as he had settled in Tom Brown, their keeper, called to make his number. Two dogs, stiff-legged with hackles raised, would be a fair description of our attitudes.

Gamekeepers often regard naturalists as fuddy-duddy eccentrics, hell-bent on ruining the keeper's livelihood by harbouring 'vermin' which will slaughter the pheasants on which his reputation is built. They think that we are airy-fairy 'book-men' who have filled our heads with theory gained from other people's knowledge, but that we would be quite incapable of putting into practice what we preach. Their firm belief that boffinery is indistinguishable from buffoonery is all too often right. Little men with big Adam's apples, knobbly knees and butterfly nets are not figures of fun in the countryside without good cause.

For my part, I know enough keepers to harbour few illusions about professions of faith in the virtues of predators of any sort. Hannam hated all creatures with a curved bill or canine teeth. He would have expected anyone to be certified insane for criticising him for doing his best to obliterate anything from an eagle to a barn owl or a weasel to an otter. In his day that was accepted practice and the Old Squire, who presided on the local magistrate's bench, would have had every sympathy with him.

Keepering is a solitary and exceptionally traditional profession where trade secrets are handed down verbally from generation to generation. Techniques have not changed much since old Hannam's day in spite of the fact that most landowners now appreciate other things than game upon their land. All sportsmen now genuinely agree that the use of steel gins and pole traps for the genocide of predators is socially unacceptable. By no means all syndicate shooters have yet been converted to the doctrine, partly perhaps because many of them are so urban that they have no personal experience and it is more comfortable to remain in ignorance. Rents are now so high that hard-headed businessmen dislike the idea of their hard-earned brass being squandered on pheasants that do not have the opportunity to fly over their guns. Tom Brown is employed by a syndicate, so small wonder we regarded each other with mutual suspicion.

My first impression was that he was a keeper through and through. A powerfully-built man in neat tweed plus fours—however rough the job in hand may be. When I later learned that he had done nine years professional boxing, it slotted perfectly into the image I had formed. Poachers would find him a tough nut to crack. In spite of his rugged air, he has the natural courteous good manners of genuine countrymen and, long before he worked for shooting syndicates, he had gained experience working for the gentry on great estates. Hannam would have greeted Tom Brown as an equal and my experience of such men provided enough in common to convince us both that we should be unwise to underrate each other, and that we had also trodden much common ground.

That first morning, in my study, I showed him photographs, not from other people's books, but taken on my land. I showed him a picture of Bill Brock scratching at my window, not to escape, but to break his way *into* my study, and I gave him my book about 'my' badger's exploits. I showed him the deserted sett opposite my study window, where cubs once played; and wild deer came to within a few yards of us when I rattled my corn bucket. Because he knew by experience what patience this entailed, he was visibly impressed. He told me he didn't mind badgers at all and that I need have no fear of harm befalling mine by any deed of his. For my part, I promised to return the compliment with 'his' pheasants. It was a good beginning.

During the first few weeks after Tom arrived, badgers made several half-hearted attempts to colonise my setts. Bedding would appear outside the entrances for a few consecutive nights or there would be substantial piles of excavated earth. But the working always stopped again as suddenly as they began, and I came to the conclusion they had probably used my earths as temporary lodging when something disturbed them where they had been before. As soon as things settled back to normal they left without paying the bill by so much as giving me a glimpse of their black and white stripes.

When I went to feed the hens, one spring morning, the fox-trap had gone off. The large cage which I had built into the perimeter fence has a sliding steel shutter as entrance and a treadle platform at the far end. It has an upper story which opens into the hen run and I encourage a few bantams to roost there.

Any fox, with evil designs on my poultry, naturally slinks round the boundary fence to see if anyone has left a door open—and they have. Through the sliding shutter of the cage trap the fox smells, hears and sees the bantams perched in safety over the wire mesh roof of the cage. If he goes to investigate, and treads on the wooden treadle, the steel shutter slams behind him—and he is waiting for me to greet him in the morning.

Not having had any particular incentive to control foxes for the previous three years, I had not bothered to persuade bantams to roost above the cage and it was therefore unbaited, so I was surprised the trap had sprung and went over to investigate. I could see, from fifty yards away, that it contained a large animal and thought, at first, that it must be a stray dog. When I got closer, I was simply delighted to discover that it was the first badger I had seen alive on my land for more than two years. After feasting my eyes on him (or her!) for a couple of minutes, I prepared to open the steel shutter to let him go. Before doing so, I fetched Jess to share my pleasure and stationed her with field glasses at a vantage point where she could overlook the intersection of five rides. By noting the direction the badger retreated and watching for him to cross first one ride and then another, she should be able to get a pretty accurate idea of where he was making for.

He was in no hurry to exchange what he seemed to regard as the security of the cage for exposure to danger in the world outside. He stayed perfectly still for a few moments, testing every air eddy with his sensitive nose. I had flattened myself against a tree trunk, twenty or thirty yards downwind, so that he could neither hear me, smell me, nor focus me with his short-sighted eyes. When he calculated that the coast was clear, he hesitated at the mouth of the trapdoor for a few moments, to double check, and then he ambled off as if tomorrow would do. He was in no hurry, but his springy, bear-like gait covered the ground in a leisurely but deceptively efficient way. Twenty seconds after he had left the trap, he went to ground in the house sett opposite my study window. I see a good many wild creatures under great stress in the course of my work, but I never cease to marvel at the immense dignity of most animals when the pressure is really on. I should like to believe that I have the guts to behave as well, or think as quickly if ever I land in a really tight corner.

Although he took refuge in the sett, thereby proving that he had a comprehensive grasp of the local geography, he didn't stay there for long. He took no bedding in, and within a couple of days, there were no visible signs that it had been occupied. Nevertheless, it was encouraging. It indicated that local badgers were visiting often enough to know the territory well so that, when their population climbed back to normal, there was no reason why we should not enjoy their company regularly again.

In about June, I noticed feathers and bones and desiccated rabbit skins outside the holes of the sett at Primrose Dell. Badgers don't carry food back to their setts so, knowing there must be a litter of fox cubs there, I went to see Tom Brown. Before I'd finished telling him, he'd sent Andy, his young assistant keeper, to fetch a terrier from across the yard and the shotguns from the house. We piled into his Land Rover and were back at Primrose Dell within ten minutes.

The decision to let him put his terrier down the hole was not as simple as it seems. Although I didn't think there was a badger there, I had given the place such a wide berth to avoid disturbance that I hadn't inspected it as closely as I should have liked. I knew there were fox cubs, because I'd seen them there—but foxes and badgers sometimes share the same earth and the fact that I had not seen badgers was not conclusive. There was just a chance that putting the terrier into the sett might disturb a badger too. If I'd wanted to play it really safe, I should have left well alone and risked no disturbance. Foxes don't do me that much harm anyway.

On the other hand, I had promised Tom that he if he played ball by taking care not to harm my badgers, I would do all in my power to help him get a decent stock of pheasants. So far, I knew he was co-operating because badgers were visiting my wood from his beat and I had checked that his setts had not been intefered with. As yet, he had no proof that my word is as good as my bond.

He sized up the chances when he got to the sett and I told him which way the fox would bolt. So he placed Andy to cover one side, popped his terrier down the hole, cocked his own gun—and we all waited silently. Nothing happened for a bit. Then, deep underground I heard the high-pitched rasping voice of the terrier 'speaking' to quarry which is holed-up and defying. We didn't dare to breathe aloud lest we convinced the fox—if fox it was— that risks below ground, from a terrier its own size, were less than the perils of running the gauntlet of professional marksmanship.

The fox must have shifted because I felt, more than heard, the

rumble of subterranean movement somewhere under my feet and the next second she exploded from the thicket. Tom Brown's gun barked out and stopped her. Between them, he and Andy also shot the six cubs, about the size of cats, that followed.

Tough on the foxes, you may think, but there are a thousand sheep up on the farm and foxes are not welcome guests among either lambs or pheasants. So far as Tom Brown was concerned, it worked wonders because it was the first hard evidence he had had that I should honour my side of the bargain.

By that time I had collected the eggs from the pheasants I'd caught up in spring and hatched them under bantams. The birds that laid them had been set free to go back in the wood and lay a last clutch to hatch for themselves, so I was glad the foxes were out of the way for their sake too. And, lastly, I was glad because my artificial sett was vacant once more, should the badgers take a fancy to it.

Although I try to keep the wood as a bird sanctuary for birds rather than bird watchers, I share my pleasures, so far as I can without inconvenience to the creatures for which I find sanctuary. One way of doing so is to encapsulate some of them on the television screen so that millions can see them for the price of one session with the TV cameras. A moment's reflection indicates that the cameras have to be concealed so well that they cause little disturbance for the simple reason that shy creatures would not hang round to be filmed if they realised what was afoot. The snag in exposing the place to millions, even on the screen, is that a tiny percentage of them are determined to come and see for themselves and are pretty thick-skinned about taking my polite 'No' for an answer. Fortunately, one of the few blessings with which Nature endowed me is an even thicker skin, so that the harder I am pressed the more obdurate I become!

Among the exceptions I make are a few girls taking biology at the local girls' boarding school, occasional post-graduate students, and scientists specialising in some creature that thrives here. So when a professional biologist I knew slightly telephoned to say a colleague of his, a university lecturer, was a distinguished authority on micro-beetles, and that some very rare ones might still be in my wood, I was duly flattered. Apparently the tiny beetles on which he was an 'authority'—whatever that might be—could only survive under the bark of ancient oak trees, such as once thrived in the area of Needwood Forest where I live, and the scientist wanted to check whether species which had not been reported since last century were still around.

In due course, my visitors arrived and I piloted them down the wood to show them where the few ancient oaks to survive weather and timber merchants through the centuries were still standing. When I left them, I asked them to call at the house on their way home. That was about eleven in the morning and I didn't see them again till tea-time. When they turned up at my study window, I asked if they had found any rarities. They said they didn't know. The micro-beetles in which they were interested were so minute as to be difficult to see with the naked eye. But they had collected about twenty pounds of material which they would put through a fine sieve when they got back to the lab, so they would let me know what they found in due course.

Popular imagination associates sportsmen with damage to the species they hunt or shoot—or at least to the predators which prey upon their quarry. The wrong sort of gamekeeper can decimate wide areas of what he considers to be the enemies of game, and fishermen entangle hundreds of birds on broken and discarded fishing lines. Few people would suffer the smallest pang of doubt about the wisdom of welcoming 'distinguished authorities' on pinhead-sized beetles. What, after all, could be more harmless and innocent than a duet of dedicated bug-hunters? Who should be more welcome to the freedom of a wood managed as a wildlife sanctuary?

Then I had niggling doubts about the 'twenty pounds of material' stuffed into their haversack for examination in the lab. You could get a lot of little beetles in twenty pounds of almost anything. I regretted my lack of curiosity in not asking what it was.

Next morning, when I took the dogs up the wood, I wandered up to one of the ancient oaks in the hope of seeing some rarity myself. At first I thought that pheasants had been scratching at the foot of the tree. The leafmould seemed to have been turned over for yards around. It took some time to dawn on me that the litter was not leafmould. It was chunks of bark, prised off my favourite oak. I could not believe my eyes, for a gang of vandals would cause less incurable destruction. There was less chance of restoring bark to the base of that old tree than of putting Humpty Dumpty back on the wall again.

I stormed back to the house and telephoned the man who'd asked to come. I demanded to know why he and his academic mate, whose name I never discovered, had vandalised my wood. He doubtless regards himself as a respectable biologist so he took serious umbrage. He wasn't used to being called a beetlemaniac he said, and anyway, how did I think they could find beetles under the bark without stripping it off? We had too little in common to hold a dialogue so I told him I wasn't surprised his pal's beetles were rare if folk like him destroyed what habitat there was to prove their presence.

It isn't only keepers or chemical sprays or bureaucrats who destroy our heritage, even naturalists are not above suspicion, although they maintain that such damage may be justified in the cause of increasing knowledge. I suppose that we are both entitled to our point of view, but for this reason I don't allow bird watchers to put rings on the legs of 'my' birds. They might cause a few casualties when they are netting them and I have come across birds whose legs have been chafed, even by the rings that were correctly applied. When nestlings are ringed just before they are fledged, it is sometimes impossible to avoid scaring the young birds, so that they 'explode' in all directions from the nest before they are strong enough on the wing to return. With some species such as herons, a youngster that falls (or flutters) from the nest but is unable to fly back will almost inevitably starve, as the parents will not fly down into the wood to find it.

At about this time, a stranger called at the door and asked to see me. 'I am the River Board fisheries officer,' he said, so I asked him what I could do for him. 'It's what I can do for you,' he said. 'I've just been listening to a radio programme where you were complaining that your pool was very acid. Perhaps I can help?'

The experience of finding a civil servant actually looking for work was so refreshing that we had some coffee on the strength of it and went down to the pool in high spirits.

The water flows in via a ditch that goes right through the wood, draining about forty acres of peaty oak leafmould, so that it is likely to be pretty acid. When the river board chap took a sample, he blenched and said it was about strong enough to top up car batteries. Figuratively speaking, of course!

But it did explain the fact why very few water weeds grew there and, because of the absence of plants, there wasn't much pond life in the way of water beetles, freshwater shrimps, sticklebacks or other attractive food for birds like dabchicks, whose absence I'd been lamenting in my broadcast.

So it was decided that he should take away a sample of the water, get it accurately analysed in the lab. and tell me what to add to the pool to produce the degree of neutrality that would support plants to attract the wildlife I coveted.

The advice came back that I should put in a ton of ground lime for starters, and some limestone chippings in the feeder ditch so that, once the bulk of the water was all right, the fresh supply from the ditch could leach out enough lime to avoid undoing the initial good we did.

It didn't work out according to plan. Conservation rarely does. Instead of the usual pair of Canada geese that nest on the pool's island, a flock of twenty-five turned up. They grazed the pool side of the paddock as close as the centre court at Wimbledon and chopped out the young grass I'd planted on my new deer lawn as effectively as a herbicide rated high in the *Approved Products for Farmers and Growers* booklet.

Canada goose populations have been exploding over the last few years, causing complaints from farmers which have encouraged the men from the Ministry to mount an investigation. I had heard they had been dyeing some pink, in the Midlands, in an attempt to monitor their wanderings. Having seen no more pink geese than pink elephants myself, I cannot vouch for the story, but although there were no pink ones in our lot, they had nearly all been fitted with rings on their legs. There were metal rings with numbers on and various combinations of coloured rings, none of which solved my problem of too many Canada geese. They chobbled the grazing that I had reserved for the deer and destroyed several hundredweight of water weeds I'd put in the pool after liming it according to the instructions of the fisheries officer.

I made a complicated corral in which to catch them up and we transferred them into a Land Rover and dumped them on another pool, thirty miles away. I have often wondered how many of those numbered rings turned up in unexpected places.

The experiment in which we controlled the acidity of the pool by adding lime, fired the imaginations of the two biology girls who had been up from the school for the past year. They are a delightfully keen couple and it has always been my ambition for some of these girls to do work here that is original and significant enough for them to write a paper that would be printed by the Zoological Society. To have their name in the 'respectable' literature for original research, while still at school, would be quite a feather in their caps.

I had suggested a project to them the previous year that had turned out to be a monumental flop. It had struck me that it would be interesting to monitor the effect of grazing by animals of various sizes and capacity. So I enclosed a patch of ground in a clearing with cattle fencing, through which deer could not pass but smaller animals could. The girls took an accurate census of the grasses and other plants inside this enclosure and on a 'control' patch immediately outside the fence where everything was free to graze.

During the summer, they hoped to note the difference in growth of vegetation inside and outside the enclosure, and this would be some yardstick of the effect the deer were having on clearings in the wood, and what we could expect on patches from which the deer were excluded.

As a refinement, I enclosed a patch within the enclosure with rabbit-proof netting and a small patch, inside that, with mouse-proof netting. In theory, the girls would be able to assess the effect on the vegetation of deer, rabbits and mice.

Theory and practice are often incompatible bed fellows. What I had overlooked was that the clearing I had chosen had only just been made in what, for centuries, had been mature and ancient woodland, with the exception of the last few years when the Corsican pines had been there. Giant mare's-tail is one of the plants that can lie dormant in old woodland for generations and, when conditions are right, its recovery is spectacular.

Conditions in our enclosure were obviously better than right. Such a jungle of giant mares'-tail sprung up that all other herbage was swamped and the only conclusion from the experiment was that neither deer nor rabbits nor mice appeared capable of curbing regenerative powers of the prehistoric plant, which seems to be invincible.

It was therefore pretty important to find an alternative project which would give them a chance to leave school with the taste of success on their lips. When they showed interest in getting more life in the pool, their biology mistress and I invited the volunteer from the River Board to stretch his advisory services, which he seemed delighted to do. Meanwhile, an official from another government department had asked permission to take a soil sample every ten acres, for some long-term national soil survey that is going on all over the country. So we press-ganged him to show the girls how to check the soil analysis of the catchment area that feeds the other two small pools in the wood. One will be left alone, and used as a 'control', to be the yardstick to measure the effects on the other when we deliberately change the chemical analysis of the water by adding lime to sweeten its acidity. The girls will monitor the plants and beetles, fish and frogs and newts to see what differences to life in the pool the acidity of the water makes.

There were spasmodic signs of badgers working in our wood during the whole of Tom's first spring and summer. Cynics might not have been surprised because both he and Andy were so involved with rearing pheasants that there couldn't have been much time left over to deal with 'vermin'. Nor was there any great urgency to do so because there were few wild pheasants in the wood when they arrived and theirs had not yet wandered from their safe release pens. The time for me to worry, the knowing ones said, was when his birds were out in the wood and he felt the cold draught of a few losses.

I never showed such pessimism. I've made my living in a pretty hard school and have had fair experience of summing up people. Tom struck me as a tough character who wouldn't suffer fools gladly but, once there was mutual respect, would be a grand ally in a tight corner. Nevertheless, I did have cause to bite my nails early in September.

The first thing I noticed in September was that the sett in front of the study window had been opened by a couple of trial boreholes, no more than eighteen inches deep, and two or three yards from the 'official' entrance I had made. They had been used by rabbits but had not been excavated enough to admit anything larger. These new holes might have been made by foxes digging out a nest of rabbits from the single hole, or 'stop' where the doe had left them. They might as easily have been made by badgers but there were no footprints plain enough to convert guesses into certainty. Nor were the holes deep enough for either a fox or badger to have taken up residence. Within a week, the main trunk entrance had been excavated and there were wisps of bracken trailing back into the wood, indicating that bedding had been carried in.

It is impossible to describe my elation at having a badger back in residence, in the very sett which had housed the cubs on which I had pinned such hopes. There had been no badgers living in my wood for almost three years and I had barred no holds to get them back. Although I take great pride in getting on well with my neighbours, I had fought a ruthless campaign despite the fact that I had had no more than the circumstantial evidence of finding one body in a snare. There was never any proof who had set that snare, nor if it had been set for fox or for badger. Now that I had a badger back, I had no regrets for getting tough.

I never went near the sett, but inspected it through binoculars from a distance that was safe by any standards, so that it was some time before I even got a clue about the status of my lodger. Then I saw foot prints in the mud beside the ditch, and was not surprised

to see that they were very small. I reckoned that a last year's cub had colonised my sett, probably a cub kicked out of one of the big setts around, either because of overcrowding or because it was a surplus boar. I called Tom in, as he was passing the house one day, ostensibly to share my delight with him—but also to make sure that he knew that I knew that I'd got a badger in the sett. If anything should change his mind about badgers—and I had no means of knowing what his employer's instructions might be—I didn't want to risk him knocking one off under the delusion that I wouldn't notice.

I needn't have bothered. He was as pleased for me as I was myself because, as so many of the better keepers are, he is a keen naturalist and far from one of the kill-everything-but-pheasants school. When the shooting season began, and his birds came acorning in my wood, I gave him a key so that he and Andy could come in when they liked and 'dog' them out again—and there aren't many keepers for whom I would do that!

The temptations to sit by the sett to get hard proof that my new tenant was really living there, as opposed to making casual nightly visits, was almost irresistible, but I was so determined not to scare him off through any fault of mine that I didn't fall. A practical minor consideration was that badgers don't often come out till after dark when autumn nights draw in.

One night in November, at about half past ten when I was

feeding the dogs, I heard a shindy up the wood. It horrified me because, although I hadn't heard it for more than ten long years, the first agonising screech kindled memories as sharp as yesterday.

The last time I had heard that sound was during the first season I had Bill Brock, my hand-reared boar, who had almost been killed for trespassing onto the territory of a wild boar.

Small wonder, then, that an encore of the same refrain tangled my guts in knots of apprehension. The hubbub was coming from the far bank of the pool, about a hundred yards away and, as I listened, it became obvious that it was a running battle, skirmishing across the open glade, diagonally away from me. There was nothing I could do about it, though the journalist in me urged to rush to the house for my tape recorder and then to go over towards the noise in the hopes of capturing it on tape.

The realist, who shares the back of my mind, told me not to waste my time. Long before I'd got a tape laced-up, the beast getting the thick end of the stick would either have escaped or died. I really must fulfill my good intentions of having everything always at the ready for such eventualities.

As things were, I froze horror-stricken, listening helplessly as the grappling badgers fought their way across the wood, and then their screams faded into the distance. There was no means of knowing exactly what had been going on, but I guessed that it was some sort of territorial quarrel and, since it takes at least two to make a quarrel, the inference was that badgers in the area were on the increase and disputing their rights.

For a day or so after that, there were no signs of activity at the house sett and I was just beginning to think that some hulking great bully-badger had made an isolated expedition into our wood, beaten up the resident and driven him off, when I found a pile of fresh bedding at the sett entrance. The fresh badger tracks in the mud along the edge of the ditch had not been made by the familiar small feet whose tracks I'd seen all autumn. The back feet of these prints were two and a half inches wide and two and three-quarters long. A big brock by any standards. I am precise about the measurements because I was so impressed that I made a plaster of Paris cast and have just checked the dimensions with calipers. So the theory of an invasive bully-boy might not have been far out, but instead of casual trespass, it looked as if he'd driven off 'my' cub and squatted in the sett.

When my pointer Tick was a puppy, she would 'point' at almost any living thing. The chap I bought her from told me she had been 'pointing' bumble bees at four weeks old and, although I dismissed the tale as sales-patter then, I believed it in retrospect. When she comes down the wood, I let her potter ten or fifteen yards ahead and, every now and then, she stops, with foot raised, staring into a bush or tussock of grass or thick cover. She stays, frozen immobile, either until I tell her to get in and flush it, or go over to see for myself what she has found.

Her expression, when 'on point' is a fixed hypnotic glare. When I became involved with *One Man and His Dog*, the shepherds told me that a good sheep dog needs a 'strong eye' to master his sheep. Sure enough, when I watched them closely, I could see that they were almost in a trance of concentration and that they had the same hypnotic expression that Tick has when she finds a bird or rabbit. It came as no surprise to learn that there is a dash of pointer blood in many of the best working sheep dogs.

Thinking it over, I wondered if, in return, Tick shared any of the sheep dog instincts to round-up and herd a flock. Sheep dog puppies often start their training by 'herding' ducks or poultry, so I amused myself training my bitch to drive the hens into the pen at night when I went to shut them safe from foxes. 'Training' overstretches it because she took to it as naturally as a sheep dog pup to sheep. She would 'get round' them at a majestic sweep of my arm, inch towards them as slowly as I liked, stop, when I told her or raised my hand, or fluster them when I said, 'Get to them. Make them go.'

It had been a short step to encourage her to do the same with pheasants, which will rarely fly when they can walk. Before Tom arrived, we amused ourselves by rounding them up, and walking whole batches right across the wood. When they reached the opposite boundary to where they had entered, Tick did my farmer-neighbours a good turn by 'making them go' towards their corn or coverts.

My relationship with Tom turned things on their head. Instead of driving his pheasants away, we drive them back so that what could be one of the worst areas on his shoot for 'holding' birds is probably one of the best.

When the shooting season is over, I live-trap as many of the pheasants in my wood as I can. My previous practice has been to rear thirty or forty poults, and I shall do so again. I establish them in the wood, and give them enough subsidiary feed to hold them, because their gaudy gaiety delights my eyes. At the turn of the year, I trap up the surplus cocks for the deep freeze, and a cock to six hens for a laying pen to supply fertile eggs for next year's stock before I let them go again.

When the season ends, I catch up every bird I can, which practically 'drains' the wood—leaving nothing for the foxes. Every evening young Andy comes round to collect the hens and take them for Tom's laying pen. One of Andy's main jobs, after Christmas, is to trap up their own birds because, left to herself, a hen pheasant would only lay one clutch of fifteen eggs or so before going broody to hatch them.

In large laying pens, safe from disturbance, and with plenty of good food and security, it is possible to coax about forty eggs from each bird. These are hatched in incubators and the chicks are reared in brooders as they would be in the poultry industry. Not my idea of the sort of birds to shoot for sport, but each one to his taste.

Meanwhile, with his birds safely penned from foxes and the eggs immune from carrion crows, jays and magpies, the modern keeper can have a few weeks to get the vermin down and to do any repairs to his release and rearing pens. When he has collected all the eggs he wants to hatch, he will turn the hen pheasants out in the wood again, in time for them to lay one more clutch in a nest of their own choosing and hatch a brood of chicks for themselves.

At this stage, Andy brings back the hens I have 'lent' him so that I can return them to their own territory in my wood to hatch one last clutch of eggs for me.

You can't work as closely as that with people without getting to know them pretty well. Andy is young, amusing and packed with enthusiasm. Even so, he might have a job to catch his own full quota of hens for the simple reason that so many of them pass from his beat over the boundary into my wood. Perhaps it was no bad thing, in their first year, to demonstrate that I am capable of putting theory into practice. I know perfectly well that if a keeper on my boundary chooses to get nasty with my badgers, I shall soon have no badgers for him to get nasty with. It is equally important that he appreciates what would happen to his pheasants if he did.

The other side of the coin is that sportsmen and conservationists can be of immense mutual benefit, however different their points of view may be.

Gone are the days when every keeper really did have to exterminate all predators in order to rear his game. Pheasants and partridges were mainly vulnerable during the breeding and rearing season, when crows took the eggs, foxes took the sitting birds and stoats, hawks, owls, jays and magpies preyed on the chicks. Nowadays the hens are safe in laying pens, the eggs are safe in incubators, the chicks are safe in brooders and the poults in release pens. When the birds are strong enough to fly out into the wood, they ought to have enough sense to roost aloft and keep out of harm's way. In this context, as I've mentioned previously, badgers can actually help by disturbing birds roosting in ground cover so that they are forced to fly up to safe perches.

Rats or too many stoats or foxes, and carrion crows, jays and grey squirrels still have to be controlled and I would be the last to quarrel with any keepers that did so. The fact that vermin are now allowed to increase to the point where they run riot is of as much benefit to song birds as it is to game.

In 1978/79, when we had the first real winter for fifteen years, I took every opportunity of knowing what was about instead of only making deductions from clues of tufts of hair at gaps through fences, droppings and food remains, tracks and holes.

The big badger was definitely established in the house sett and I followed his tracks through the snow for almost a mile in each direction. It gave some clue of the badger's vulnerability because anyone with evil intent, far out of the area that I control, could have caught him in a snare, shot him, poisoned him or gassed him if he'd gone down a sett on unfriendly land. It would, of course, have been illegal, but the publicity surrounding the West Country extermination campaign by the men from the Ministry has given people elsewhere, who don't like badgers, all the excuse they need,

With most animals, the size of territory is, to some extent, inversely proportional to the available food supply. The more plentiful the food, the smaller the territory needed, so I decided to increase the food supply for my badger by giving subsidiary food. Bill Brock loved golden syrup and we used to buy it in 15-lb. tins for sixteen honest English shillings, but I reckoned it would now need a cheque book to buy a tin that big. The question was academic because the stuff was unobtainable in the hard weather because the lorry drivers were on strike and so were the sugar refiners.

I managed to get some molasses, used in the manufacture of cattle cake, diluted an egg cupful with boiling water and poured it over a dish of flaked maize. Andy, who was observing the operation, said it smelled so good, he thought he'd move in as a lodger. The problem now was where to put it so that crows or pheasants or wild duck or deer wouldn't scoff it before the badger came out.

Starting off by putting it in the centre of a huge clump of rhododendrons, I was delighted to see the sweetened maize had gone by morning. There were badger prints in the snow—but also the prints of almost everything else that might have competed for free grub. There wasn't any snow in the bush itself to supply evidence from the footprints.

When I had confined Bill Brock and his sow by the house, I had to give them subsidiary feed as the six acres of their enclosure was not large enough to supply all the natural food they needed. So I had made a low wire-netted frame, about three feet by four and fifteen inches high, that could only be entered through a swinging badger-gate. Both my tame badgers were well used to the badger-gate into the wood and, having no fear, they blundered nightly in and out of the frame cage to feed. The whole contraption looked like a cage trap and the wire mesh was too fine to admit rats, so that the food was reserved exclusively for my invited guests. Although I thought my wild badger would be far too suspicious to risk getting caught, I put the feeding cage down by the rhododendron clump, and fastened the badger-gate wide open to leave a gap through which diners could pass freely in and out.

The second night my bait went. I had put it only just inside the cage so that a badger could stand safely outside and feed by sticking his head just through the open gate. There was no means of knowing whether a duck—or even a deer—had pushed his head in first, so each night I put the food further and further from the gate till it was impossible for anything to take it without venturing right inside.

At this stage, I eliminated other possibilities by letting the gate swing-to and moving the food close to it again. Now, nothing could get it without actually pushing the swinging gate open and reaching inside. Within a week the food was so far from the entrance that it was inaccessible except to a creature that opened the gate, pushed past until it could swing shut and went to the far end of the cage. To clinch my diagnosis one might, I moved the cage away from the rhododendron, about four feet further, onto clear snow. Next morning, the food had gone and the interior of the cage had been paddled by fresh badger footprints. I had

persuaded a wild badger to live in my artificial sett and feed from a covered cage that excluded competition. Life had rarely seemed so good.

Andy had been intrigued by the experiment. Trained to cull predators, not encourage them, he had doubtless regarded my absorbing interest in wildlife as somewhat eccentric. But you can't be an efficient keeper without a good knowledge of natural history—and his interests are far wider than the tame pheasants his employers shoot. He was sceptical when I was prepared to spend weeks on what must have seemed the impossible task of persuading a shy wild animal to enter a constricted and possibly dangerous enclosure in search of food it could never have met in the wild. When I succeeded he was almost as enthusiastic as I was and turned up, next day, with Tom so that he too could see the set-up.

Tom had not met a naturalist before who was prepared to help his work instead of criticising it. He was pleased with the hen pheasants I had caught for Andy—and he is not the sort of chap to accept good turns without repaying them. He was genuinely delighted by my success with badgers so I pointed out that it would not be possible without his co-operation. It was 'our' success, not mine.

While the snow was lying thick, I had another pleasant surprise. Tracking the wanderings of 'my' big boar, I noticed that his large footprints often ran closely parallel to a set of tracks not much more than half their size. I wondered if he had followed the trail of a trespasser or if a trespasser had followed his.

Then it dawned on me that I saw the same two tracks so often that it was just possible that they might not be following each other but moving around together. There was just the chance that a bachelor boar had found a mate and my mind went back to the November night when I had heard a battle. Perhaps it hadn't been a battle at all. Perhaps the original occupant of the house sett had been a sow and not a cub. Perhaps the row I had heard had been amorous love-play instead of territorial aggression. The presence of of cubs within sight of the window again would more than compensate for all the unpleasantries and anxieties of the last three years. Tom added to my hopes by tracing both sets of footprints to the same sett and his eyes lit up in the hopes that *we* (not I!) would be able to badger-watch from my window.

It remains to be seen whether such hopes materialise or evaporate as fantasy, but of one thing I am confident. If things don't break our way it will be through no fault of Tom and Andy. I hope their reign here is long and successful because I should hate to have to start all over again.

The encouraging signs are that my neighbour, when he let the shoot, was considerate enough to take great pains to select tenants he thought would cooperate with the work I am doing and that the syndicate he chose are doing all in their power to allow Tom and me to work together—and what better prospect for the future could there be that there are at last badgers in my wood again.

So I am inching the feeding cage gradually nearer to the house so that, as days draw out, and badgers are active while there is still light enough to enjoy them, we may see a grey form crossing the ride at suppertime. Perhaps there will be a pair of grey forms—or even a sow and her cubs.

I am looking forward to putting a micro-switch to the badger-gate of the cage and wiring it up to the barograph in my study so that they will clock-in and out at mealtimes and record the precise times of their activity. To make sure we miss none of the fun, I will put a pilot light in circuit and mount it on the television to warn us when to switch off the shadow in favour of the far more exciting substance—just as I had done with Bill so many years before.

What a wonderful world it could be with just a little more give-and-take by the conflicting interests in the countryside.

Postscript

It is easy enough to claim that my case was exceptional. Most people, as interested in the welfare of wildlife do not start with my advantages to help them to arrange a marriage between sport and conservation. I have been brought up with keepers and understand their point of view so that we can start off with mutual respect. Because I have had practical experience of their problems, perhaps I am inclined to be less critical of predator control than some of my friends who are purist conservationists.

If—or when—the crunch point comes, as it did when I believed the local keeper was as hard on badgers as he claimed, the cards are stacked my side. My wood is quiet and undisturbed; it has lashings of acorns and blackberries and hawthorn, and the wide variety of food and cover pheasants love as much as the threatened species for which I try to provide a sanctuary. So, when the chips are down, I can milk a large area of pheasants as easily as any neighbouring keeper can clear my badgers from his beat.

That is a last resort and life is far pleasanter with Tom and Andy. There are plenty of keepers like them because theirs is such a solitary way of life, so close to the basics of quiet places, that few men take it on who do not have a wider interest than partridges and pheasants.

The occasional rogue keeper, the kill-everything-but-game lout, is best dealt with by attacking not him but his master. If you find a pole-trap set or an illegal gin, photograph it and fetch the police, the RSPCA or the RSPB, and make quite certain that any summons issued is taken out against employer as well as the man who set it.

The most likely types to employ keepers because they advertise themselves as 'good vermin catchers' are the mini-tycoons who have made some brass and can fiddle their shooting costs to avoid tax, by claiming the outlay is 'expenses for entertaining foreign customers' or 'a company shoot' to be paid for before profit is assessed. Such shoots are treated as status symbols by the gin-and-jag brigade and there is no surer way of going down in the world—after having climbed up—than to land in the spotlight of publicity, convicted of using steel gins or pole-traps or destroying rare, protected species.

I know perfectly well that the boss man is unlikely to be aware that a bad keeper is using such devices, because the chances are that he never goes near the shoot except on shooting days, or to be shown only what the keeper wants him to see of his pheasants being reared. These fellows rarely walk more than a hundred yards from their Range Rovers on fine summer days or raise their backsides off their shooting sticks till driven birds appear in front of beaters.

But they value their images as sporting gents and if they land in court through their keeper's misdemeanour one week, they'll have another keeper next. His contract of service is likely to include a clause to discourage repeating his predecessor's offence.

My own experience is that most keepers now do at least as much good as harm to the wildlife of the countryside and even the villains, who get their profession a bad name, can only influence a limited area round their beats. Gone are the days when vast tracts of the English countryside were owned by a chain of neighbouring landowners, rich enough to keeper their estates intensively, so that predators really could be wiped out over huge areas.

The odd baddie, nowadays, is a terrible nuisance to his neighbours who try to encourage wildlife, but the problem is still a local one.

Conservationists themselves are not snow-white. They cause insecurity and disturbance by photography and bird ringing and putting pressures on the creatures they profess to love, simply because too many of them want to enjoy them. Ramblers and runners, motorists and fishermen and horse riders are all destroying the seclusion that shy creatures need to thrive.

But the biggest threat of all, far exceeding the depredations of the sporting landowners of last century, or the leisured class of this, are farmers with their modern methods. Many of them deplore such trends as bitterly as any of the critics—but there is nothing they can do about it. Mammoth machines need prairies of space to make them economic and labour costs have spiralled till labour-intensive methods lead only to bankruptcy. So hedges are grubbed out and little pools filled in to make endless stretches of plough and pasture—which are kept almost clinically weed-and-insect-free by deluging the land with modern chemicals.

Some of these are so fiendishly dangerous to wildlife that, as well as destroying the natural food of many harmless species of insect, bird and animal, they pose the risk of poisoning for whatever goes on the land after such miracles of science have been applied.

As I have shown, some of the stuff in the catalogue approved by the Ministry of Agriculture for farmers and growers, should never be spewed over the fair face of England. The urgent necessity is for research in to safer alternatives—and the only way to get that is to apply the enormous pressure of public opinion.

Don't go for the farmers. They can only use what is advised and what is available. The place to apply pressure is on the Ministry itself. Bureaucrats are allergic to publicity and, just as the keeper's Achilles' heel is his boss, the Men from the Ministry's weak spot is the Minister himself. By writing to him—never to lower levels— and persuading MPs to ask questions in the House which will attract maximum adverse publicity in the media, there is some chance of applying pressure where it will be most effective.

Until then, I would rather have a coven of cats, a 'bad' gamekeeper, or a gane of poachers in my wood than one little man from the Ministry.

Index